DIRECTING TELEVISION AND FILM

WADSWORTH SERIES IN TELEVISION AND FILM

D I R E C T I N G
TELEVISION AND FILM

A L A N   A.   A R M E R
CALIFORNIA STATE UNIVERSITY, NORTHRIDGE

WADSWORTH PUBLISHING COMPANY
BELMONT, CALIFORNIA
A DIVISION OF WADSWORTH, INC.

Senior Editor: **Rebecca Hayden**
Production Editor: **Leland Moss**
Designer: **Paula Shuhert**
Print Buyer: **Barbara Britton**
Copy Editor: **Anne Draus**
Technical Illustrator: **Lisa Sliter**
Cover Designer: **Paula Shuhert**
Cover Photographer: **Dow/Clement Photography**
Compositor: **Thompson Type**

Printed in the United States of America
1 2 3 4 5 6 7 8 9 10—90 89 88 87 86

ISBN 0-534-05202-9

Library of Congress Cataloging in Publication Data

Armer, Alan A.
   Directing television and film.

   Bibliography: p.
   Includes index.
   1. Television—Production and direction.   2. Moving-pictures—Production and direction.   I. Title.
PN1992.75.A76   1986   791.43′0233   85-3237
ISBN 0-534-05202-9

FOR ELAINE

P R E F A C E

This is a book about directing.

It is not a production manual. It will not help you disassemble an electronic switcher, determine the gamma rating of Eastman's newest color film, nor design a more sensitive omnidirectional microphone.

This book assumes you already know something about switchers, microphones, and color film. If you don't, don't panic. Ninety percent of the material that follows is self-explanatory. If you've studied television or film production, so much the better.

When I made the transition from the entertainment industry to academia and undertook the teaching of two directing courses, I began a search for an appropriate text. I discovered that while many excellent books have been written on the subject—describing what directors do, how they do it, the problems they encounter, the techniques they employ, and the various facets of the fascinating world they work in—none of the books provided sufficient insight into *why* directors do the things they do. The thinking. The theory. This book is an attempt to provide the *why* of directing.

Since many readers will ultimately find careers in local television stations or cable outlets, the volume embraces two directorial areas: fiction and nonfiction. (We cannot call the latter "nondramatic" since much nonfiction is intensely dramatic.) The two fields are closely related; many of the basic principles of fiction apply forcefully to nonfiction. Theories relating to the staging of performers and camera become foundation stones for day-to-day television programming. Principles of emphasis apply as much to a newscast or cooking show as they do to *Star Wars*. Therefore, I encourage you to read the pages in the "Fiction" section before undertaking the "Nonfiction" material. Perhaps *encourage* is too weak a word; I recommend, urge, (almost) insist that you read "Fiction" first.

The book is divided into three sections. Part One, dealing with basics, examines what kind of creature the director is, the elements with which he or she fashions a show, and the principles of visual composition that help directors create dynamic pictures.

Part Two, discussing fiction, explores such bedrock areas as the script and the elements necessary to make any drama come to life; the magic that changes actors into dimensional characters; how directors create movement for actors, externalizing their thoughts and emotions; how cameras should photograph the action; and the surprising nature of dramatic suspense.

Part Three, exploring nonfiction, discusses five prominent program elements or television genres from a director's perspective: commercials, news, interviews, demonstrations, and music shows.

In preparing this book, I spoke with a number of directors to get their opinions in certain key professional areas: What is a director? Where does he or she come from? How does a person become a director? The most practical of their answers appear in the first chapter. In seeking the definition of a director, I discovered that certain characteristics or abilities cropped up again and again. Among them: leadership, taste, sensitivity, dramatic or technical expertise, and organization.

This book cannot make you a leader. It probably won't do much for your taste or sensitivity either. But it will provide you with the theory necessary to stage a dramatic scene or to prepare a newscast. It will guide you through the selection of camera angles. It will help you counsel performers in a broad spectrum of program forms. It will offer insights into the subtleties of creating mood and atmosphere. It will give advice on how to handle yourself in the directorial arena.

Of the characteristics necessary in a director, organization is critical. Confidence, security, feeling good about yourself, all arise from *preparation*—doing your professional homework. Had Thomas Edison been a director (and he would have made a good one!), he would have declared, "Good directing is 98 percent preparation and 2 percent inspiration." As much as any other factor, meticulous preparation is responsible for the success of most directors. So important is this concept that I repeat it endlessly in the chapters to come.

Fact of life: No book in the world can transform you into a director. Not even this one—although we certainly try! Practical, in-the-trenches experience is essential. But this book does provide reassuring signposts that will guide you on the appropriate path.

I wish you well. And when cast and crew assemble and the dream is ready to come alive, I hope that it will be *your* voice uttering the classic word that makes the magic happen . . . "Action!"

ACKNOWLEDGMENTS

I would like to express my deep appreciation to the following television and film professionals for sharing their expertise, opinions, experiences, and personal anecdotes—and for helping me get my act together: Michael Armer, Tony Asher, Tom Burrows, Ben Brady, George Eckstein, Dick Fleischer, Walter E. Grauman, Delbert Mann, Walter Mirisch, Jay Roper, and Sidney Salkow.

My appreciation also to the executives at KHJ-TV who helped in the preparation of television news material in Chapter 11: Program Director Walt Baker, News Director Stephany Brady, Executive Producer Bill Northrup, and Director Chris Stegner.

My thanks to the good people at Wadsworth Publishing Company for their friendliness, their eminently sensible suggestions, and their professionalism. In particular, I'm grateful to Senior Editor Becky Hayden for her continuing support and guidance; to Production Editor Leland Moss for his patience and resourcefulness; to Designer Paula Shuhert for her creativity; and to Editorial Assistant Naomi Brown for her thoughtfulness.

My appreciation to those generous academicians who took the time to review the manuscript, contributing far more than criticisms or assessments; their questions made me dig for significant answers. Their proffered nuggets of knowledge added richness to the text. Thanks to Graeme A. Bond, University of Miami; E. Scott Bryce, St. Cloud State University; Peter Dart, NcNeese State University; Garland C. Elmore, Indiana University, Indianapolis; Donald G. Godfrey, Southern Utah State College; David Irving, New York University; Kenneth K. Jones, San Diego State University; and John W. Young, University of California, Los Angeles.

My gratitude and love to all of the students in all of my classes. They stimulate me and brighten my life. Special thanks to Terry Spalding, Venessia Valentino, and Tim Sharman, who allowed me to include their pictures here.

C O N T E N T S

Contents

DIRECTING TELEVISION AND FILM

PART 1   *The Basics*

C   H   A   P   T   E   R   1

What is a director?

You walk into a television studio or motion picture soundstage. Overhead, electricians are making final adjustments on lights. In one mirrored corner, makeup artists apply the finishing touches to performers' faces while hairdressers brush and spray the performers' hair. Near the lighted set, the camera crew scratches chalk lines on the floor, marking camera positions for the upcoming scene.

Within the set, a dozen crew members politely but relentlessly question an Authority Figure about props, script, costume, production schedule, retakes, location, and so on. The Authority Figure answers quickly, waves them away, and then nods to someone offstage. As you watch, the assistant director brings the cast into the set. The Authority Figure whispers a few final instructions and then a bell clangs for silence. Outside the soundstage, a red light blinks a warning to passers-by. Inside, a camera assistant holds a slate in front of the camera. Someone calls, "Speed." And then the Authority Figure speaks the two-syllable word that will bring the characters to life.

In television and film, such authority figures are the spine of any production pattern. They organize, assemble, interpret, and dramatize the elements of a show. Most conspicuously, they create order out of chaos. We call them *directors* because they direct the activities of a wide-ranging group of technical experts and craftspeople as well as the efforts of creative artists. To complicate matters, many so-called technicians are also artists; many artists are also technicians (for example, directors of photography, editors, art directors, and

If they changed all the rules and they said, "You've got to stand in line and pay money to do this work," I would be the first guy in line.   WILLIAM FRIEDKIN[1]

special effects experts). Therefore, because they straddle two diverse worlds, the technical and the artistic, directors may be considered artist-technicians.

Art has often been defined as *communication*. In television and film (popular art), directors stand at the center of the communication process, shaping and transmitting the message from its Sender (writer/originator) to its Receiver (audience). The director shapes a program or film message through the manipulation of technical and artistic elements, seeking to maximize their effect upon the audience. If the director interprets the message with skill and sensitivity, the audience will become emotionally or intellectually involved. Generally, the greater the degree of audience involvement, the more successful the film or program.

Awareness of audience needs is seldom in the front of a director's mind. Directors cannot act on (or even be aware of) a thousand disparate spectator preferences or prejudices. They can only please themselves. When staging a scene, directors necessarily become its most critical audience. In relying on personal taste, they must hope that their dramatic judgments and directorial styles reflect today's world and today's audiences. When directors find that

---

[1]*Directing the Film: Film Directors on Their Art*, ed. Eric Sherman (Boston: Little, Brown, 1976), p. 3.

they are no longer in the mainstream of today's world, they must update their taste—or get out of the business.

This chapter will examine the chemistry of directors, the nature of their world, and how they function in that world—in other words, the thinking, the theory, and the logic behind a director's actions. This examination comprises six primary categories:

- THE DIRECTOR EMERGES: a capsule history of the director's contribution to theater, film, and TV

- PORTRAIT OF A DIRECTOR: an examination of the artist, the technician, and the parent-psychiatrist

- THE DIRECTOR AT WORK: a study of two professional worlds—"live" or videotape (directing from a control booth or in the field) and film (its applications in motion pictures and TV)

- CHARACTERISTICS OF GOOD DIRECTORS: the opinions of professionals on the qualities necessary for directorial success

- THE APPEAL OF DIRECTING: reasons why so many students and entertainment industry professionals aspire to direct

- WHERE DIRECTORS COME FROM: an exploration of the paths that take directors to their chosen careers

THE DIRECTOR EMERGES

Anyone involved in the production aspect of television or film would find it difficult to imagine a show without a director. Production patterns have become so incredibly complex in recent years that a set such as the one described at the beginning of this chapter would instantly degenerate into chaos without an authority figure to provide leadership and structure. Consequently, most people believe that directors have always been with us. Not so. Through most of drama's long history, no one was minding the store.

> When the director did finally appear toward the end of the
> nineteenth century, he filled so pressing a need that he quickly
> pre-empted the hegemony that had rested for centuries with
> playwrights and actors. . . . The appearance of the director ushered

in a new and original theatrical epoch. His experiments, his failures, and his triumphs set and sustained the stage.[2]

In the brief century of their existence, directors have dominated the shaping (or reshaping) of four major entertainment forms: the stage, motion pictures, radio, and television.

When the great director-innovators (Stanislavski, Appia, Reinhardt, and others) first appeared, the theater was shapeless and without a point of view.

> They insisted that if theater was to retrieve its unique, primitive, communal power, a director would have to impose a point of view that would integrate play, production, and spectators. By his interpretation a director would weld a harmonious art and a cohesive audience out of the disturbing diversity increasingly apparent in our urban, industrial mass society.[3]

In American theater, audiences became increasingly unwilling to suspend their disbelief; they demanded more and more realism. Directors attempted to satisfy this need by doing away with flimsy canvas flats and constructing a lifelike, architecturally solid stage world. At the turn of the century, herds of sheep, locomotive engines, and portions of restaurants appeared on the American stage, but audiences were still dissatisfied. Motion pictures provided the reality they were looking for—but stage traditions did not die easily.

Early film directors, unsure of their new medium, borrowed theatrical techniques. The stationary camera watched proceedings from an audience position, as if through a proscenium arch. Actors moved laterally across a stage, at a distance. Their gestures and makeup were exaggerated, as if for the benefit of spectators at the rear of the house.

But innovative directors soon broke out of the mold, experimenting, defining new forms, and creating a cinematic language. Edwin Porter, D. W. Griffith, Sergei Eisenstein, and others moved the camera closer, higher, lower, panning and tilting, dollying and trucking, making it a participant in dramatic action rather than a spectator. They established the motion picture as an art form in its own right, evoking mood from lighting, creating new dimensions in character and plot, and evolving editing techniques still in use today.

In the late 1920s, the introduction of sound fascinated and perplexed

---

[2]Toby Cole and Helen Krich Chinoy, *Directors on Directing* (Indianapolis: Bobbs-Merrill, 1976), p. 3. Used with permission.

[3]Cole and Chinoy, p. 4. Used with permission.

a new generation of directors. Radio directors discovered the technique of creating pictures in their listeners' imaginations solely through the use of sound. Silent film directors, unused to actors who actually spoke words, stepped aside for stage directors, since the latter were acknowledged experts with the spoken word. Stage directors tried their hand briefly at film but failed because they lacked experience in cinematic techniques. They didn't understand the raw power of the visual image and returned audiences to the lukewarm custard of "proscenium arch cinema." Stage-trained directors gave way rather quickly to a dynamic new breed (Lubitsch, Hitchcock, Mamoulian, and others) who were able to combine sound and image effectively, each now enriching the other, creating new cinematic dimensions.

When television emerged in the late 1940s, its directors sensibly borrowed techniques from motion pictures. Since live television cameras were extremely mobile, many early TV directors developed a fluidity of movement in their shots, tracking actors as they moved about a set, gliding from two shots into closeups into three shots. They preferred moving their cameras to actors (or actors to camera) rather than frequent cutting from angle to angle. When many of those TV directors later made the transition into film, they carried those techniques with them, further enriching that medium.[4]

WHAT IS A DIRECTOR?

A portrait of a director displays many colors. It is multidimensional, resembling certain Picasso paintings in which the spectator views a model's face simultaneously from two or three angles. Expressed another way, a director becomes many things to many people: parent, priest, psychiatrist, friend, writer, actor, photographer, costumer, electronics wizard, musician, graphics artist, and a dozen more.

Directors' work embraces two worlds, the artistic and the technical, which is why this chapter initially defined directors as artist-technicians. Let us begin our portrait with those two definitions, which are by no means mutually exclusive.

The Artist

In drama the script is usually a director's first artistic consideration. Good directors know that a fine picture is seldom possible without a fine script.

---

[4]Film aficionados will recognize that such camera mobility was actually pioneered in film (by Max Ophuls and others) years before the arrival of TV.

Their taste, experience, and sensitivity enable them to recognize the potential that sometimes appears even in a mediocre script. When a script requires additional work—which is usually the case—directors seldom rewrite it themselves. Instead, they seek the services of the best writer available who will shape their vision on paper. The ability to understand script structure, to analyze its progression, to recognize potholes, to build colorful, dimensional characters, and to help create pungent dialog, all define the director as artist.

In nonfictional television or film also, the script marks a show's parameters for success and therefore merits the director's earliest attention. The director's artistic perceptions must combine with drawing board craftsmanship. Does the script accomplish its primary purpose? Can production values be improved? Does the show include humor? Does it build logically? Can the elements of showmanship be enhanced? (See Chapter 2.) If its purpose is educational, is the message understandable and vivid? The ability to conceptualize the transition from words to picture also defines the director as artist. The script contains the seeds of pictures that will take form first in the director's imagination and later on a soundstage.

The sensitive director has a salon photographer's understanding of pictorial composition. Such a director knows from which vantage point a scene should be shot, from a high angle or low, past foreground trees or with the horizon tilted. Such a director has a painter's sense of color, coordinating sets, costumes, and photographic tones to create specific emotional responses.

Directors of drama understand the artistry of acting, not just intellectually but on a deeply intuitive level. They may hate actors or love them, but directors surely understand them. In casting, directors search for more than acting ability and appropriate physical characteristics; they search for subtleties in style that will enrich a story, as well as chemistries between actors that will add dimension.

Recognizing actors' weaknesses, directors protect them. Recognizing their strengths, directors accept no less than their best efforts. (Surprisingly often, directors have themselves acted, extending their artistry to still another dimension.) But good directors understand performers of all types and talents: singers, dancers, comedians, mimes, and minstrels. They support them and bully them and inspire them to perform their best.

The director's artistry also extends to other facets of production. On one of television's earliest dramatic series, "Matinee Theater," the executive producer required all of his directors to design their own sets. His theory: Sets and their dressing are so closely related to a director's staging that both should be designed by the same person. While such an assumption has some validity, it is undeniable that *art directors* make enormous contributions to TV and film. They design all sets. They are instrumental in planning the "look" of a show. The best art directors have learned to think like directors. Accordingly, they design settings that offer multiple options for effective staging.

Not surprisingly, directors of drama often make major contributions to a set's design. Because they have studied their characters, they usually understand them better than an art director does. Since a setting necessarily reflects the characters who inhabit it, the director is better prepared to supply this added dimension. Also, because directors understand their characters, they are prepared to evaluate the characters' tastes in furniture, books, paintings, and accessories—thus functioning in another artistic capacity, that of *set dresser*.

The director's artistic functions also include editing, special effects, costume design, makeup, hairdressing, as well as designing graphics for titles and credits.

The Technician

Successful directing requires more than just minimal understanding of the technical aspects of video and film. Artsy-craftsy directors who try to bluff their way through a project with neither technical know-how nor the desire to acquire it find that first, they communicate ineffectively with experts on their crew and second, because of that communications breakdown, their project has suffered a loss of quality. Directors with an understanding of technical subtleties and current technological advances can discuss those subtleties with crew specialists, thereby providing an extra degree of polish for their show.

Whether in film or video, directors' technical expertise functions first at the planning stage, in choosing production equipment. Such decisions, usually discussed at length with crew members and finalized at a production meeting, include choice of camera and lenses, film, lighting options, sound equipment, special effects, crew size, crew members, switching needs, microwave link, and so on.

In video, production patterns vary enormously, from a one- or two-person *ENG* (electronic news gathering) unit on location to a studio "special" with a crew of 100. Crew size depends on the director's technical needs, the scope of his or her production plans, and the nature of the program. Once production begins, a director's technical knowledge must encompass dozens of specialized areas, from color saturation to microphone characteristics, from computer-generated graphics to postproduction editing. In motion pictures, electronic aspects are replaced by a wide range of film-related technologies, beginning with camera and film characteristics and concluding with *ADR* (automated dialog replacement), the *dubbing* of music and sound effects (integrating them with dialog into a composite track), and an analysis of answer print color values at the processing laboratory. An *answer print* or "first trial composite" represents the laboratory's first attempt at balancing color values from scene to scene in a film that contains the final dubbed sound track.

The Parent-Psychiatrist

In any organization requiring the closely integrated services of skilled specialists operating in a pressure-cooker atmosphere, an authority figure is needed to prevent the pressure cooker from exploding. In film and video, where temperament frequently is part of the artistic equation and where enormous talent often conceals the most fragile of egos, such an authority figure must be a master of diplomacy.

Because skills and personalities are diverse, conflicts arise. Because problems are subjective, they elicit widely divergent solutions, again promoting conflict. Because the pressures of limited time and money foster insecurity, voices become unsteady, tempers flare, performers quit, and directors consider changing professions.

Successful directors control the divergent elements of a production company in the same way a mother or father raises a family—with discipline and love. Directors who are themselves well prepared set an example for others in their company. Directors who announce the rules up front, establishing a clearly defined production pattern, enable everyone to find some degree of security and comfort in that structure. Crew members and performers prefer to work on a relaxed, happy set. By their own demeanor directors establish the mood: A happy set reflects a secure, confident, businesslike director; a nervous set often reflects a tense, uneasy director.

Most of a director's discipline problems originate in the performers. Since actors must make the greatest ego commitment, exposing themselves to the possible ridicule of strangers, they are the most insecure. When temperamental conflicts arise, often there's an underlying reason. Maybe performers have personal problems. Perhaps they need more guidance or clarification—or love. After the director has provided these, if the performers continue to make imperious demands, they will lose the respect of their peers. Most performers pride themselves on their professionalism. Awareness of that pride is a director's strongest disciplinary weapon.

Directors don't need psychiatric training, but they do need practical common sense and insight—the ability to look inside a performer's mind to ascertain the real reason for unprofessional behavior. Sometimes television performers drag their heels because their roles don't seem as juicy as those of other series stars. They rebel because they feel their talents are being overlooked or (worse!) have been judged deficient.

In both motion pictures and television, performers sometimes behave inappropriately because of unresolved conflicts with the producer, perhaps over money or billing or the size of their dressing rooms. Script problems are also common, as are disagreements over a characterization. Both should be resolved, whenever possible, prior to production. Occasionally, personal problems—the loss of a parent, ill health, or a fight with a lover—interfere with concentration.

No book can provide easy answers to the myriad of personal or personality problems that disrupt a set or inhibit a performance. Wise directors begin with compassion and understanding, resolving problems that can be resolved and establishing priorities. The first priority: Turn off the outside world. Each performer and crew member must focus 100 percent attention within the dramatic arena. Such an edict is not always easy to enforce. The director may need the wisdom of Solomon, the kindness of St. Francis of Assisi, and the unyielding discipline of an army sergeant.

THE DIRECTOR AT WORK

When directing a "live" television program (sports broadcasts, award shows, special events), the director sits in a control booth, surrounded by electronic gadgetry and facing an array of video screens. Performers and cameras are some distance away, connected to the director through the umbilical cord of program lines. When videotaping a major program such as a drama, the director works in much the same fashion as in a live show—from the nerve center of a control room. Minor programming, such as segments of news shows and magazine formats, may originate in the field with the director utilizing a single lightweight camera.

In film, the director also stands beside a single camera, a whisper away from performers. (A notable exception to this is the multicamera comedy show.) The film is later processed, screened, edited on moviolas, and screened again. (A *moviola* is a device used for viewing and editing film.) Videotape from a field operation is also edited in postproduction. In live television and major taped programs (directed from a control booth), editing is performed simultaneously, as the program takes place.[5]

Technologies differ widely between film and TV. Specific directorial functions also differ. But the theory behind their utilization remains *exactly the same*. The principles that determine whether a film producer makes $50 million at the box office or loses his shirt, whether a TV program garners a Nielsen rating of 50 or 5, whether audiences laugh, cry, or yawn, are fundamentally the same in both media. Those principles relate to concepts of showmanship that were true 2,000 years ago and will be equally true in the year 4000.

---

[5]The described procedures are those most commonly used; exceptions and modifications occur daily.

Directing "Live" or Videotape

The TV director works for many bosses: local stations, cable outlets, commercial or public broadcasting networks, plus independent production companies that create programming or commercials. Within that employment spectrum, program content ranges broadly from drama to commercials, from music to news, from kidvid to special events.

Two types of directors function within the still burgeoning television market: the specialist who has refined his or her talents in a specific program type, and the multifaceted director who is capable of handling cooking shows and symphony orchestra broadcasts with equal grace and style. Successful TV specialists include Marty Passetta, who excels at awards programs; Marc Breslow, who focuses on game shows; and Jeff Margolis, who concentrates on music programs. Multifaceted directors frequently work on the staffs of local television and cable stations. In time, because of unique talents or the caprices of destiny, these directors become more and more adept at a particular program type and make their transition into the ranks of the specialists.

Whether directors work from a control booth or beside a single field camera, their first consideration always must be what happens *in front of the camera*. Film school students and those in directing or production classes often tend to concentrate on hardware: control booth gadgetry, the camera, lighting, microphones, and other production paraphernalia. Such fascination is understandable; these are wondrous toys that smack of professionalism. On a TV stage, the size and raw power of the technology seem to dwarf performers.

Such misplaced emphasis immediately becomes apparent when you consider program material from the audience's perspective. Audiences generally remain unaware of microphone characteristics or subtleties of lighting. Most are (consciously) blind to cuts, oblivious of dissolves, unaware of camera moves. They become involved with *performers*. If they can see those performers and hear them clearly, all other aspects become secondary. Such cold reality is often traumatic for students who excel at television's technological aspects.

Control Booth Operation.
Once TV directors have staged program action to their satisfaction, they then position their electronic cameras. Directors of drama follow an almost identical pattern. The action usually is meticulously rehearsed, first with actors ("dry") and then with cameras. The director assigns specific shots to each of the camera operators who may jot these down on a *shot sheet* or use shot sheets already prepared by the director.

In awards shows, rehearsal is necessarily limited since the show's outcome is unknown. The host and awards presenters receive a briefing on entrances and exits and what generally will be expected of them. Their spoken material is checked on cue cards or teleprompters, and final changes in copy are made. The director assigns specific shots or angles to each camera. Sometimes lettered cards substitute in rehearsal for nominated performers, giving camera operators the chance to know in advance where each star will sit. Lavish production numbers, of course, are carefully rehearsed, sometimes for many weeks prior to the air date.

In sports and special events, very little may be rehearsed. Each camera is assigned a position and a general area of coverage. Because they usually are complicated, technical aspects of such shows are double and triple checked. In special events, the director often works from an outline rather than a script. Frequently the planned sequence of events changes at the last minute so directors must be able to replan their camera coverage, extemporizing to fit the redesigned program pattern.

Prior to airtime, the director takes his or her place in the control booth (whether in the studio or in a van), making sure that all program elements are ready and standing by. When the broadcast begins, the director cues performers and then edits the action as it occurs by *cutting* between cameras. The director selects those angles that most effectively reveal or dramatize the action, emphasizing the most significant aspects. Thus, in drama, the director might cut from a full shot on camera 2 to closeups of individual actors on cameras 1 and 3. In a live or taped commercial, the director might cut from a medium shot of a saleswoman to an extreme closeup of the product she is pitching. The director executes such cuts by cueing a *technical director* (TD), usually seated to the right. The TD uses a versatile electronic *switcher* to accomplish a wide variety of transitions between shots, such as cuts, dissolves, and wipes. The switcher also allows one picture to be superimposed upon or within another, that is, *matting* or *keying*. In some stations, directors do their own switching.

Elsewhere in the control booth (usually off to the director's left) sits the audio control engineer who manipulates the sound portions of a program: either music or dialog originating from the stage and picked up by microphones or sound originating in the booth, such as recordings, cassettes, or cartridges ("carts"). The show's producer also usually sits in the control booth.

Single-Camera Operation—Drama.   When dramatic programs are videotaped in the field, away from a controlled studio situation, they usually are recorded with a single camera, a technique called *EFP* (electronic field production). EFP resembles the motion picture pattern more than television recording, because editing is performed at the conclusion of production rather than concurrently. The advantage of EFP over a multiple-camera technique is that each angle can be individually rehearsed for maximum effectiveness, assuring clean sound, superior lighting, controlled photographic composition, and optimum performance. The major disadvantage of such an operation is that it is time consuming. Additionally, editing becomes a major cost consideration since all of the individual angles (and there may be hundreds!) must be assembled with an eye to logical progression as well as dramatic effectiveness.

As in motion pictures, each scene is photographed angle by angle. Thus, if a director decides that a scene must play in a master (wide) angle, two over-shoulder shots, and two closeups, the scene must be photographed five separate times: once for the master, once for each of the over-shoulder shots, and once for each closeup. The videotape director may screen a "take" at its conclusion, making sure that the scene has the necessary impact. If not, he or she will record another.

For more information on the single-camera pattern in drama, read Chapters 4 through 8, which cover the subject more extensively.

Single-Camera Operation—ENG. A far more economical use of the single-camera operation is *ENG*, electronic news gathering, usually operated by two people. It is a compact, portable operation utilizing a videotape recorder that may be taken anywhere instantly, with a minimum of equipment. Because of its great mobility, ENG is ideal for news operations. Its only drawback is that its picture and sound quality is lower than that of film or EFP. **NO LONGER SO.**

For other than major news breaks, most local station ENG operations have no designated director. They are staged by a field producer or an associate producer or by the talent, usually a member of the station's news team. For aspiring directors, such a position affords excellent practical experience in a wide variety of entertainment arenas. ENG is also used to provide segments of programs other than news. Local station magazine format shows, in particular, utilize ENG, recording a broad cross section of feature stories for five, sometimes six, half-hour programs per week. The production staff smilingly refers to its production quality as "down and dirty,"[6] knowing that they will be able to enhance it in postproduction through effective editing and use of optical effects.

Directing Film

The film director works in both television and motion pictures. Television films primarily include half-hour or hour segments for continuing network series, TV movies ranging from ninety minutes to eight hours in length, commercials, animated children's shows (that is, animated films for children,

---

[6]As quoted by John Gordon, associate producer for KABC's "Sportsline" magazine format program.

not films for animated children!), and some documentaries. Motion picture films, intended for theatrical exhibition, usually run from 90 to 120 minutes. While they deal in both comedy and drama, movie producers slant their story lines primarily to audiences between the ages of 14 to 24.

There is relatively little difference in the mechanics of filming a motion picture feature and a television feature or even a TV series segment. The differences lie in the budgets and the subject matter.

Motion Pictures.   Since motion picture budgets usually are substantially larger than those provided for television films, movie directors have the luxury of better writers, actors, composers, editors, and camera crew, increased production scope, and more time. Increased production scope implies the use of elaborate sets, distant locations, special effects, animation—whatever will enhance the film's visual imagery. While the extra production time may not appear as impressive or significant as some other budgetary dividends, any experienced director, if given a choice, will almost certainly opt for it. There never seems to be enough time, either in production or in preparation. TV series directors seeking quality, impatient at sausage-factory production practices, eye the leisurely (to them) motion picture schedules wistfully.

The second major difference between television and feature films concerns subject matter. Attending a motion picture is not inexpensive. In order to coax spectators out of their homes, movie producers feel they must offer story material and production elements that patrons cannot receive free in their living rooms. Directors therefore work with more sexually explicit scenes than are possible in TV, with more overt violence than is permitted by network censors, and with stories that are (sometimes) more sophisticated than the lowest-common-denominator programming of television. Because motion picture studios often have more dollars to spend, they are able to employ more prestigious directors, actors, and writers, more luxurious scenery, and more exotic locations. Longer shooting schedules allow directors more latitude in their search for perfection.

Movies are said to be a "director's medium." Since movie directors are primarily responsible for making a story work, for breathing life into its characters, for creating the mood and style that will attract audiences, they are given a strong voice in structuring and polishing the script, in selecting a cast, and in shaping the production pattern.

Television.   While it has become fashionable to deprecate series television, it nevertheless provides directors with basic training of incalculable value. After-school specials, Saturday morning children's shows, filmed programming of every size, shape, or budget, all offer valuable in-the-trenches experience, preparing directors for more challenging and more prestigious television or motion picture features. By working within limited hours and limited budgets, TV directors are forced to use their imaginations, to find more economical ways of planning and staging material. That is, they must limit the number of sets, cast and extras, and camera *set-ups* (camera positions and arrangements of lights) through resourceful staging of the actors' movements within a set. If a scene can be staged in two angles rather than three, for example, the director can probably save half an hour or more. On a tight schedule, an extra half hour is solid gold.

Three Phases of Directing Film

It might be illuminating to follow the activities of a television series director through film's three traditional phases: preparation, production, and post-production. Since television's production pattern generally parallels that of motion pictures, such detail will (more or less) describe the entire film spectrum. Let's make our prototypical director a young woman named Sara.

Sara's odyssey begins when her agent makes a deal with the production company that packages a television series called "Buckeye." She will direct one episode: six days of preparation, seven days of filming. She must report to the studio on thus and such a date. If the company likes her work, it may exercise an option for two additional segments, dates to be arranged.

Preparation.   A script arrives at Sara's home the day before she is due to report. She opens the cover. The title page states, "Rough Draft—Limited Distribution." As she reads the material, Sara understands why distribution is limited. The script is awkward and amateurish. Her heart sinks. This has been a quality series. Why are they sticking her with a second-rate script? She reads quickly, trying to get an overall impression. Not a bad concept, but it needs work. Lots of work. Can the script possibly be pulled together in the limited time remaining? She reads it again, more slowly this time, making notes as she goes, trying to visualize the characters.

The following morning she reports to the producer and discovers that he has already given the writer many of her suggested changes. He's bright and likeable, trying to soothe her concerns with assurances that the writer will complete all revisions in a couple of days. He asks if Sara is familiar with the show. Yes, she has watched it but would like to screen a couple of episodes in order to more completely familiarize herself with the show's characters, style, and production pattern. Sara also wants to see how much *camera coverage* other directors provided—how many different angles in each scene—so that she can give the production company what it expects.

That first day Sara meets the casting director, a middle-aged woman of considerable experience. They discuss the characters at some length, suggesting possible actors for some of the key roles. The casting director will check salaries and availabilities. When she has answers—and a more complete list of choices—she will schedule a meeting. Perhaps tomorrow.

Sara also meets her *assistant director*, an intense young man, and the *unit manager*, a gruff, outspoken film veteran who shakes his head, grumbling that the "limited distribution" script is considerably over budget, totally unrealistic. He implies that it will probably never be filmed. The assistant director gives Sara a covert wink, as if to say, "Don't worry about him. He's paid to worry."

The assistant has broken down the rough draft script and put it "on the board." That is, he has converted the script into a series of cardboard strips, one strip for each scene. Each strip lists scene numbers, whether day or night, length of scene, which characters appear, probable number of extras, stunts, and special effects. The strips are then arranged on a production board, all scenes in the same locale grouped together. As much as possible, scenes for each character are also grouped together for economy; the more days an actor works, the more money it costs. Location days usually are placed at the front of the schedule so that bad weather will allow the company an escape hatch—to move indoors. (If location shots were placed at the end of the schedule, rain would leave the company nowhere to go since all soundstage material would already have been filmed.)

Sara goes over the board with her assistant, suggesting several changes for the benefit of actors and performance. Like most directors, Sara prefers to save the most demanding material for late in the schedule, to give actors a chance to absorb their characters, to "get into" their roles. For this reason, she prefers to shoot as much in sequence as possible.

The assistant has already looked at a number of possible sites for location sequences. To save Sara unnecessary work, he has eliminated those that were obviously wrong, narrowing choices to two or three for each location.

Sara visits each location with her assistant and the art director, selecting those that seem most appropriate to the script and would bring color or richness to the show (*production values*). For each day's work, she tries to find locations that are close to each other so as to avoid long (and therefore costly) moves. The assistant takes Polaroid photographs of each location so that the producer may subsequently approve or disapprove the director's choices. (When producers have time, they accompany directors in scouting locations.) Sara discusses with the art director how to conceal prominent advertising material that might cause network problems. She arranges for signs to be made, identifying locations per the script's requirements. Her happiest discovery is that her assistant is both perceptive and dependable. His location choices all were excellent. She will be able to delegate authority with confidence.

Sara's first real problem occurs at the casting session next day. The casting director and the producer try to convince her to use a certain actor as the guest lead. Sara is not a fan of this actor. She realizes she has seen him act only once, in an inferior play on Broadway. But she knows that if this part is not cast superbly, the whole show could fall apart. So Sara asks to see film of other roles this actor has played. When the film is screened for her later, she's still not convinced that the actor is good enough. She asks if he will read for her. The casting director is horrified. This actor is too important to read for a part. Sara is adamant. Finally, the casting director calls the actor's agent and pleads her case. The agent grudgingly agrees to ask the actor if he will read. Later, after a lukewarm office reading, the producer grins ruefully and acknowledges that they can probably find someone better. Sara has been burned too often, taking someone's word about an actor. No matter where she works, if an actor is recommended and she doesn't know the actor's work, she doesn't pretend familiarity; she demands to see film.

The following day the script revisions arrive. Sara reads them with some apprehension. They're an improvement, but the script is still a long way from where it should be. The producer sends for the writer. With Sara, they go through the script, page by page—in some scenes, line by line—refining, suggesting additional rewrites, consolidating, trying to solve the script's creative problems as well as its budgetary ones.

When they are finished, the writer prepares to go home to complete his work. The producer grins, takes him by the arm, and ushers him to an office. He must complete the rewrites here. "*Here?*" the writer screams, complaining loudly that he has eight hours' work to do. Maybe more. The producer puts an arm about his shoulders, promising to have dinner sent in—a thick juicy steak, french fries, even exotic dancers if that will make him happy—but the writer must finish here, tonight, so that the script can be speeded to the mimeograph department.

When the mimeographed scripts are delivered the next day, Sara breathes a sigh of relief. In spite of apparent mental anguish, the writer did an excellent job. For the first time, Sara begins to believe that this can be a good show.

The production pattern of most television series is that director A films one program while director B prepares the next. While director A is shooting, Sara visits the soundstage in order to meet the *cinematographer*—in charge of the camera crew—and the star. The latter, a handsome but relatively inexperienced actor, is cordial. Sara watches him work, realizing that he will require extra attention. Since he hasn't yet read the next script, she gives the star a capsule description. The purpose of her visit is primarily social, so that when she begins her show two days hence, the star and crew will accept her as a member of the family.

After their agents have worked out financial and billing details, all cast members visit the wardrobe department. It is here that most actors will meet Sara for the first time. Sara has already discussed with the wardrobe person the number of "changes" (of costume) each character will have. Now each wardrobe item is evaluated for fit, color, appropriateness to the character, suitability to the scene's action, and so on. If a costume is scheduled for a fight (or other action) sequence, it probably will have to be "doubled," that is, there will have to be several identical costumes on hand since one or more may become damaged.

As the production date looms closer, casting is completed, locations are confirmed, and set plans are okayed. The story editor or the producer gives the script a final polish. The unit manager calls a production meeting that all members of the production team attend. The cinematographer will get there if possible but must give first priority to the show now being filmed. At the meeting, Sara goes through the script page by page, describing her specific needs. Although she has already discussed properties, set plans and dressing, picture cars, stunts, and other production requirements with the people concerned, she now reinforces each of her needs, clarifying areas of confusion, making certain that each department head understands what is expected during production so that there will be no last-minute problems. (Some problems will inevitably surface later, but production meetings reduce their quantity and severity.)

On the eve of production, Sara studies each scene to be shot the next day. She makes rough sketches of contemplated action and business (see Chapter 6). She considers ways in which she can *cover* (photograph) the action effectively. Additionally, since she must shoot six location pages tomorrow, she estimates where she must be at each point during the day. Since a major scene is to be filmed in the morning, she must allow extra time for it. She will thus appear to be behind schedule—for a while. But she plans shortcuts for some unimportant scenes later in the day, where she can sacrifice coverage (and thus gain time), thereby finishing the day on schedule. If she can finish her major scene by 3:00 P.M., she will be home free—for the day. She plans to inform her assistant of her plans while driving out to location.

Sara wants to work for this company again. She knows from experience that giving the producer an excellent picture is only part of the equation. If she has gone over budget, spending company money recklessly, she will not be invited back. (Occasionally, when directors appear either irresponsible or insufficiently prepared, they are replaced in the middle of filming a picture.) But if the picture is solid and finishes reasonably close to budget, everyone will be satisfied. A production manager once told Sara that most budgets contain a small amount of padding, a layer of protection for contingencies.

Production.   As soon as the crew arrives at location the next morning, Sara gives her first set-up or camera position to the cinematographer and then tentatively walks it through with the cast, exploring the action for logic, determining if it seems comfortable for the actors. The star has not been scheduled until later; he worked late the previous night and is entitled to ten hours before his next call. The assistant director has tried to provide him with additional time off since the star carries a tremendous work load.

Sara is delighted with the crew. They are fast and efficient, giving her more time than she expected. The star is due to arrive at 10:00 A.M. At 10:30 he still hasn't arrived. His first scene (the major scene of the day) should be shot at 11:00. At 11:05 the star arrives. He looks terrible, has a throbbing headache and puffy eyes. Sara gives her assistant a reproving look; he never told her the star drinks. She welcomes the star warmly, gets him coffee, mentally restages the big scene. Now she decides to shoot her master angle from behind the star, saving his closeups until he feels better.

While the company waits for the star to finish his makeup, Sara rehearses with the rest of the cast. Then she goes over to talk it through with the star, quietly and privately. He has problems with a couple of lines. She offers alternatives that he accepts and they decide to shoot the closeups both ways, as written and as revised, to give the producer a choice.

At 11:45 the star is ready for rehearsal. But by the time cast and crew are prepared to film the master angle, the crew must break for lunch. They've been on the job six hours. If they don't break, there will be a meal penalty, an extra and unnecessary expense. Sara makes a practical decision. It would ultimately cost more money to break for lunch, come back, rehearse the master angle again (the actors would be cold), and then shoot it. Better to pay the meal penalty and shoot the scene now. Concealing her apprehension, she tells the assistant her decision. He grins, good idea. They shoot the master scene. It's too slow. They shoot it again. Halfway through, the star blows a line. No matter. Rather than shoot the entire scene again, they pick it up, beginning just before the flubbed line. The scene goes beautifully. Sara is thrilled and they break for lunch.

Sara completes coverage for her master scene at 3:25 P.M. Her assistant had pleaded with her to sacrifice some of her intended coverage for that scene in order to make up lost time, but she had been adamant; the material was too important. She would be happy to sacrifice somewhere else. She is aware now that they will lose daylight at about 5:15. They may not finish the day's work. Sara gulps, retains her composure, and pushes on.

The company *wraps*—finishes for the day—at 5:15. One short sequence was not filmed. They will try to pick it up tomorrow. It will add to tomorrow's burden, but Sara knows she will be able to handle it. Most importantly, in spite of problems, she got through the first day, filming excellent material, missing only one short, unimportant sequence. When she pretends concern for the missing sequence, the assistant laughs. Who does she think she's kidding?

Postproduction.   When they return from location at the end of the second day (yes, Sara picked up the missing sequence), Sara, her cinematographer, and her assistant grab sandwiches and run to a projection room to look at the *dailies*, the film shot the previous day. The editor watches with them although he ran the footage earlier with the producer. How did the producer like it? He was ecstatic.

As they watch, Sara discusses the film with the editor, preferring certain takes, suggesting certain patterns in putting scenes together. Later, after the editor has assembled the total footage into a *rough cut*, Sara will return to evaluate the assemblage, making sure that the editor has put the film together according to her vision. If not, she will suggest certain changes to be made before the producer again views the footage. The Directors Guild contract guarantees directors the right of "first cut" although, in television, directors are often so busy that they voluntarily relinquish the privilege.

Within a week after the producer views the assembled footage, the business affairs office contacts Sara's agent, exercising its option for her to direct two additional films. They also have a question: Would Sara be interested in directing other films for the same studio?

CHARACTERISTICS OF GOOD DIRECTORS

Ask any group of directors—television or film, drama or nondrama—about the qualities necessary to become successful in their craft. Some will specify imagination or leadership. Others will cite showmanship or sensitivity or the ability to organize. All, of course, are prime attributes of the successful director. Some are inherent; others can be acquired, at least in some degree.

Taste

In preparing this book, I recorded conversations with a number of TV and film directors, asking each which qualities he or she felt are most necessary in a director. The answer voiced most often was *taste*. Most interviewees quickly assured me that taste is only a part of the total equation, but the brightest, most imaginative, most organized director without taste could not succeed.

How do aspiring directors acquire taste? By stimulating themselves through exposure to a variety of entertainment forms: by reading the works of fine authors, listening to fine music, viewing fine art, seeing fine plays or movies. Whether in college or out, such exposure to the brightest creative minds of all time gives us the opportunity to enrich our imaginations—and our taste.

Exposure to the work of today's most creative talents also keeps our taste *current*. Every year styles change imperceptibly—in clothing, music, stories, and a dozen other areas. Because these changes occur so slowly, we are only dimly aware of them. If we isolate ourselves, they pass us by; we become old-fashioned in our tastes and behavior. Remember a motion picture that you raved about ten years ago. When you view it again, perhaps on video cassette, it probably appears dated.

Expertise

Students frequently complain that many directors succeed because of luck. There can be no question that luck is a factor in achieving any goal. But most of us are given more than one opportunity to demonstrate our creative talents or abilities. Yes, luck opens a door for us—but we must have the expertise that will take us past the threshold.

Expertise in the various arts and crafts comes primarily from three sources: from study, from curiosity, and from experience.

Study.   Universities and film schools generally provide an excellent background in cameras, film or videotape characteristics, video control panels, and sound equipment. Many offer courses in acting, script writing, aesthetics, and directing. In 1984, over a thousand colleges and universities offered courses in film or television production techniques. And those departments seem to be proliferating. Books such as this provide additional insights.

Curiosity.   A healthy curiosity frequently grows out of the need to succeed. It pushes aspiring directors beyond the knowledge acquired in school or in books. It provides them with the impetus to poke their noses into TV stations or motion picture sets, to visit companies shooting on location, to talk to cast and crew members, to wangle jobs as assistants to the assistants, or to seek out industry members when they speak in public. It takes them to little theater groups where, working for little or no money, they can gain insights into the subtleties of acting and the intricacies of directing on a legitimate stage.

Curiosity sparks an interest in unusual theatrical films and television shows, thus encouraging aspiring directors to learn from the finest teachers in the world, the directors themselves. Critical viewing may reveal how directors use their cameras and how they stage action. Students may discover the latest developments in special film or video effects. They can listen to dialog, trying to figure out what makes it effective. Or to musical scores, to guess why the composer wrote a specific kind of music as a background for a specific kind of scene. They can study acting, learning how fine actors build dimensional and involving characters.

Here's a tip: When possible, see a show *twice*. The first time, in spite of good intentions, we all tend to watch as pure audience. We get involved in the story, worry for the hero, and completely forget our original purpose. But the second time, we can watch as students, critically observing how the director has manipulated the show's elements.

Curiosity also drives many aspiring directors to create their own shows, on videotape or film, with or without synchronized sound. Such a project can be expensive, but it can also prove enormously enriching because it contributes experience.

Curiosity, of course, is not limited to aspiring directors. Professional directors ask questions relentlessly in order to expand their skills. They read trade and technical journals and attend seminars on new technologies. They attend private screenings by avant-garde directors to soak up new techniques. And they experiment constantly with their own techniques. One of the entertainment industry's most effective methods of generating audience excitement is through expansion into the deep space of new technologies. Directors must continue to educate themselves—or abandon their trade.

Experience.   NBC news director Jay Roper expressed the opinion that students should try to ally themselves with a TV or film operation *while* they're in school—even if the job is menial. "When students wait until after they graduate to interface with the world, it's too late. They have to be already working part time somewhere in the industry. They need to see what's going on." Getting a foot in the door early, Roper believes, provides students with an additional learning experience as well as with professional contacts that may prove valuable later.

One Director's Perspective

While many believe that imagination and perseverance are necessary qualities in a director, Walter Grauman's definitions of them may provide additional insights:

Q. What specific qualities distinguish most good directors?

A. A number of things. Imagination. Even to the point, maybe, that some people say they're a little crazy. They don't see things quite the way the average person sees them. I think they see them filtered through a slightly bizarre or twisted perspective.

Q. What else?

A. Tenacity. Obstinate tenacity. To stick with whatever a director sees and senses or imagines in his own mind. The biggest treachery that a director faces is betraying himself because he listens to other people's opinions and advice. If you're wrong, you're wrong. But if you're right, you're right by yourself.

Educational Background

In addressing one of my directing classes, former Directors Guild of America president Delbert Mann cited the need for a well-rounded liberal arts background. He mentioned such areas as history, literature, drama, and political science as requirements for a successful director. Mann's views have been echoed by a number of other directors. Interestingly, most valued such learning above technical or production know-how. In my own experience, the majority of good directors are well-read. They know what's going on in the world; they're acquainted with Tennessee Williams and with Molière; they can cite batting averages in the National League. But they also know lens and film characteristics, lighting techniques, and the latest wrinkles in computerized special effects. Since, by definition, directors are both artists and technicians, both aspects must be nurtured.

Both Richard Fleischer and Delbert Mann attended Yale Drama School. Both feel that their experience as actors proved enormously valuable in their careers as dramatic directors. According to Fleischer,

> The most important advice that I ever give to students interested in being directors—not technicians, but directors—is to get theatrical training. If they had to choose between film school or drama school, I would strongly urge them to go to the drama school. The most important function that a director has is to get performances from actors. And getting performances means that you have to communicate with actors and understand them and know what their problems are and know how to relate to them and talk to them.
>
> I have great respect for actors. I think every director should act at some time in his career. Doesn't have to be a good actor. He just has to act, to put himself in the actor's situation and understand the problems that an actor has—and also face the experience of being directed, somebody telling you how to act.

A classic story from the early days of live television concerns an arrogant and relatively inexperienced director who was having difficulty in staging a dramatic scene. After a number of awkward trials and errors, the actors began to grow impatient. Trying to help, one of them suggested another way of staging the scene. Instead of being grateful, the director snapped: "Don't tell me how to direct! Do I tell you how to act?" Veteran directors guffaw at the story, aware that a dramatic director's most essential function is "telling performers how to act."

Fleischer added a postscript to his thoughts on acting. Knowledge of writing and dramatic structure is "equally important. Writing courses for directors are absolutely necessary. If a scene isn't working, you have to realize *why* the scene isn't working. If it's because of the dialog or if the structure is wrong, then you have to figure out answers and fix it."

THE APPEAL OF DIRECTING

Directing is what everyone in the film or television business wants to do. Most film editors, producers, assistant directors, writers, and network vice-presidents in their secret hearts would instantly trade places with a director. Most students in most college production courses view directing as their ultimate goal.

There are several reasons for such wide appeal. Directing is enormously gratifying to the ego. As indicated at the beginning of this chapter, a director is the authority figure to whom everyone looks for answers. He or she is the prime mover on the set, the maker of miracles, wielder of power, source of creative inspiration, solver of problems, a Super Being who has stepped down from Mount Olympus in order to create Truth and Beauty.

In addition to its ego gratification, directing also offers the opportunity to exercise real creative control over a project. To the uninitiated, creative control doesn't appear to be a critical factor. After all, doesn't a writer have creative control? Or an actor? Or a producer? In fact, none of them does. In each case, someone higher on the executive ladder, someone with more "clout," is capable of wresting control away. To artists who genuinely care about the integrity of their work, such distortions can be worse than frustrating; they can be agony.

Finally, because directing requires a state of continual alertness and concentration, it is exhilarating. It is being 100 percent alive. Some have compared directing to mountain climbing. The sheer difficulty of the climb challenges and seduces you. Ignore the smallest detail and you hurtle to your death. And yet the view from the top is mind bending! Here is Delbert Mann again:

> I love the job of directing. I love the responsibility—the sense that it is on my shoulders to do. I'm one of the lucky people of the world to be able to make a living doing what I like to do best. I'm also awfully glad that none of my kids wanted to go into the film business.

WHERE DIRECTORS COME FROM

Directors seldom start out as directors. They approach their careers from many directions. In live television, floor managers normally "graduate" to become directors. In film, such in-line promotion seldom happens; when assistant directors move up the ladder, they usually become unit managers or production managers.

Where, then, do film directors come from? From any of a dozen affiliated arts and crafts. Since a director controls the expenditure of hundreds of thousands (and perhaps millions) of dollars as well as the fate of a project, untested directors are not selected lightly. Even in episodic television, normally cautious producers, anxious to protect the security of each episode, eager to gain the greatest quality in the least amount of production time, would never, never buy the services of an inexperienced director. Unless . . .

Unless the director happened to be the producer's boss. Unless the director happened to be the producer. Unless the director happened to be one of the series stars, contractually guaranteed the right to direct an episode. Unless the director happened to be an excellent writer whose services the producer desperately needs. (The writer agrees to write three episodes in exchange for guess what?) Unless the originally scheduled director "falls out of the schedule" at the last minute, becoming sick or otherwise unavailable. Then the desperate producer, suddenly under the gun, must find a director wherever possible and as quickly as possible. Under such circumstances, producers sometimes are forced to take chances on newcomers.

Film editors sometimes become directors (such as Robert Wise). So do actors (D. W. Griffith, Charlie Chaplin, Orson Welles), cinematographers or artists from other visually oriented fields (Stanley Kubrick, Haskell Wexler), writers (Robert Towne), and art directors (Marvin Chomsky). And sometimes directors become directors. That is to say, small-time directors become big-time directors (Steven Spielberg, George Lucas). Directors with minimal experience catch fire on successful low-budget films and find that they are suddenly in demand.

With increasing frequency, directors seem to be emerging from college film departments. Steven Spielberg, director of *Jaws, Close Encounters of the Third Kind, E.T., the Extra Terrestrial,* and other record-breaking films, graduated from the film department of California State University, Long Beach. A cinema buff, Spielberg had been producing, directing, and acting in his own films since childhood. While in college he directed a student film that was later screened by executives at Universal Studios. They were sufficiently impressed that they gave him the chance to direct some episodic television at Universal. Because his talent was extraordinary, Spielberg was soon directing TV movies. One of the most successful, *Duel,* was later released as a feature film in Europe. On the strength of *Duel* and other TV films, Zanuck-Brown offered Spielberg the opportunity to direct *Jaws,* which has grossed well over $100 million to date.

George Lucas, director of *American Graffiti* and creator, director, and/or producer of the *Star Wars* trilogy and the Indiana Jones series, came from the cinema department at the University of Southern California. His student film,

THX 1138, later was expanded to feature length by Warner Brothers and became the launching pad for *American Graffiti.*

The executive producer of *American Graffiti,* Francis Ford Coppola, graduated from the film department at UCLA. The script he had written for a Master of Arts degree became his first feature, *You're a Big Boy Now.* Later he directed *Godfather I* and *II, Apocalypse Now,* and others. A number of other current directors also emerged from university film schools, among them Martin Scorsese, John Milius, Paul Schrader, and Brian DePalma.

CHAPTER HIGHLIGHTS

- Directors communicate concepts to an audience through the manipulation of creative and technological elements. When they interpret the message skillfully, audiences become emotionally or intellectually involved.

- Until a century ago, directors *per se* did not exist. They emerged toward the end of the nineteenth century, integrating play, production, and spectators, taking over the functions that previously had belonged to playwrights and actors. Early motion picture directors borrowed stage techniques. Edwin Porter, D. W. Griffith, and others discovered new cinematic techniques that gave film a form and style of its own. When television emerged, its directors borrowed techniques from motion picture production.

- Directors play many roles: artist, technician, and parent-psychiatrist. As an artist, the director must be writer, photographer, editor, actor, and set designer—able to function creatively in each of these essential areas. As a technician, the director must be able to communicate knowledgeably with experts and crew members regarding choice and use of equipment and subtleties in production techniques. As a parent-psychiatrist, the director must assume the role of a wise and loving authority figure, resolving personality conflicts and disciplining performers whose conduct becomes unprofessional.

- Directors of "live" or videotape programs work in two essential patterns. Sometimes they operate from a control booth in a studio or van, facing a bank of video screens. Then the director selects (edits) those pictures that dramatize the action most effectively, cueing a technical director to cut between cameras. At other times, directors use a versatile ENG (electronic news gathering) unit in the field when recording on-the-spot interviews or fast-breaking news stories.

- Film directors work in two primary fields: TV and motion pictures. The differences between the two fields lie in budget and subject matter. Since movie theaters charge admission, motion picture studios usually offer patrons what they cannot receive free at home: lavish production, more explicit sex or violence, and greater story sophistication. A TV series director functions in three areas: preproduction, production, and postproduction. Preproduction covers such essential bases as story and casting conferences, location scouting, wardrobe, set design, and a production meeting. Production concerns the actual physical shooting of the project, either on location or on a soundstage. Postproduction involves working with an editor, assembling the film into a "first cut."

- Certain characteristics are common to most good directors: taste, imagination, leadership, sensitivity, a sense of showmanship, and tenacity. Some of these may be acquired through study or practical experience. Others are inherent. Many directors cite the need for a strong liberal arts background, giving such an education higher priority than technical or production training. For drama, experienced directors proclaim the importance of acting experience in order to empathize with actors and to understand their problems. Knowledge of writing and of dramatic structure are also important.

- Directors emerge from a variety of fields. In live television, they often move up from the ranks. Many film directors previously worked as actors, cinematographers, film editors, or art directors. More and more, today's directors are graduating from film schools.

C   H   A   P   T   E   R   2

Elements of entertainment

Certain facets of human nature have caused people to assemble in groups since our ancestors first sat by a campfire to hear a tribal wiseman narrate myths and legends. Those same elemental needs took audiences to see the ritual ballad dances that predate Greek drama, to watch gladiators fight for their lives in Roman circuses, to wonder in darkened parlors at hand-drawn lantern slides projected by candlelight onto a wall. Those needs for entertainment constitute the raw materials with which a director shapes a program.

Gregariousness may be a part of those audience needs, but it is not a requisite—although comedy shows certainly play more successfully to groups than to individuals. One reason why television sitcoms so frequently include a laugh track is to give viewers at home the comfortable reassurance of others also present, who join the viewers in savoring the program's humor.

In order for directors to stage a program effectively—to make intelligent decisions regarding script, camera, music, and other key production elements—they must understand the nature of that program's attraction for audiences. They must understand the nature of entertainment itself.

In the past century, entertainment forms have become so diverse that formulating any exact definition of entertainment is difficult. As cable channels proliferate and television audiences expand worldwide, such complexity grows even more difficult to assess and define. Communications scholar Stefan Melnik describes a system of evaluating entertainment that he calls the

The film's job is to make the audience "help itself," not to "entertain" it. To grip, not to amuse. To furnish the audience with cartridges, not to dissipate the energies that it brought into the theater. "Entertainment" is not really an innocuous term: beneath it is a quite concrete, active process.   SERGEI EISENSTEIN[1]

"Uses and Gratifications" approach.[2] Melnik theorizes that all media functions must be evaluated in terms of *receiver needs.* Since the director stands at the center of the communication process, interpreting the Sender's message in such a way that the Receiver will be intellectually or emotionally gratified, Melnik's approach seems appropriate. Thus, an analysis of audience needs and expectations will begin our examination of the elements of showmanship.

Audience needs have been categorized by researchers into the following general classifications:

1. To increase aesthetic, pleasurable, and emotional experience
2. To gain information, knowledge, and understanding
3. To decrease the pressure of personal, professional, or social problems
4. To strengthen contacts with family and friends[3]

---

[1]*Film Form—Essays in Film Theory* (New York: Meridian Books, 1957), p. 84.

[2]*Entertainment—a Cross-Cultural Examination,* ed. Heinz-Dietrich Fischer and Stefan Melnik (New York: Hastings House, 1979).

[3]Adapted from Elihu Katz and Michael Gurevitch, "On the Use of Mass Media for Important Things," *American Sociological Review* 38, no. 2 (1973): 166–67.

Expressed in simpler terms, in the first three categories audiences seek *pleasure, information*, and *escape*. Since so many television viewers and radio listeners (for example, shut-ins or senior citizens) use the media to relieve loneliness, the fourth category must expand beyond the social experience of enjoying entertainment in the company of others and be considered a need for *companionship*.

Within each major category we will examine the program forms and entertainment elements most likely to be encountered by directors in traditional film and television. Inevitably, some elements overlap from category to category.

PLEASURE

Of the four major entertainment categories, *pleasure* contains the greatest number of components with which directors can deal directly. Watching television or a movie represents passive play—a pleasure-seeking activity. An understanding of the elements that provide pleasure enables directors to enrich their program material, thereby making it more appealing to audiences. These elements include:

- SPECTACLE: possessing sensual appeal for audiences through sound, motion, and color

- SURVIVAL (also known as *conflict*): providing the basis for drama, sports, and game shows because it evokes primal urges in viewers

- MALE-FEMALE CHEMISTRY: stimulating viewers through appeal to their sex drives

- ORDER/SYMMETRY: appealing to that facet of human nature which seeks equilibrium and harmony and which delights in the poetry of visual or organizational rhythm

- SURPRISE AND HUMOR: providing freshness and discovery through the unexpected

Some combination of these components of pleasure appears in every successful television program or feature motion picture ever produced.

Spectacle

One of my favorite high school teachers once told me the secret of the popularity of his chemistry classes. He prevented lectures from becoming dull or boring by performing illustrative experiments featuring fire and smoke, liquids that changed colors, occasional small explosions, or terrible smells. Such spectacular effects invariably brought his students to life.

From infancy we're fascinated with sights and sounds that appeal primarily to the senses. Although the word *spectacle* literally refers only to the visual, I will use the term here in a wider interpretation—to describe all elements of extraordinary sensual appeal, primarily *sound, motion,* and *color.* Examine a baby's toys and notice how they incorporate these elements: the rattle (sound); the mobile with slowly rotating plastic animals (color, motion); music boxes (sound); wind-up animals (color, motion); celluloid whirligigs that spin in the wind (color, motion).

As we grow older, the same spectacular elements continue to attract us. We explode firecrackers on the Fourth of July and watch skyrockets spray colored plumes across the sky. We hold kaleidoscopes to our eyes, observing the myriad color forms in constantly changing patterns. We watch parades, fascinated by costumed marching bands, strutting drum majorettes, and floats festooned with flowers and pretty girls. We attend the circus to enjoy its clowns, trapeze artists, trained animal acts, and garish music: an extravaganza of sound, motion, and color.

Spectacle, as defined here, is not limited to the bright, the dazzling, the upbeat. It also contains darker elements of sensual appeal such as those in (1) the awesome natural forces of thunder and lightning, raging fires, floods, and windstorms, and (2) the contravention of natural laws. The second category includes such fantasy elements as magic and illusion, witchcraft, demonology, and ghosts and spirits. Such traditional magician's fare as floating a figure in air, sawing a woman in half, or making an elephant disappear continue to fascinate us because they defy logic and the laws of nature. Such entertainment is part *spectacle* (contravention of nature) and part *puzzle.* We gasp at a feat of levitation and simultaneously wonder how it is done.

If the term *spectacle* describes elements of sensual appeal, why do we accept such spectacular creatures as witches, demons, and ghosts as appealing? Because in the entertainment world it is *safe* to be frightened by them. When twenty-foot sharks or poltergeists or demons terrorize us, it is a delicious fear that we experience. Why else would audiences flock to theaters to see so-called horror films? The apprehension, the fear, the shock become acceptable because the more practical side of our minds remains aware that we are spectators in a theater. When the terror grows too intense, a safety valve reminds us it is all make-believe. The terror is thus doubly enjoyed: We experience the thrill of an intense emotional experience, yet we are secure in our comfortable seats. We may reassure ourselves at any time merely by glancing around the theater at other audience members and smiling as they recoil from the screen's images.

Similarly, when we watch floods or hurricanes on the six o'clock news or tornadoes in a television movie, we may be awed by nature's spectacular displays while we remain isolated and indestructible in our warm living rooms. If anxiety should overwhelm us, we can always change the channel or turn off the set.

Spectacle adds luster to a motion picture or television program. Like other elements of audience appeal, it cannot compensate for content that is ill-conceived, but it does tend to make such content more palatable. Let us examine a few different program types and determine how the element of spectacle fits into each.

Sports.   Almost nowhere is the element of spectacle more evident than in the field of sports. Its marching bands, cheerleaders, card stunts, electronic displays, blaring music, and costumes are the apotheosis of sound, motion, and color. The wise director automatically *covers* (photographs) such elements, aware of the sensual appeal they add to a sportscast. Yet the athletic contest itself contains strong spectacular elements (as well as compelling elements of conflict) and must remain the primary focus of attention. The delightful fringe color enhances the contest's drama; it does not replace it. An astute sound engineer can maintain fringe color by keeping viewers aware of essential sound (cheers, band music, voices on the playing field) when cameras are directed elsewhere.

Newscasts.   In newscasts, the element of spectacle equates with *visuals.* Audiences want to see newsworthy events. Presenting a visual—videotape, film, or even a still photograph—is preferable to showing a stationary seated figure, a "talking head," merely describing the event. The former is dynamic, the latter static. The first creates a sense of physical presence at a news event; the second is little better than reading about it in a newspaper.

Conscious of the need for visuals, newscast producers frequently include stories for which film or tape is available and minimize or abandon those without. Such awareness of the importance of visuals makes a more entertaining newscast but frequently distorts the relative values of news stories, failing to provide a balanced perspective on world or local happenings. If there's film, a story gets aired. Without film, it often doesn't.

A modern version of Bishop Berkeley's dictum prevails. If a tree fell in the forest, he wrote, and no one was there to hear it, it would make no sound. So it is with television news. Events may take place— important events by any standard—and if there is no camera and correspondent present to record it, it is not "news" and at least 50% of our countrymen will never learn of it.[4]

[4]Frank Mankiewicz and Joel Swerdlow, *Remote Control* (New York: Ballantine Books, 1979), p. 99.

The dilemma is an old one: integrity versus commerce. In terms of television news, the dilemma involves choosing a balanced perspective on world events or stories that assume disproportionate importance because of available tape or film footage. Because each TV station struggles to seduce viewers away from competing channels, commerce frequently wins. (See Chapter 11 for more on visuals in the news program.)

Drama.   Lavish spectacle has become an intrinsic part of most feature motion pictures and a factor in their soaring production costs. In decades past, Hollywood studios manufactured as a part of their total output a number of low-budget B pictures called "programmers" containing relatively few elements of spectacle. With the emergence of television in the 1940s, Hollywood relinquished that portion of its production package to its new competitor. What was left had to be powerful enough to attract a mass audience, offering theatergoers what they could not see on the tube: expensive production values, star names, explicit sex, and/or violence.

The term *production value* approximates *spectacle* and includes those elements of a motion picture or television show that combine to give a rich or handsome impression, implying that no production corners have been cut. The term relates to use of actual locations, elaborate sets, costumes, special effects, stunts, chases, perhaps even extravagant makeup or hairdressing.

In the early years of television, audiences grew rapidly. Drama, largely, was live; production values were minimal, which was fine with viewers. They were thrilled to be watching drama in their living rooms without paying admission. As live television was replaced by film, the use of minimal production values survived—for a while. Then, as audiences became more sophisticated, production values improved. "Naked City" and "The Untouchables" were the first television series to offer night-for-night photography, extensive location shooting, and movie-quality sets. (*Night-for-night photography* is just what its name implies: shooting night scenes at night rather than the less time-consuming practice of photographing such scenes in the daytime and making them appear to be shot at night through use of filters.) Other series quickly followed suit.

In recent years, the element of spectacle has probably been abused (or perhaps overused) more frequently in TV series that in any other entertainment form. Television directors or producers, perhaps compensating for the lack of substantial story or character values, have repeatedly resorted to such affordable sound, motion, and color elements as car chases, fights, stunts, and special effects. Emphasis on such elements often is fostered by pressure from networks in their continuing struggle to win Nielsen rating points.

Responding to TV's new expensive look, the fragmented motion picture industry expanded its horizons, reaching new heights of spectacle with science fiction films (the *Star Wars* and *Star Trek* trilogies, *Alien, Close Encounters of the*

Third Kind), fantasy adventure (*Superman, Raiders of the Lost Ark, Temple of Doom*), and horror epics (*Amityville Horror, Poltergeist*). These films explored new areas of spectacle in the awesomeness of deep space and alien life forms; they reached new frontiers of technical sophistication in computerized miniaturization and special effects photography.

From a director's point of view, spectacle usually enriches a project. Successful directors are like kids in a candy store; they want to cram their projects with as much richness as possible (including not just spectacle, but also good actors, crew, writers, and so on). Production values are desirable when they legitimately relate to the script and its theme. However, if spectacular elements simply call attention to themselves, distorting the honesty of a dramatic situation, they must be arbitrarily rejected.

For example, if a script tells the intimate story of a love that emerges between two charming old people, *simplicity* would probably be the keynote for directorial treatment. Lighting, staging, costumes, locations, and music would all reflect the intimate mood. Soaring helicopter shots and tympany drums would seem jarringly out of place.

A noteworthy exception to the requirement for honesty is when a director works with a less-than-mediocre script or (alas) a hopelessly inadequate cast. Such a project appears doomed unless the director can add sufficient theatricality to make it attractive. In such a case, the director is justified in using whatever elements of sound, motion, or color he or she can cram into the project, creating an illusory sense of excitement.

Music Programs.   In 1984, music video (or *MTV*) exploded onto television screens, exploiting the elements of color and motion (and certainly sound) as never before. Appealing primarily to young audiences, these enormously visual rock, country, or soul numbers include bizarre imagery, computer graphics, dancing, singing or dramatic action, kaleidoscopic or hallucinatory special effects, with few limits set on the nature of subject matter except that it relate generally to the theme or flavor of the music or its lyric content. In some cases, the presentations lean so heavily on the element of spectacle that they wander far from the musical content, apparently exploiting effect for its own sake. More than almost any other entertainment form, music video programs offer directors the opportunity to exercise their imaginations almost without restriction.

More traditional music programs cannot use the elements of sound, motion, and color so flamboyantly. Directors of symphony orchestra broadcasts find more muted elements of spectacle in the settings, in the impact of close angles on musical instruments, and in whatever drama the conductor may impart. Vocal numbers on musical variety shows sometimes include spectacle in their settings and in visual or special effects, such as smoke, flashing lights, overlapping images, and so on. (See Chapter 13 for more on music shows.)

Commercials.   With the exception of a few major feature films, no "entertainment" form utilizes spectacle more consistently and more effectively than television commercials. It has almost become a cliché that they frequently outshine the programs that surround them.

A couple of decades ago the advertising industry was agog when a canned soup company filmed a thirty-second commercial featuring Ann Miller and other dancers for a cost of approximately $250,000. Today, such a figure is not uncommon. The cost factor on handsomely mounted one-minute commercials can run between $300,000 and $500,000 apiece.

Why do advertisers spend such staggering sums of money on commercials? For two reasons. The first is obvious and relates directly to the chapter premise: to add sensual appeal and thereby attract audiences. Aware that television viewers often use commercial breaks for such practical purposes as going to the bathroom or getting a beer from the refrigerator, advertisers must first attract before they can sell.

The second reason why advertisers spend such enormous sums is that rich production values "attach" to a product. Images of attractive, fun-loving teenagers playing ball, painting a sailboat, or enjoying a picnic, enhanced by a lively jingle, create an ambience of exhilaration, of warm acceptance in a joyous male-female relationship. In the audience minds, those images become inextricably involved with the product itself. Ultimately, the ambience *becomes* the product; the two are inseparable. The sales message, by inference, becomes, "Buy our product and participate in this joyous lifestyle."

Survival

In *The Dragons of Eden*, Carl Sagan discusses a survey of the dreams of college students. The dream most frequently reported concerns a fear of falling.

> The fear of falling seems clearly connected with our arboreal origins
> and is a fear we apparently share with other primates. If you live in
> a tree, the easiest way to die is simply to forget the danger of falling.[5]

The second most frequent dream reported by college students is that of *being pursued or attacked*. Like the dream of falling, the second dream directly

---

[5]Carl Sagan, *The Dragons of Eden* (New York: Ballantine Books, 1977), p. 158.

concerns survival. Steeped in race memory, it relates to a time when nightmarish reptiles warred with predatory mammals, when all of life was a carnivoral carnival: Kill or be killed, eat or be eaten.

The battle rages on in our subconscious, tormenting us yet in dreams, sublimating itself in games and contests. We have replaced tooth and claw with more acceptable forms of mayhem. We still participate in the life-and-death struggle but vicariously now, by extension. Watch the faces of fans at a boxing match, howling for blood, inflamed at the smell of death.

Observe puppies at play. They fight with each other endlessly, growling, biting, attacking, lunging for the throat, retreating, and attacking again—but seldom hurting each other. For them, as for humans and other animals, conflict is play; play is conflict. Such play creates an exhilarating tension. It is the game of survival—with the element of life or death removed. The game of survival appears in a hundred relatively civilized forms—political, economic, or social. It is the social form that interests us here, specifically, of course, television and motion pictures.

The struggle for survival manifests itself most frequently in the form of *conflict*. So attractive is conflict that it pervades all forms of drama, sports activities, quiz and game shows, many documentaries, even radio and television commercials. The need for conflict lies buried so deeply within us that we seek it out, even when unaware of the identities of the participants. Note the crowds that instantly gather when a fight erupts at a ball game or on a street corner. We watch commercials we would otherwise ignore simply because a husband fights with his wife over use of a deodorant or because two jocks argue over the attributes of a light beer. We watch bad movies, tepid commercials, sports broadcasts in which we have no rooting position largely because their gladiators are at war; our primordial instincts smell blood.

In drama more than in sports, we participate vicariously by identifying with protagonists—it is *we* who fight to survive, struggling with modern saber-toothed tigers. In quiz and game shows, we sometimes identify with participants, but more often we actively enter the contest, competing with them, trying to win (vicariously) the Cadillac Eldorado or the trip to Tahiti.

Aware directors recognize the enormous appeal of conflict for audiences. With that insight, they must then assess the show's format, deciding whether or not the element of conflict logically pertains. (That choice, of course, begins with the producer and administrative staff.) The role of conflict in drama, sports, and quiz or game shows is universally accepted; its function in other entertainment forms often goes unrecognized. Finally, the director must search for methods of incorporating conflict within the show's legitimate parameters.

How, for example, could the director of a cooking show utilize conflict as a way of attracting viewers? Most traditionally, homemakers could be invited to mail in favorite recipes as part of a competition (conflict among viewers), winners receiving a prize or appearing on the show as a guest. Some years ago I directed a cooking show with two hosts, husband and wife. We maintained a continuing sense of competition between them as each struggled to outcook, outperform, or outmaneuver the other, each teasing the other for small failures. It was good humored and loving. But it *was* conflict.

In newscasts, friendly rivalry between the anchorperson and the station's sports personality also provides conflict. Differing points of view about upcoming football games or the effectiveness of the home team's players stimulate viewers and motivate them to take positions of their own.

Conflict doesn't have to be angry, filled with threats or violence. As we will discover in Chapter 4, it can be *internal*. Thus, the hostess of a cooking show might wage fights with herself, trying to break herself of certain habits (such as sneaking tastes before a dish is completed). Internal struggles in a program can be delightful, especially those involving foibles that viewers recognize in themselves.

When elements of conflict already exist in drama or a program format, it becomes the director's responsibility to make certain that they are not lost or minimized. In some cases, it is possible to add conflict to a dramatic scene where none exists, not by rewriting dialog but simply through performance. I recall a scene in a foreign feature film in which a government official questioned a young lady. Such an expository scene, clarifying final story details, usually is dull. The director made this one entertaining by giving the official a predatory manner. With glance, gesture, and innuendo, he insinuated a message that was never part of the dialog. The official was clearly interested in seduction; the lady would have none of it. The superimposed pattern was not dishonest. It provided subtle conflict in a scene that otherwise would have lacked it.

In sports programs and quiz or game shows, the participants are already clearly at war. Through the announcers or emcees, the competitive elements may be reinforced, making spectators aware that beneath the fun and good humor lies a battle between gladiators.

Male-Female Relationship

Because nature has implanted within us the curious and compelling magnetism represented by sexuality, many of the so-called "rules" of showmanship may be bent, broken, or knocked slightly askew. Graceless dancers, voiceless singers, and emotionless actresses have attracted and held (primarily male) audiences because of sexual appeal. For several decades, women who were neither dancers, singers, nor actresses pranced about a stage in time (more or less) to musical accompaniment, displaying nothing more artistic than their bare physical dimensions. Stripteasers or exotic dancers demonstrated that personal involvement takes many forms. The spectators' voyeuristic pleasure belongs to the category of spectacle or sensual appeal, that is, satisfaction in viewing, sexual stimulation and arousal, and projection of self into a fantasy dream.

In the American theater, the only plays able to survive extended engagements with just two characters have focused on a pairing of the sexes. These include *Two for the Seesaw, Same Time Next Year,* and *Voice of the Turtle.* Viewers usually identify with the character of their own sex, experiencing the mating ritual vicariously. Identification in the case of male-female chemistry assumes such power that otherwise rigid rules of dramatic storytelling frequently go out the window. For instance, professional writers accept the validity of establishing a story problem early in order to "hook" an audience. Yet when an attractive male pursues an attractive female (or vice versa), audiences delight in the chase to such a degree that they are willing to suspend their usual expectations. The relatively routine situation of a boy and a girl flirting at an amusement park can be extended on videotape or film, if not indefinitely then certainly for twice the time a nonsexual encounter would take.

Television Commercials.   Several seasons ago, advertisements for blue jeans gained prominence as TV's most overt sexual expression. Young ladies thrust their denim-clad *derrières* into the camera, thus proclaiming the snugness and sensuality of the product. Billboard, newspaper, and magazine advertisements echoed the motif: The male-female relationship, brashly displayed on beaches, horseback, and mountaintops, would reach new heights in sensuality if only the participants wore designer jeans. Jeans manufacturers had discovered what cosmetics, deodorant, mouthwash, and a dozen other companies knew all along: The way to sell a product is through the promise of a richer, more sexually fulfilling life.

Sports.   Directors of sportscasts, aware of the nature of their predominantly male audience, sprinkle *honey shots* throughout their coverage: glimpses of attractive female cheerleaders doing their sensual routines for the home team. Sports director Andy Sidaris in the PBS program "Seconds to Go" was asked how he got the idea for honey shots. "I remember when I was seventeen, every time I looked at a girl I'd just tremble. And I thought, 'If I'm like that, maybe other people are, too.' And you know what? They are. They sure as hell are!"

Motion Pictures.   When television replaced the feature film as provider of mass entertainment, the movie companies faced the problem of enticing audiences out of their comfortable living rooms and into theaters. Research discovered that the bulk of the movie audience consisted of a surprisingly narrow age grouping: 14 to 24. Can you guess what males and females in that age group usually have on their minds? Certainly not Middle East politics! Their fascination with members of the opposite sex simultaneously provided motion picture producers with an answer to television competition as well as with a new focus for story material. In the sixties and seventies both domestic and foreign films for the first time featured frontal nudity as well as depictions of the sex act itself. There seems to be a diminution of such explicitness in the eighties, perhaps because audiences have become desensitized.

Miscellanea.   Songs, whether rock 'n' roll or old-time ballads, continue to deal with love and romance, the male-female relationship. Today's songs reflect today's culture in a more casual acceptance of sexual intercourse as a physical expression of love. The emergence of magazines such as *Playboy* and *Penthouse*, featuring graphic nudity and articles and stories dealing with sex-related issues, is another demonstration of modern cultural acceptance of more liberal standards of conduct.

Directors don't have to read textbooks to discover that sex sells tickets. Nor do most directors require lessons in good taste. Yet an awareness of the necessity for taste and a proper balance of values should remain paramount in the director's mind. Bare cleavage is expected in an advertisement specifically designed for *Playboy* magazine yet is totally out of place for a TV anchorwoman. Sensual kissing might fit the format of an adult film yet would be ludicrous in a Saturday morning kids' cartoon. The key to a proper balance often is *understatement;* the human imagination remains the richest dramatic source. If the mind is allowed to provide the unseen, the unseen acquires sensuality and dramatic power. By suggesting rather than showing, the director allows the spectator to participate.

Order/Symmetry

In the 1930s, America demonstrated its depression jitters through a jigsaw puzzle craze. Bleary-eyed citizens spent hours, days, sometimes weeks painstakingly assembling hundreds (or thousands) of tiny, intricately shaped puzzle pieces. When they were finished, they had a picture of rather ordinary scenic beauty in which they promptly lost interest. Why such tremendous effort for such meager reward? Because of a fundamental psychological human need to seek order, to put Humpty Dumpty together again. Possibly the economic disarray of the thirties was responsible for the intensity of that need during that time. If Americans could not restore a world that had been riven by an economic jigsaw, they would quietly restore order where they could.

Jigsaw puzzles are still sold in game stores. While the craze died decades ago, the human needs responsible for it persist. Those needs today are gratified by dozens of different puzzle forms—and by literary and entertainment forms containing elements of the puzzle. Prominent are the whodunits: private eye or police shows in which the spectator discovers a world in disequilibrium. A murder has been committed. Order cannot be restored until the various pieces of the puzzle have been put together and the murderer has been unmasked. In horror films, a monster or a supernatural being commits a series of atrocities, creating a rupture in the dramatic equilibrium. Once the ghosts have been driven away or the monster destroyed, order is restored.

By definition, all drama concerns disequilibrium. In the classic pattern, a ruthless antagonist fights to keep the hero from reaching a worthwhile goal, creating emotional *sturm und drang*. The problem worsens; the viewer's worry grows; the problem resolves; equilibrium is restored. Even in films that end unhappily, some measure of equilibrium usually is achieved: The hero regains his honor, a wife finds new respect for her husband, and so on.

Directors frequently gratify the audience's need for order or symmetry through rhythm. As we will discuss in the next chapter, *rhythm* in the visual media implies repetition. Artists use this principle in paintings, aware of the sensual pleasure in viewing the repetition of a line or form: trees, archways, a shadow pattern. When composing a shot, visually aware directors search for such rhythms in their staging of actors and in their choice of scenery and locales. A *raking* (side angle) shot of several faces, for example, provides a repeated profile, diminishing in size, that is visually pleasurable. Such shots are often used when photographing symphony orchestras, the camera angling down a row of cellists, the succession of virtually identical forms creating a visual pattern that is highly pleasing.

Repetition need not be solely visual. In music, a *leitmotif* is a recurring theme usually associated with a character or a concept (such as a love theme) that builds audience familiarity and emotion with each replaying. The song "As Time Goes By" in *Casablanca* demonstrates the leitmotif principle dramatically. Recurring themes (motifs) may also occur in dialog, gaining impact with each new reading (for example, "Here's looking at you, kid," also from *Casablanca*). Similarly, locales may be revisited for additional impact as when in a love story the lovers return to their own private place (the small Chinese restaurant where they first met). In the motion picture *Greystoke*, Tarzan encountered death again and again among members of his primate family. He registered grief each time by placing the animal's "hand" atop his head. Through repetition, the gesture gained emotionality. When, late in the film, Tarzan's grandfather died and the apeman repeated the same grieving gesture, the effect was devastating. Such personal actions, called *business*, often reinforce the dramatic content of scenes. As a recurring motif, the action brings a sense of symmetry to a dramatic program.

While symmetry tends to provide a comfortable and soothing state of mind, there are times when viewers enjoy being startled.

Surprise and Humor

How often have you watched a television program and said out loud the exact line a character was going to utter? How often have you predicted with accuracy the outcome of a movie or a twist in its plot? Such familiarity arises, of course, from repeated exposure to identical dialog and plot patterns.

For hikers, a new trail promises adventure and the excitement of discovery. Hiking the same path again and again produces only boredom. The ability to predict a show's outcome reveals an oft-travelled entertainment path that will inevitably lose viewers. In entertainment as in art, innovation usually is welcome; freshness of concept or execution causes spectators to sit up and pay attention.

Clichés appear in many areas of entertainment. In drama, they begin with the script. When directors are offered clichéd material, they have two options: to try to freshen dialog, characters, or plot through a rewrite or to refuse the project altogether. Stereotypes also extend to casting. We have all seen an actor play the same character in a variety of shows. Such casting is lazy. The director, casting director, or producer is taking the easy, expected path by hiring the most obvious actor for a part without bothering to stretch his or her imagination.

When a television program becomes successful, its producers tend to cling to the story patterns that generated its success. While such patterns hold audiences for a while, eventually they become tiresome. The program's producers must either relinquish their security blanket, providing variety and surprise by deviating from expected patterns, or lose their audience.

Directors fall into stereotypical patterns of their own. For years, both on the stage and in film, whenever directors needed a piece of business they would instruct the actor to light a cigarette. Cigarette business has lately been replaced by drinking business. Watch three or four television soap operas. See how often the cast members pour drinks, sip thoughtfully at those drinks, add ice, or refill the drinks. Directors under pressure (like anyone under pressure) sometimes grab at quick, easy answers. Easy answers are usually clichés.

Patterns of staging and camera coverage also become stereotyped. Recently I spent several weeks on jury duty. Day after day, standby jurors watched television soaps. There was little else to do. In scene after scene, the staging was virtually identical: An actor entered (full shot), encountering another; as they approached each other, the director covered the action in over-the-shoulder shots; as they confronted each other, tension building, the director used closeups. When one of the characters exited, the director held close on the face of the actor remaining. A moment later, the director cut to another scene where other actors walked through an (almost) identical pattern. Of course I was far more conscious of staging similarities than were the other standby jurors. They watched with casual interest, smiling occasionally; it was a way to pass the time.

Dramatic surprise is closely related to humor. When we expect a story to go in one direction and it unexpectedly veers in another, we are fooled; we laugh, perhaps in embarrassment at having guessed wrong. Charlie Chaplin used this principle repeatedly in his films. In *The Immigrant*, the audience discovers him on an ocean liner that tips dizzily back and forth in a storm. Poor Charlie is leaning far over the railing. After a moment he appears with a fish on his line. Instead of being sick as we had guessed, Charlie has been fishing! We laugh because we are surprised. In another film, we discover Charlie expertly spinning the combination dial on a huge safe. When the safe finally opens, he takes out a mop and bucket. Instead of being an executive as we had expected, Charlie is the janitor. He has fooled us again—and we laugh.

Humor constitutes another significant element of showmanship, another valuable directorial tool. One effective way of creating appeal in a character or performer is to provide him or her with moments in which to display humor. Audiences love to laugh. Anyone who gives them the opportunity becomes endearing. Of course, there is considerable difference between laughing *with* a performer and laughing *at* a performer. Performers with the capability of laughing at themselves become especially appealing.

Conscious of the power of humor to attract audiences, directors can provide performers with opportunities to display the brand of humor best suited to their personalities. In the fierce competition among television stations, newscast producers have encouraged members of their news teams to intersperse personal observations throughout the news stories and to find humor wherever possible. Their aim: to allow newscasters to become people rather than robots. By displaying a sense of humor, newscasters become real, dimensional, and infinitely more appealing.

INFORMATION

When we seek information voluntarily, we are motivated by an often demeaned human characteristic, curiosity. Present in all of us in varying degrees, curiosity takes two forms: morbid and healthy. The two cannot always be separated; one sometimes contains traces of the other; they may be inextricably interwoven.

Morbid Curiosity

An early memory: breaking my parents' edict not to cross streets so that I could sneak glimpses of the recluse who lived in the next block. She was an albino. In youngsters, such curiosity represents an understandable fascination with the different, the apparently aberrant, and is part of the learning process. Fascination with the different continues as we grow older. We visit freak shows at circuses. We try not to stare at the beggar without legs or the old man with a hump on his back.

Morbid curiosity becomes almost obsessive in our attraction to the grisly and macabre. Watch spectators gather in excitement at the scene of an automobile accident and stare compulsively at the injured; if a bone protrudes through torn flesh, so much the better! Fascination with the grisly is part of our attraction to horror films such as *The Texas Chain Saw Massacre*.

Fascination with the macabre sets up a curiously conflicting reaction in most of us: We are simultaneously attracted and repelled. Squeamish spectators of horror films cover their eyes during particularly gruesome moments, sneaking glimpses at the screen through cracks between fingers. Part of our revulsion at the sight of a cadaver grows from this reminder of our own mortality. And our fascination perhaps signifies relief that the deceased is not us. Like freak shows, cadavers occupy a shadowed niche in our culture that is labelled "forbidden." Like Pandora, we strive to see the unseeable.

Fascination with the different also takes us to strange lands to watch Indian fakirs and Arabian camel drivers, to stare at the sphinx and pyramids and such awesome natural spectacles as volcanoes or the Grand Canyon. Then curiosity loses its morbidity, reflecting the healthy desire to learn or discover.

Healthy Curiosity

The pioneering need to find out what's on the other side of the mountain has been responsible for humanity's greatest explorations. It took Columbus to the new world. It sends astronauts into space. It leads scientists into explorations of the atom and the nature of disease.

The need to learn prompts us to read the morning newspaper, to buy books or magazines, to visit foreign countries. It sends students to universities. It provides the motivation for watching educational and documentary films and some of TV's panel and game shows. Realistically, the desire to learn is often mixed with self-interest. Knowledge helps us climb the social or professional ladder, to gain respect from peers. When we watch "Wall Street Week" on TV, we may use some of the information to plan purchases or sales of securities. When we watch a documentary or panel show, we acquire knowledge that we may casually drop into conversations with friends, impressing them with our awareness of what's going on in the world. We watch instructional or industrial films usually to gain specific information that will help in our careers or hobbies.

Learning is not limited to educational programs. A significant fringe effect of drama is that audiences appraise the actions and appearances of role models, sometimes modifying their own actions and appearances to conform. Many find (or hope to find) solutions to personal problems in televised drama, adapting the solutions chosen by TV or movie role models to their own life situations.[6] Such learning is not always positive or beneficial. Evidence gathered by H. J. Eysenck and D. K. B. Nias[7] and other researchers indicates that the mentally unstable in our society often imitate violent or aggressive actions taken by characters in TV and film. Directors must therefore be aware of a responsibility to their audience and to society, especially when role models undertake illegal or immoral actions. Life, apparently, does imitate art.

ESCAPE

During the great depression of the 1930s, attendance at motion picture theaters remained surprisingly strong. One-fourth of all factory workers were unemployed. Banks failed by the hundreds. Life savings went down the drain. Businessmen leaped from office buildings. Yet it was possible to escape from that world for a while and buy a dream. The more intense the pain, the more necessary it became to retreat into the theater's opiate darkness and become someone else. After 1932, weekly attendance figures rose to 80 million admissions per week and remained close to that figure for the rest of the decade. The more shattering life became, the more urgent became the need to live vicariously in another, more exciting world as another, more glamorous person.

During World War II, the same motivations recurred, this time grounded in fear and loneliness. Loved ones were away in the armed services; there was a chance they might not return. The friendly neighborhood movie theater offered respite, picturing the world not the way it was but the way viewers wanted it to be. Attendance during the war years climbed to 85 million per week, the highest in industry history, with the exception of 1946.

The Random House dictionary defines entertainment as diversion. To divert is to turn aside or distract from a serious occupation. Thus, when TV and film entertain, they take spectators' minds away from real cares and

---

[6]Erik Barnouw traces such attempts at problem solving back to radio soap operas in *The Golden Web* (New York: Oxford University Press, 1968), p. 97.

[7]*Sex, Violence and the Media* (New York: Harper & Row, 1978).

worries. Escape is the only entertainment element over which the director has no *direct* control. Remember, the categories are defined in accordance with audience needs. Directors have relatively little control over a spectator's ability to hide from life's pressures. The capability for escape is individual and personal, varying from viewer to viewer, depending on the gravity of life's pressures and the spectator's facility at submerging himself or herself in a fantasy world.

Indirectly, however, directors contribute enormously to audience escape. When we turn on our television sets or visit the movies, it is not for the purpose of viewing reality. Reality can be dull, dreary, boring. Go stand on a street corner and watch the passersby. Mildly diverting for a minute or two, they offer you none of the entertainment elements: spectacle, information, escape, or companionship. The parade of drab, disinterested people passes you by without involving you, either intellectually or emotionally.

Reality can also be painful. Witness the increasing numbers of battered wives, abused children, rapes, and homicides, and the rising tide of suicide.

No, it is not reality we seek in movies and TV. It is the *illusion* of reality—to use Alfred Hitchcock's phrase, life "from which we have wiped the stains of boredom." The stories that we watch are more structured than life, more economical in their dialog, scenes, and characters, more intense in their emotional stirrings. (See Chapter 4 for more on drama versus real life.) And yet the master illusionist (also known as a director) is usually able to convince us that we are watching life. And in a sense we are, for good drama always contains the *essence* of life. The master illusionist allows us to escape from boredom or desperation by fashioning intense emotional experiences and by performing his or her art with such sensitivity and skill that we taste the pain and joy and passion of those experiences.

COMPANIONSHIP

People often perceive or use radio and television programs as a permanent switched-on source of background noise or flickering images without really paying attention to what is going on.[8]

Companionship takes two forms: active and passive. The passive form described in the quotation occurs whenever entertainment provides a background to other activities. Thus, the term may be applied to television but not to motion pictures seen in the theater. When entertainment provides passive

---

[8]Fischer and Melnik, p. 16. Used with permission.

companionship, the nature of the program is secondary to the mere presence of sound (music, news, or drama) relieving loneliness, helping to fill an empty home, or enlivening a dreary office.

The active form of companionship occurs when viewers make the TV set or motion picture screen their primary focus. Such viewing may be interspersed with conversation or snacks or (as in the case of television) trips to the telephone, kitchen, or bathroom, but the viewer's primary purpose is to relate to characters on the screen. Whether the spectator greets old friends as in soap operas or television series or meets new ones as in TV or theatrical movies, the feeling of companionship arises from a unidirectional personal relationship.

Personal Relationship

Involvement with a character or performer is the fundamental basis for drama as well as most other entertainment forms: *People relate to people.* Audiences applaud fireworks displays, delighted at the sound, motion, and color. Performing seals and trained elephants amuse them. They gasp and "oooh" and "aaah" at light shows and dancing waters displays. But seldom do audiences become genuinely emotionally involved unless it is with human performers or performers exhibiting markedly human characteristics.

Wherever we go, in the arts or in our daily lives, we seek people, driven (perhaps narcissistically) to find a mirror image of ourselves. When I go to a museum exhibiting nonrepresentational paintings, I invariably seek (and find!) human forms or faces in the tangle of colors.

So acute is this need for identification that when a motion picture or TV program includes no actors at all, as in some *avant-garde* films, the spectator strives to find some vestige of the human presence or, failing that, invests animals or machines with human characteristics. Walt Disney created a dynasty from anthropomorphism. For half a century he devised creatures that physically resembled animals but who fell in love, ate spaghetti, primped in front of mirrors, smiled, got drunk, lusted, wept, and laughed. Disney's animals exhibited such clearly definable human characteristics that we could instantly identify with them.

Drama.   In drama, audiences identify with a protagonist or hero. If there is no identification—some genuine emotional involvement—then the writer, the director, or the actor has failed. The spectator-protagonist relationship often becomes profound, with audiences actually experiencing the protagonist's emotions: agonizing over his or her problems, rejoicing in the victories. Under ideal circumstances, the spectator loses orientation and sense of personal identity for the duration of the drama.

Psychologists and communications scholars have speculated on the reasons why audiences find such deep personal involvement in drama. Since "plays exist to create emotional response in an audience,"[9] the most accepted theory suggests that such emotional response affords a catharsis of guilts. Most of us during our lifetimes commit deeds of which we are less than proud. In order to continue to function, we push our guilty feelings deep into the subconscious where they fester, creating neuroses. When we watch drama, identifying strongly with a protagonist, agonizing as he or she suffers, we are able to exorcise some of the demons that torment us. This accounts for the pleasurable sense of release we experience when a story resolves.

> When we find ourselves deeply moved by a story, with an intensity
> we can hardly understand, it is because we have secretly accepted
> it as our own, *identifying* ourselves with the people in it. Identifi-
> cation—this is the mechanism that taps imprisoned emotions. If
> [audiences] weep, it is not for the heroine but for themselves. If
> they laugh, it is not because the hero's tensions are being relieved,
> but their own.[10]

Newscasts.   While spectacle elements of sound, motion, and color will attract an audience's attention and hold it briefly, *human elements* generally will hold that attention far longer. Fires or floods provide temporary excitement on the six o'clock news, but a feature on a homeless family or a mother who has lost her child creates more substantial involvement. A mother who has lost her child, of course, represents drama in its purest form—a reminder that these categories necessarily overlap. Elements indigenous to one may apply just as significantly to another.

Because of the competition that has arisen between television stations, selection of a newscast host or anchorperson has become critically important. Some hosts attract viewers; others seem abrasive. While journalistic experience is essential, other characteristics appear equally significant: dramatic ability, a pleasing appearance, and personal charm. What is charm? Simply the capability of creating involvement in the spectator, a caring reaction, rapport. Of course, charm isn't limited to anchormen and women.

Performers.   Personal charm is a prime requisite in show business and an asset in every aspect of life. When we buy life insurance from salespeople whom we trust, they probably manifest that same elusive characteristic. Realistically,

---

[9]From Yale's venerated George Pierce Baker in *Dramatic Technique* (New York: Houghton Mifflin, 1919), p. 43.

[10]Erik Barnouw, *Mass Communication* (New York: Rinehart, 1956), p. 56.

newscast hosts, comedians, singers, and dancers are also salespeople. The product they sell is themselves. If they are successful on television, we laugh or applaud. If not, we press the magic remote control button that sends them to oblivion.

Such personal appeal often seems related to energy. We are attracted to life and repelled by death. We are drawn to people who bubble with humor, high spirits, and dynamism. We edge nervously away from the "grey people," entombed within themselves. Musicians who play their instruments vibrantly, who radiate joy and enthusiasm, usually draw crowds. Musicians who are far superior in technical expertise yet who play stolidly, in impassive concentration, seldom create audience excitement.

The display of energy ("aliveness") is a part of showmanship; it stimulates a responsive aliveness in those who watch, sweeping them into the performer's mood, creating a sense of participation. Designers of the TV commercial, "Coke adds life," were certainly aware that life ("aliveness") constitutes a quality of enormous appeal when they equated the soft drink with that appeal.

A word of warning: A director's goal should not be the stimulation of artificial aliveness, encouraging performers to wear masks of gaiety, simulating emotions they do not feel. Most audiences are sensitive to false smiles and phoney mannerisms.

The director's goal should be threefold: (1) to encourage the performer to *feel*, actually to experience the exhilaration attendant to a public performance, (2) to *magnify* that exhilaration, and (3) to *externalize* it. Watch great singers, dancers, and instrumentalists. See how their faces and body movements reflect the varying musical moods. You empathize with them because of their sensitivity, their ability to feel the humor or sadness or exaltation of the music. You are caught up in their moods because they have not merely reacted to an external stimulus; they have become one with it, expressing the stimulus with all of the physical instruments at their command, externalizing moods and emotions through facial expression, gesture, and body movement. In order to project those feelings across a distance to a spectator, they must magnify them; the greater the distance, the greater the degree of magnification necessary.

A final factor, *authority*, relates to performers' ability to involve us as companions. Unfortunately, authority is a characteristic that directors can seldom instill. More usually, it grows with experience, relating closely to personal confidence. When some performers appear before a camera, the viewer worries, detecting a sense of nervousness or disquiet or perhaps only an inability to control the audience. Such lack of authority sometimes disappears with experience. Not always. A performer with authority "takes over." Johnny Carson and Joan Rivers demonstrate superb control of their audiences. They are comfortable, secure—or at least they convey that impression to the audience. When circumstances go awry, they take advantage of those mishaps, clowning, reassuring the audience through their own sense of security.

Directors can help performers gain authority by offering support and reassurance, bolstering their egos. Confidence is contagious. If a director exudes easy assurance, a sense of control, the performer will absorb it and demonstrate it. Similarly, if a director becomes upset or nervous, shouting at crew or cast members, that instability is communicated to the performer and often erases any composure he or she might have acquired.

An insecure performer can be protected from external factors that might exacerbate his or her insecurity. By double-checking each of the elements that will touch the performer (music, other performers, floor manager) and making sure that each has been meticulously instructed or rehearsed, the director can surround the performer with an atmosphere of certainty, a sense of control, a feeling that everyone on the production team knows exactly what will transpire. Such an atmosphere is vastly reassuring.

Companionship versus Escape

As indicated earlier, the separate elements of entertainment—pleasure, information, escape, companionship—overlap and support each other. When we form personal relationships with screen characters or performers, we enter their world, leaving our own pressurized world behind. Thus, the element of escape inevitably becomes a component of companionship; companionship becomes an element of escape.

ABOUT ENTERTAINMENT—A POSTSCRIPT

Pretelevision Hollywood films were occasionally criticized for their slickness: lustrous photography, unblemished dialog, rapturous music, and a predictable, structured, mass-appeal plot that sometimes left connoisseurs and critics dissatisfied. The films were glossy, appealing to worldwide audiences, yet they often lacked sensitivity and substance. They seemed to be all form and little content.

This chapter's discussion of the ingredients of showmanship does not imply that quality shows can be achieved merely by adding one part spectacle to three parts humor; mix well and add a pinch of conflict. Such an assumption would be absurd. Beneath the elements of audience appeal must lie the concrete foundation of *concept*. Without a substantial concept, most shows will eventually fail, no matter how glossy their production values.

By definition, shows also require someone to see them. When a Sender lacks a Receiver, communication fails. When a director or a producer finds that magic equation in which entertainment elements are appropriate to a concept, enriching the concept and simultaneously attracting an audience, genuine communication will have been achieved.

CHAPTER HIGHLIGHTS

- In order to function effectively, directors should understand the timeless elements of audience appeal that are present in all entertainment forms. Mass media researchers have divided the entertainment function into four, sometimes overlapping categories: pleasure, information, escape, and companionship.

- A major ingredient of **pleasure** is *spectacle*, consisting of elements that appeal primarily to our senses, essentially sound, color, and motion. We enjoy such elements in circuses, fireworks displays, and parades, but they also appear in sports (marching bands, costumes, gyrating cheerleaders), in drama and commercials through use of colorful locations, lavish sets, dancing, and singing, and in newscasts through concentration on visual elements.

- A second component of pleasure is *survival* (conflict), which carries subconscious memories of our primitive ancestry and the need to kill or be killed. This primal force is reflected in athletic contests, in quiz and game shows, and in traditional drama in which a protagonist wages war against an adversary.

- *Symmetry* is another ingredient of pleasure. Some facet of the human mind seeks order. It is part of our fascination with puzzles. Most drama by definition creates a state of disequilibrium. Part of the spectator's pleasure, especially in whodunits, is in seeing equilibrium restored. Audiences enjoy the symmetry of certain rhythms in drama: in the repetition of musical or visual motifs, of significant phrases, of locales, and of actions by characters.

- *Male-female chemistry* appeals to another primal urge, the sex drive. Because of its raw power, it has become enormously persuasive in commercials, in attracting audiences to sensual performers or to stories accentuating the male-female relationship. Directors must understand the need for taste in the staging of sexually implicit relationships and the power of the human imagination to provide unseen detail.

- The final component of pleasure is *humor and surprise*. For an audience, knowing what to expect diminishes suspense. Stereotypical stories, dialog, casting, or directorial patterns quickly lose spectators. Unexpected twists and turns often produce humor by fooling the audience and causing them to laugh (at themselves) for having guessed incorrectly.

- The second major function of entertainment is to provide **information**. This function gratifies the viewer's curiosity. Morbid curiosity drives us to seek out the deviant, the grisly, the visceral, and the forbidden. It compels us to stare at accident victims and corpses and to attend violence-ridden movies. The compulsion is double-edged: We are simultaneously repelled and attracted. Curiosity also contains a healthier aspect that drives us to learn and discover. This aspect takes us to college, sends us to seminars, and makes us watch educational programs. It is frequently based on self-interest, the need to improve our status in society.

- The third function of entertainment is **escape**, the need to seek diversion from the pressures of everyday life. History reveals that at times of greatest societal stress (such as wars, depressions), movie attendance increases. Short of striving to make characters or performers involving, directors can do relatively little to help audiences find escape. The need and the capability lie within the spectator.

- The fourth category of entertainment, **companionship**, recognizes its capability of relieving loneliness. Passive companionship is non-directed; the TV simply provides a background for other activities. In the active form, the viewer directs attention at a television or motion picture screen, seeking emotional involvement with characters, thereby hoping to lose awareness of self and life's pressures.

- Audiences relate to people with whom they can identify. In newscasts they become emotionally involved in human interest stories far more than in displays of fire or flood. They become involved with performers (singers, comedians, dancers, musicians) who display such characteristics as personal charm, energy, and authority.

- It should not be assumed that mere inclusion of traditional entertainment elements will ensure a show's success. Beneath conflict or spectacle or humor must lie the bedrock of a story worth telling.

C H A P T E R 3

Thinking visually

Students of drama, trained in traditions of the stage, often tend to approach the craft of television or film directing with disproportionate emphasis on the spoken word. In theater, much of the dramatic development occurs solely through dialog. Because of spatial limitations, major dramatic events happen offstage rather than on; they are described rather than shown.

The transition from theatrical stage to the more visually oriented media of film and television requires a major change in emphasis. Such a change involves (1) learning principles of visual composition, (2) learning to "think visually," and (3) learning to use these principles to communicate a message. The first is relatively easy, but the last two require practice; they are developed skills.

Many art students (and some teachers) are reluctant to reduce composition to a set of mathematical principles. Since beauty lies in the eye of the beholder, they claim, composition must remain personal, varying from subject to subject and from artist to artist. It cannot be absolute. Students who chaff at the burden of discipline welcome such a view. While it contains an indisputable element of truth, this viewpoint ignores the fact that certain arrangements of line and form and color have pleased the eye since the beginning of time. Harmony, balance, and rhythm have fundamental and continuing emotional appeal. The laws that govern them may be ignored—but at some risk.

Those laws, while directly applicable to salon photographs and paintings, must be modified for TV and film drama in accordance with certain classic

Two and two make four. But a picture to be worth remembering must add up to more than the sum of its parts.   ALBIN HENNING[1]

principles of emphasis. Whether characters face the audience or look away, for example, affects the weight of their positions within a frame. Also, there are occasions when a director deliberately violates the laws of balance for dramatic effect, or when composition must be subordinated to mood or atmosphere or to a character's state of mind. We will discuss the principles of emphasis at length in Chapters 6 and 7.

This chapter will describe some of the elements of visual composition—balance, dominance, and rhythm—and will apply those principles of composition to the director's staging of actors and camera. We won't attempt to examine all such principles or to discuss them in depth; such an examination would require a textbook of its own.[2] Instead we'll discuss those few principles of visual composition most likely to help aspiring directors achieve the emphasis, pictorial balance, and emotional impact they desire. The second part of the chapter will suggest methods by which a director might develop or acquire a visual sense as well as exercises designed to expedite the process.

---

[1]As quoted by Fritz Henning in *Concept and Composition* (Cincinnati: North Light, 1983), p. 4.

[2]See Herbert Zettl's *Sight, Sound, Motion* (Belmont, Calif.: Wadsworth, 1973).

VISUAL COMPOSITION

> A composition is a harmonious arrangement of two or more elements, one of which dominates all others in interest. Because of the greater attraction this element has for the eye, it becomes a focal point which we call the center of interest or climax.[3]

We start with a blank screen. In television its proportions are exactly three units high and four units wide, the same proportions that once shaped the motion picture screen. Upon the surface of this blank screen we will place shapes, lines, textures, and colors. By their arrangement, we will create balance or imbalance, harmony or disharmony, depending entirely on the psychological mood we intend to generate.

Because of its smaller screen size, television usually requires greater simplicity in its compositions than do motion pictures. The need for a single, dominant focus of interest becomes more critical. Secondary interests cannot be allowed to detract from the primary subject matter. Also, since the television screen is divided into 525 lines, a picture containing dozens of small shapes begins to lose definition. Such a picture would emerge crisp and clear on a gigantic movie screen. Recall some of the biblical epics you have seen replayed on television with thousands of extras, horses, and elaborate costumes. Remember how difficult it became in many scenes to distinguish detail? Think of the many times you have seen dresses or neckties with small stripes or intricate patterns that seemed to swim dizzily back and forth, moving stroboscopically between the lines of your TV screen.

A single, dominant focus of interest. But where should we place it?

BALANCE

In Figure 3.1 the focus of interest has been placed dead center. Strictly speaking, such a placement does not constitute a composition since it involves only a single mass. But since television and film so often use a single figure within a frame (for example, closeups), let us temporarily expand our definition of composition. While center placement is stable and comfortable, many

---

[3]A. Thornton Bishop, *Composition and Rendering* (New York: John Wiley & Sons, 1933), p. 13.

Figure 3.1   Placing an object in the exact center of a frame does not represent a composition. Compositions require two or more elements.

artists arbitrarily rule it out, regarding it as static. Like many of the rules of visual composition, this one has been broken frequently and with great success by artists ranging from Leonardo da Vinci to Andrew Wyeth.

In Figure 3.2 the mass has been placed above center. Now the space around it is divided unequally and is therefore more interesting than in Figure 3.1. The space below the mass has a weight of its own and seems to support it. The arrangement in Figure 3.2 corresponds to the head position in TV or film closeups; in most closeups, however, the head is supported by the shoulders, presenting a stable, solid triangular form.

Above-center placement of a face in closeups is acceptable and appropriate whenever the performer relates directly to the audience, looking into the camera lens. Such positioning is customary in commercial pitches, instructional shows, newscasts, and for hosts of game or quiz shows. In drama, such eye-to-eye contact with the audience has generally been regarded as taboo since it implies awareness of the spectator's (camera's) presence and thus breaches the illusion of a fourth wall. Eye-to-eye contact thus makes the spectator a participant instead of an unseen observer. In a dramatic context, glancing into the camera lens would be appropriate only if an actor were to step out of character and speak to the audience in "asides."

Figure 3.2   Placing the mass above center divides the space un-equally, making the arrangement less static, more interesting.

Adjusting the Balance

When photographing a closeup in drama, it is customary to "lead" actors, allowing slightly more space in front of them than behind—or more space in the direction in which they are looking. When characters stare off to the left or right, they create additional weight on that side of the frame and the director must allow extra space to accommodate it. Then the head is no longer equidistant from the sides of the frame, as shown by the position in Figure 3.3. Here again, the white space assumes a weight of its own, balancing and supporting the head.

While allowing additional space in front of a figure has become more or less standard in dramatic closeups, the practice has been ignored as often as observed by the world's great artists, confirming again that compositional rules can only be regarded as guidelines. Notice in Figure 3.4 how the artist (El Greco) has actually minimized the space in front of Saint Andrew, deliberately creating an uncomfortable tension in the viewer, echoing the despair on the apostle's face. Directors can use the same technique, intentionally creating a crowded or cramped frame. For example, characters may feel that dramatic circumstances have hemmed them in, confining or restricting them. By crowding characters within a frame, the director conveys to the audience a sense of claustrophobia.

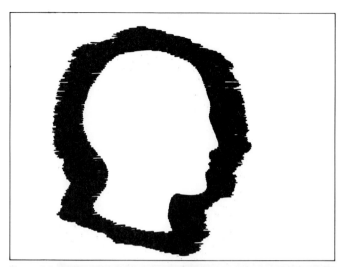

Figure 3.3   Characters create additional weight in the frame when they glance (or face) in a specific direction. It is therefore customary to "lead" characters, allowing extra space in front of them in order to maintain pictorial balance.

The Golden Mean

Throughout history, artists have searched for a mathematical formula that would provide the basis for perfect design. One of these formulas, sometimes referred to as the *Golden Mean*, was first postulated by the Greek mathematician Euclid (although some historians have credited Pythagoras with the discovery).

In the language of geometry: A straight line is said to have been cut in extreme and mean ratio when as the whole line is to the greater segment, so is the greater segment to the lesser. In Figure 3.5, line AC is as proportionate to CB as CB is to AB. Those who advocate the Golden Mean theory in art believe that the proportions provide an ideal basis for the placement of figures within a frame—at the intersections of lines. Many photography schools teach the principle far more simply: They draw lines dividing the frame into equal thirds, horizontally and vertically. The intersections of lines almost exactly coincide with the Golden Mean. In Figure 3.6, Monet's *Beach at Honfleur*, the lines of the cliff and shore intersect at the lighthouse, fastening our attention there, very close to the Golden Mean. Notice that Monet has placed the figure of a man also close to the Golden Mean.

In a more complex composition (Figure 3.7), Pierre Bonnard has grouped his ladies in the lower righthand corner of the canvas. Their looks seem to

Figure 3.4 In El Greco's painting of *The Apostle Saint Andrew,* the artist deliberately reduced the space in front of the figure, creating tension. (The Los Angeles County Museum of Art: Los Angeles County Funds. Used with permission.)

converge (focusing our attention) near the fisherman sprawled over the parapet—close to the Golden Mean.

In traditional over-the-shoulder shots, the position of the favored actor's head approximates the Golden Mean. As shown in Figure 3.8, the figure facing the camera acquires additional emphasis simply because he or she faces the viewers while the foreground character does not. Before you leap to the conclusion that a geometric formula provides a convenient solution to all compositional problems, note that illustrator-author Fritz Henning[4] measured

[4]Fritz Henning, *Concept and Composition* (Cincinnati: North Light, 1983), p. 98.

Figure 3.5   The intersection of lines designates the Golden Mean, one of four positions in the frame said to represent the aesthetically perfect focus of interest.

hundreds of reproductions of great paintings to determine if their centers of interest coincided with the Golden Mean. He found that extremely few of them did.

The Two-Shot

In Figure 3.9 two masses share a frame, equidistant from the center and of equal size and weight. Now we have a true composition, but a static one. Thornton Bishop's definition (earlier in this chapter) states that in every composition one element must dominate. Since neither of the masses dominates in Figure 3.9, the composition becomes dull and flat, its focus of interest divided. This figure reflects drama's standard, flat two-shot in which two characters face each other, sharing the frame equally as the camera photographs them in profile. While directors frequently use such a shot, it lacks depth and dynamics; it is static. Interestingly, as the heads approach each other and the camera frame tightens, the shot becomes increasingly dynamic. The increased size of the subject matter together with the loss of dead space creates impact.

Figure 3.6   In Claude Monet's *Beach at Honfleur,* the lighthouse is located near the Golden Mean. The male figure falls almost exactly at another location of the Golden Mean. (The Los Angeles County Museum of Art: Gift of Mrs. Reese Hale Taylor. Used with permission.)

Herbert Zettl in *Sight, Sound, Motion* describes a magnetic pull exerted by the edges of a frame and by masses within the frame.[5] Such attraction explains the stability of an object placed at the exact center of a frame, pulled equally in all directions. Thus, gravity has no apparent effect on objects placed near the top or sides of a frame. Zettl's theory also explains the spectator's discomfort with two characters facing each other, with excessive space between them, heads crowding the edges of the frame (Figure 3.10). Instead of being magnetically attracted to each other, which would make a cohesive composition, the two figures are pulled apart by the powerful magnetic force of the frame edges.

[5]Herbert Zettl, *Sight, Sound, Motion* (Belmont, Calif.: Wadsworth, 1973), p. 122.

Figure 3.7   The intersection of lines of sight in Pierre Bonnard's *Bridge of the Carousel* falls near the Golden Mean, centering on the fisherman. (The Los Angeles County Museum of Art: Gift of Mr. and Mrs. Sidney F. Brody. Used with permission.)

Ideally, then, the figures should be held in a perfect balance, the magnetic forces pulling them toward each other exactly matching the strength of forces that pull them apart, toward the edges of the frame. When, as in Figure 3.11, the forces pulling them toward each other exceed the forces pulling them to the frame edges, the spectator is uncomfortable, feeling an urge to dolly the camera forward so as to create a perfect balance.

Balancing Images: Leverage

When the principal motif is placed farther from the center of the picture, additional secondary interests must be invented on the opposite side to establish a proper balance. Such a problem can be likened to one of leverage, where an object can be made to balance a heavier one by moving the lighter one farther from the fulcrum.

Figure 3.8   In most over-the-shoulder shots, the favored face falls near the site of the Golden Mean.

> The existence of a fulcrum is felt in all compositions where the proper balance of unequal interests is maintained.[6]

In Figure 3.12 the large mass balances the two smaller masses because the latter have been placed farther from the "fulcrum." In your mind, move the two smaller masses closer to the center of the frame and see how the large mass gradually assumes more weight. Imagine a balanced seesaw in which an adult sits on one side of the plank near the center, and a small child sits on the other side at the very end. As the child moves toward the center—or as the adult moves backward, toward the end of the plank—the seesaw loses its perfect balance. It should be noted here that drama's standard over-the-shoulder shot apparently contradicts this principle. In Figure 3.8 the large mass is situated at the edge of the frame (end of the seesaw) while the small object occupies a spot nearer the center. The reason why this seeming compositional imbalance works—why it is acceptable to our aesthetic senses—lies in the area of dramatic emphasis.

---

[6]Bishop, p. 14.

Figure 3.9   When two masses share a frame equally, the composition is static.

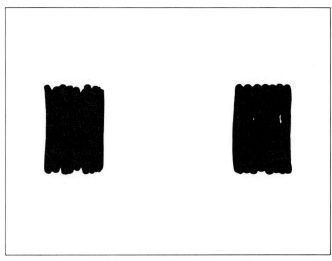

Figure 3.10   When objects are placed too near the frame's edge, the composition seems to favor the space between them. Here the masses seem to be pulled outward by the magnetism of the frame's edge.

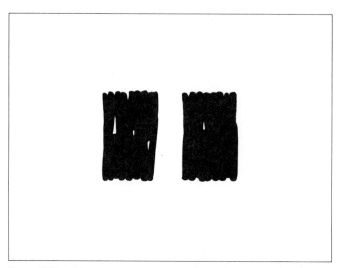

Figure 3.11   When objects are placed too close to each other, spectators become uncomfortable. Their attraction exceeds the pull of the frame edges. We want to "dolly forward," to make the pull equal.

Dramatic Emphasis

As we have indicated, figures facing the camera create far more impact than those facing away. This dramatic emphasis more than compensates for any compositional imbalance; our eyes instantly go to the character facing us. Suppose the character with back to the camera turns and faces us. We would see two faces, one very large in the foreground, the second smaller in the background and near the frame's Golden Mean. The balance in the picture changes dramatically. Because we have erased the major differences in dramatic emphasis, the large head at the frame's edge clearly dominates the picture. (See Chapters 6 and 7 for a complete discussion of dramatic emphasis.)

DOMINANCE

In drama it is not always desirable to achieve perfect balance. Just as a claustrophobic frame creates predictable psychological reactions in the spectator, so does imbalance create impressions that may help the director achieve certain dramatic effects. In most scenes one character is dominant. By deliberately creating a compositional imbalance favoring the dominant character, the director may visually strengthen that character.

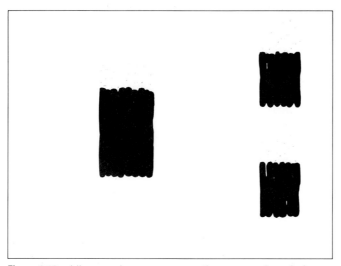

Figure 3.12   Like people on a seesaw, the masses here balance each other, the fulcrum falling near the frame's center.

Just as one theme dominates all others in a script, so must one image dominate all others in a camera frame. When secondary interests detract from the primary focus of attention, the result is clutter. When several objects vie for spectator attention, the director must determine which is of primary importance and then create dramatic or photographic emphasis. Photographic emphasis may be achieved through *contrast*, *placement*, or *line*.

Contrast

With objects of approximately equal interest, the one that contrasts with the others generally attracts attention. Contrast may be in size, color, tone, density, texture, or form or in the physical nature of an object. Viewing a picture of two children regarding a kitten, for instance, we probably fasten our gaze upon the kitten since it is different in both size and nature, other compositional aspects aside. In Figure 3.13, the portrait by John Singer Sargent, notice that even though the mother is larger and occupies a more central position in the frame, it is the boy who attracts our attention because his costume contrasts so markedly with the background.

With three or more objects, the one that contrasts with the others will gain primary attention. In Figure 3.14 note that the contrasting object may be either larger or smaller than the others.

Figure 3.13   In this John Singer Sargent *Portrait of Mrs. Edward L. Davis and her son,* our attention goes first to the boy because his sailor suit contrasts so markedly with the background. (The Los Angeles County Museum of Art: Frances and Armand Hammer Purchase Fund. Used with permission.)

Figure 3.14   With three or more objects, the one that contrasts with the others will gain attention. The contrasting object may be larger or smaller.

Placement

Other factors being equal, the object nearest the center of a picture usually attracts the greatest attention. Note that placing an object at the Golden Mean does not necessarily give it dominance; such placement is primarily aesthetic in purpose. In the advertisement for Crown Royal (Figure 3.15) the advertiser

Figure 3.15   Center placement usually provides maximum impact.
The Crown Royal bottle is also larger than the glasses and different
in form. (Warwick Advertising, Inc. Used with permission.)

has gained maximum impact by placing the bottle at center. Since it is also
larger than the two glasses and different in form and character, it demands
our attention.

Often, because of specific compositional needs or commercial requirements, an object or character cannot be placed at the center of a picture. The
object also may not provide a contrast with other elements in the picture.
Then the viewer's attention may be focused on the object through line.

Line

In nature, lines usually appear as the division between forms, such as the
horizon line separating ocean and sky or the slope of a mountain, its edge
dividing land and sky. Civilization has surrounded us with lines: streets (curbs,

painted dividing lines), telephone poles, electric wires, railroad tracks, church spires, skyscrapers, and a thousand other structures.

The nature and position of a line make strong emotional statements about the subject matter. Horizontal lines or planes generally tend to create comfortable feelings of serenity, repose, and equilibrium—all's right with the world. Vertical lines or planes provide greater strength and energy; they also suggest the spiritual, a reaching upward to the heavens, as manifested in church steeples.

The Intersection of Lines.   In photographic composition, lines represent one of the most powerful means of directing viewer attention. Their arrangement within the photographic frame determines the degree of their power. The simplest, yet most effective way of directing attention to a particular area is through the *intersection* of lines. Our eyes follow a line until it crosses another. We fix our attention there, as the director or photographer intended we should.

In drama, characters placed in doorways or windows inevitably attract attention since they are framed by intersecting vertical and horizontal lines. Figure 3.16 shows a scene from *Doctor Zhivago* with Rod Steiger and Julie Christie enclosed within a window frame. The rectangle focuses our attention on them. The rapt attention of the foreground figure further intensifies our interest. Similarly, in *Portrait of the Artist's Son* (Figure 3.17) the window frame holds out attention inside the painting even though the boy's stare tends to direct our attention outward. Notice that a second rectangle in the background, a girl enclosed within the frame of an artist's canvas, parallels the foreground window frame, echoing it and providing three rectangles of approximately equal proportions: the outline of the painting itself, the window frame, and the canvas.

In Figure 3.18, a drawing by California artist Ellen More, the powerful lines of the model's two arms form a pattern of strength and solidity that drives the viewer's eyes to their intersection at the stool top. The lines of the model's leg as well as those of the stool legs also direct our glance to the intersection.

Converging lines frequently do not physically intersect; the intersection may be implicit, actual closure taking place at infinity—in the mind of the viewer. In Figure 3.19, for example, the architectural lines of the church, as well as the converging lines of the floor, direct our view to the far archway. So powerful are these converging lines that the viewer is almost unable to resist their impetus.

A line need be neither graphic nor literal. It may be suggested. Whenever a painted figure—or a character in drama—glances in a specific direction, the look creates a line and the spectator's attention will tend to follow that line.

Figure 3.16   Frames created by intersecting lines (such as doors and windows) emphasize the subject matter they contain. In this scene from *Doctor Zhivago*, Rod Steiger and Julie Christie hold our primary attention. The observer's eye line creates additional emphasis. (An MGM release © 1965 Metro-Goldwyn-Mayer Inc. Used with permission.)

The foreground character in Figure 3.16 effectively demonstrates this principle. The closer a character is positioned to the camera, the more powerful the line of sight becomes. Such a circumstance is similar to seeing a group of people on a street corner staring upward. For a passerby, the urge to look up becomes almost irresistible. (Of course, curiosity is also a factor!) Lines also are formed by a succession of objects, placed so that the eye is led from one to another. The sailboats in Monet's *Beach at Honfleur* (Figure 3.6) form a line that directs our attention to the lighthouse.

Grouping figures so that the eye travels along them in a direction toward the center of interest is but one scheme. The attention of a human figure in a composition, directed toward the person of chief interest suggests the direction for the observer to look. The posing

Figure 3.17   In Martin Drolling's *Portrait of the Artist's Son,* the window frame directs our attention inward. Similarly, the frame of the canvas in background provides emphasis for the young girl. Her glance to the left helps to balance the strong line created by the boy's glance. Note that the violin's shape echoes the shape of the birdcage. (The Los Angeles County Museum of Art: Museum Purchase with Balch Funds by Mr. and Mrs. Allan C. Balch Collection, Mrs. Eloise Mabury Knapp, Mr. and Mrs. Will Richeson, Miss Carlotta Mabury, John Jewett Garland, Mrs. Celia Rosenberg, Mr. and Mrs. R. B. Honeyman, Bella Mabury, and Mrs. George William Davenport. Used with permission.)

of arms to define a line is frequent. In Da Vinci's *Last Supper* this scheme was followed, the gestures of the disciples being used to direct the eye of the spectator to the center figure.[7]

[7]Bishop, p. 19.

Figure 3.18   The impact of intersecting lines is demonstrated in Ellen More's powerful *Male Nude.* (Used with permission of Ellen More.)

In Figure 3.20 the group of figures surrounding Christ direct their glances at him, making it almost impossible for us to look elsewhere. *Almost* impossible. The artist (Rocco Marconi) has created subtleties in his composition that make it more complex than it first appears. While the surrounding figures compel our attention to focus on Christ, his glance leads our eyes left, past the beseeching woman to the two sinister, plotting figures at extreme left. The character directly above them, framed in a window, directs our attention back to the Christ figure, establishing a circular movement within the frame. Such is the power of the look to establish a line.

The Diagonal Line.   Of all directional lines, the diagonal is by far the strongest, the most compelling. Take a few minutes to leaf through a favorite magazine. Study the advertisements. Most use the principles of visual composition dis-

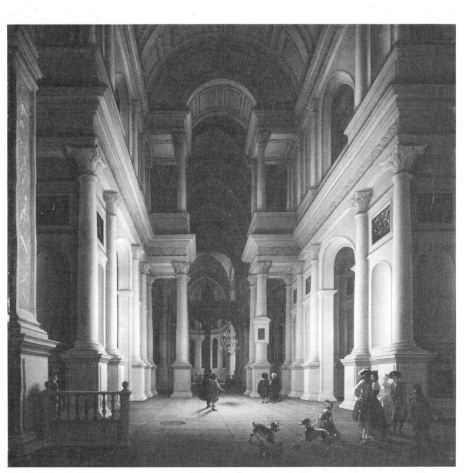

Figure 3.19   Lines may converge only in the viewer's mind but they rivet our attention nonetheless, as demonstrated in this *Interior of a Church at Night* by Dutch artists de Lorme and de Jongh. (The Los Angeles County Museum of Art: Gift of Dr. Hans Schaeffer. Used with permission.)

cussed in this chapter; many feature powerful diagonal lines to direct the reader's eyes to a product.

Many of the painters in the Dutch and Flemish schools used the diagonal line as a basic force in their compositions, allowing light from a window high in the frame to slant downward, directing our gaze and illuminating an object lower in the picture. In Figure 3.19 the architectural and floor lines in the church are diagonals, which accounts for their power in propelling our

Figure 3.20   When figures look in a specific direction, their glances create lines that direct our attention, as demonstrated in Rocco Marconi's *Christ and the Women of Canaan*. (The Los Angeles County Museum of Art: William Randolph Hearst Collection. Used with permission.)

attention forward. Also notice the strength of the diagonal lines in Figures 3.4 and 3.18.

Thus far we have discussed elements that relate to the formal compositional aspects of a picture. A compositional element that contributes to the viewer's sensual pleasure is rhythm.

RHYTHM

We recognize rhythm in the primitive dances of many cultures as well as in the crude markings on ancient Greek and Roman temples, Byzantine mosaics, and archeological relics such as vases. It is probably the oldest form of artistic expression. *Rhythm* usually implies some form of *repetition*. It is an appeal to the senses. In music rhythm implies repetition of a beat in a prescribed

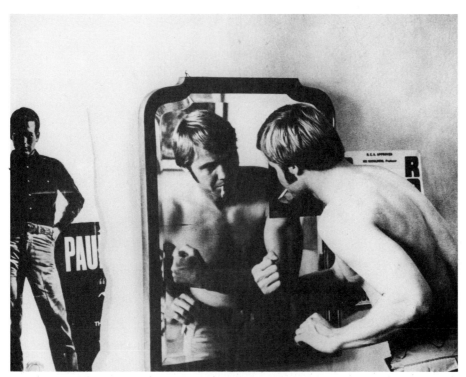

Figure 3.21   In this scene from *Midnight Cowboy*, the mirror provides a pleasing repetition of image. It also creates an inner frame, holding our attention on Jon Voight. (A UA release © 1969 Jerome Hellman Productions, Inc. Used with permission.)

cadence or repetition of a musical figure. In rhetoric it implies repetition of words or phrases (such as "of the people, by the people, and for the people"). In poetry it usually denotes a repeated metric structure (for example, iambic pentameter) or a rhyming pattern whose repetition of sound is pleasing to the ear.

In the visual media, rhythm implies a repetition of line, form, or color. In Figure 3.19 the repetition of columns and archways creates much of the painting's beauty. It is sensually pleasurable to the viewer. When composing a shot, visually aware directors often search for repetition in their staging of actors and in their choice of scenery and locales. One of the reasons we see mirror shots so often in films is that the reflections offer viewers a pleasing repetition, one image echoing the other. The shot from *Midnight Cowboy* shown in Figure 3.21 is a typical example. Note also how the mirror provides a frame for Jon Voight, holding our attention within its periphery.

Figure 3.22   This Nike ad, part of an award-winning campaign, utilizes the principle of repetition to provide sensual pleasure to the viewer. The bleacher lines also direct attention to the athlete. Note that she is positioned near the Golden Mean. (Chiat/Day Advertising. Used with permission.)

The Nike advertisement in Figure 3.22, part of a campaign celebrated for its visual effectiveness, utilizes repetition as its key motif. The repeated lines of bleacher seats lead our eyes unswervingly to the athlete wearing the Nike shoes. The artists responsible for such ads understand how most viewers will "read" such a picture, the direction in which their eyes will travel.

The Crown Royal advertisement (Figure 3.15) provides repetition in the two glasses balancing each other on opposite sides of the frame and roughly echoing the shape of the bottle itself. The ad also provides an overlay of jigsaw puzzle shapes that create a pleasing repetition of form. Picture in your mind the same advertisement without the puzzle lines. It would lose much of its appeal.

In the Diego Rivera painting *Flower Day* (Figure 3.23), the repetition of form is most evident in the profusion of lilies. But notice that the lilies themselves seem to echo the shape of the vendor's head and shoulders and their color is echoed in the costumes of the seated women. Notice the repeti-

Figure 3.23   Diego Rivera's *Flower Day* demonstrates the sensually gratifying element of repetition. Note that the two seated figures almost exactly mirror each other. The lilies endlessly repeat themselves and resemble the curves of the three heads and the foreground basket. (The Los Angeles County Museum of Art: Los Angeles County Funds. Used with permission.)

tion again in the leaves and stems in the vendor's hands and in the seated figure at the left almost exactly mirroring the figure on the right. Because repetition is far more interesting when there is variation, when one form does not *exactly* replicate the other, the seated figures are not identical. As you examine the painting further, you can find additional sensually pleasing repetitions of form.

Flower Day reinforces other compositional principles as well. The seated figures direct their gaze to the vendor, creating lines of sight that compel us to do likewise. His head gains additional emphasis because it contrasts so markedly with the flowers behind him. In this triangular composition, the vendor almost becomes a holy figure, offering a benediction to the seated figures.

READING A PICTURE

In Western civilizations, viewers' eyes generally enter the frame at the left and move to the right and downward. Perhaps this pattern of viewing emerges from the way we read a printed page, starting at the top and moving from left to right. In some Eastern cultures reading patterns are reversed, moving from right to left or in vertical lines from top to bottom. In those cultures, television or film imagery may be "read" in a different directional pattern than in the West. Examine the slanting lines in Figure 3.24.[8] Which goes uphill? Which goes down? Since most of us read a frame from left to right, you probably interpreted the first slanted line as going uphill and the second as slanting down. If your eyes had entered the frame on the right, you would probably have interpreted the lines in an opposite fashion.

German art historian Heinrich Wolfflin claimed that since we read a picture from left to right, the right side thus becomes "heavier" than the left and must be balanced by additional weight on the left.[9] If we accept Wolfflin's premise at face value, then we must conclude that in any two-shot the actor on the right side of the frame receives more spectator attention than the actor on the left. Some actors and directors disagree. They feel that a character at the left side of the frame draws more audience attention simply because we see him or her first. Actors preoccupied with their own importance frequently ask directors to stage them either at the left or the right side of the camera frame in order to focus attention on themselves and thus dominate a scene. In practice, many factors of dramatic emphasis come into play, modifying or subverting some of the principles of pictorial composition (see Chapters 6 and 7).

Some authors and critics claim that the upper portion of the frame is intrinsically heavier than the lower. When the horizon line exactly bisects a frame, the sky, being heavier, oppresses the earth, dominating figures in the lower half of the picture. John Ford in many of his Westerns used the powerful oppressive force of the sky to dramatize the frailty of his characters as they moved across the desert vastness. The sky's intimidating effect may be enhanced, of course, by placing the horizon lower in the frame, allowing the sky to occupy a major portion of pictorial space. When such a dominant sky is dark and angry, the effect becomes truly frightening.

---

[8]From Zettl, p. 129.

[9]Described by Louis Giannetti in *Understanding Movies* (Englewood Cliffs, N.J.: Prentice Hall, 1976), p. 62.

Figure 3.24   If you interpret these lines as going uphill in the first example and downhill in the second, you have demonstrated that your eyes enter the frame at the left, the usual pattern for "reading" a picture in most Western cultures.

ACQUIRING A VISUAL SENSE

Just as some musicians seem to possess an innate sense of melody, so do some directors seem to have a natural facility for composing a picture that expresses a concept or emotion in values that are strictly visual. Such talent possibly is innate, acquired through genes, but it may also be acquired through study and observation.

At the start of each semester, a few students in my writing classes despair of ever finding exciting story material. Weeks later, they are amazed to discover story possibilities everywhere—in their homes, among their friends, in newspapers, in their classes. The stories, of course, were always there. But in those few weeks the students had put on spectacles that suddenly enabled them to see: They had acquired story awareness.

Thinking visually concerns more than balance, dominance, line, and rhythm. In drama as well as in most other entertainment forms, visualization is intrinsic to the fundamental directorial task of communicating or interpreting a message. The director's primary goal is to entertain, inform, or persuade. To reach such a goal effectively, and with clarity, the director must consider the entire visual spectrum—everything that can be *seen* as opposed to everything that can be *heard*. Most significant within the visual spectrum are the performers' actions and their effectiveness in communicating (externalizing) an idea or emotion. Such actions communicate to the audience insights never possible with mere words. What performers *do* by far outweighs what they *say.*

Aspiring directors who despair of learning the principles of visual composition may take heart. Like story awareness, such knowledge can be acquired.

Education

The most obvious way to learn the principles of visual composition is to attend classes in art or in art history or both. Art classes offer acquaintance with the formal principles of color and composition, enlarging on the principles described in this chapter. Art history provides a look at the work of the great masters, instilling an awareness of visual aesthetics and compositional style and form. Either class (or both) enables one to put on magical spectacles and glimpse a world only dimly perceived before. Either awakens a new visual consciousness.

Observation

Watch the people who inhabit your world. See if you can tell what's going on inside their heads. Your clues are the actions they are frequently unaware of, little mannerisms that give them away. The punk who has been arrested for car theft, desperately trying to play it cool, surreptitiously licks his lips because his mouth is dry. The girl who tries to conceal her partial deafness turns her head slightly in conversation, the better to hear. The finest directors are sensitive to such actions (more about this in Chapters 5 and 6). So are the finest actors and writers. Genuinely creative people are almost always keen observers of the human condition.

Exercises

As a training exercise, jot down half a dozen observations every day—not just the revelatory actions taken by people around you but the thought or emotion that triggered each action. You will probably find that tension or insecurity motivates many of our mannerisms; nail biters, finger tappers, doodlers, and hair twirlers are everywhere. Society has trained us to conceal weaknesses, but inevitably they manifest themselves through some small action or gesture. An aware observer (you) may discover the clues that give us away.

Some games help build visual acuity. In my directing class I sometimes run short motion picture sequences for my students and then ask questions about them. Usually the sequences are action packed, crammed with exciting detail, so that students must struggle to absorb a variety of colorful images. Students who score poorly on early "tests" usually are delighted to discover that their visual acuity improves from week to week. Questions concern apparel of participants, their activities, details of the background, use of camera, and so forth. A familiar variation of this game is the picture puzzle, a still photograph crammed with a bizarre variety of visual elements. Students are given a few seconds to familiarize themselves with its contents and then are asked questions regarding the picture.

Another game consists of quizzing students about objects they see (or fail to see) in their everyday lives. For example, what letters are missing from the telephone dial? On traffic signals, is red at the top or bottom? What is the shape of a stop sign? Surprisingly, the most obvious answers often are the most difficult. The question missed most frequently in my classes: What is the color of the building we're sitting in? Such games teach us to be more visually aware of the world around us, an essential characteristic of the successful director.

Visual Storytelling

Television drama relies heavily on the spoken word to tell its story. Too often, instead of watching colorful dramatic incidents, we hear characters discussing them. One of the distinguishing characteristics of silent films was their ability to tell a story visually, without dialog. While many of these early films used title cards to help define a story or to paraphrase dialog, the best directors

(Chaplin, Griffith, Eisenstein) created films that were so visual in concept and form that they seldom required such crutches.

An excellent exercise in building visual awareness is to create a short script (five or six pages) totally without sound: no dialog, no narration, no music, no sound effects. You must tell your story completely with *visuals*, through actions and incidents. No title cards. No "talking heads." It should be written angle by angle, exactly as the final, edited version would appear. If you have difficulty in finding a concept, here's a hint: A chase is one dramatic pattern whose visual action tells its story.

If you're concerned that such an exercise appears to be writer oriented, don't be. A director's goal always is to find ways of visualizing. Such an exercise allies you with the great silent directors who invented actions and incidents that dramatized a concept totally without sound. Through gesture, facial expression, or business, they clearly conveyed to audiences a character's thoughts and emotions. That ability did not die with directors of silent films. Study current fine film or television drama. You will discover that today's best directors are highly skilled in the art of visualizing. In *Greystoke—the Legend of Tarzan*, 60 to 70 percent of the film was dramatized without words; actions revealed emotions, often with great sensitivity.

If the facilities are available to you and the costs not prohibitive, convert your short script into videotape or film. Often such projects become possible by enlisting the help of friends whose interests match yours. If you're a student, perhaps you can tackle such a project for a television or film production course. Directing a "visuals only" project will quickly reveal your ability to dramatize concepts or reveal hidden feelings through external actions. Not only will such a project be challenging and stimulating, but it will provide you with rich directorial experience.

If such a film or videotape seems impracticable, convert a key sequence in your script into a story board, that is, a series of drawings (frames) depicting the action angle by angle, exactly as the camera would photograph it. Then study the drawings objectively. See if they convey the story you intended.

CHAPTER HIGHLIGHTS

- While the stage uses dialog preponderantly, television and film place greater emphasis on visual elements. Aspiring TV and film directors, therefore, should learn the classic principles of visual composition as well as the ability to think visually.

- Visual composition is a harmonious arrangement of two or more elements, one of which dominates all others in interest. Because of the difference in screen size, TV compositions generally require greater simplicity than do motion pictures.

- Placement of the primary focus of interest depends upon a number of compositional factors. Many artists feel that placing the dominant object at the exact center of frame creates a static picture. Moving the object higher makes a more interesting composition; the space beneath the object tends to balance and support it. In closeups, when performers look to right or left, it is customary for the camera to lead them, that is, to allow more space in the direction in which they are looking. Sometimes directors deliberately minimize such space, using the resultant cramped or claustrophobic frame for psychological effect.

- Some artists and mathematicians consider the Golden Mean as a perfect location aesthetically for the primary focus of interest. Others dispute such a claim. When lines are drawn through a frame dividing it vertically and horizontally into equal thirds, the intersections approximately mark the Golden Mean.

- When two objects share a frame equally, they do not create a composition; one object must dominate. Profile two-shots, for example, usually lack interest.

- The balance of objects within a frame is governed by principles of leverage, much like children playing on a seesaw. Smaller objects at the edge of a frame balance larger objects closer to the center. Principles of dramatic emphasis affect such a balance. Thus, performers facing the camera create more weight than performers facing away.

- When several factors vie for attention, one must be given dominance. Such dominance may be achieved through contrast, placement, or line.

- When an object contrasts in size, color, tone, density, texture, or form with other objects in a frame, viewers' attention goes to the contrasting object. With two large objects and one small, for example, we tend to look at the small object.

- Other factors being equal, the object nearest the center of the frame usually attracts attention.

- The nature and the position of lines make strong emotional statements about subject matter. Horizontal lines suggest feelings of serenity or security. Vertical lines suggest strength or spirituality. A powerful method of directing spectator attention is through the intersection of lines. In Western cultures, the viewer's eyes usually enter a frame from the left and follow lines until they intersect with others, stopping and focusing on the intersection. Lines may be created by the direction in which characters look or by an arrangement of objects. A diagonal line is the most powerful means of directing spectator attention.

- In visual composition, rhythm usually implies repetition of forms, lines, masses, or colors. Such repetition is sensually pleasing.

- Visual consciousness can be acquired through classes in art and art history. It can also be acquired through active observation of the surrounding world, building an awareness of people and the mannerisms that reveal their thought processes. We can train ourselves with games that test our visual acuity. We can refine our visual awareness through the writing of short scripts that contain no sound elements, in which the story is revealed solely through character actions. Transferring such a script to film, videotape, or a simple storyboard will test its visual effectiveness.

C H A P T E R 4

Where drama begins: The script

*T*he cliché that film is a visual medium, only partially true, sometimes leads devotees to believe that the camera is a deity and that lenses, lighting, and fancy angles are the major determinants of a film's success. They regard the director as a visionary, a kind of miracle worker who takes camera and actors to a favorite location where they make up the story in a fever of inspiration, improvising whatever dialog may be necessary. Out of this mystic experience comes an award-winning videotape or film, something of vast artistic merit, with visual images that whisper of Truth and Beauty.

Such a view, of course, is absurd. The most creative director in the world, given the most sophisticated hardware devised by the human mind, cannot create a superb motion picture or television show without a superb script. An imaginative director can perform sleight of hand, adding theatricality and tempo to a dull script, making it seem better than it is. But unless there is substance in the word, there cannot be substance in the final product.

Ernest Lehman, one of film's most creative (and most rational) writers, puts it this way:

> I just happen to be one of those irrational persons who thinks a film cannot be any good if it isn't well written. It just *can't* be. And in all likelihood, if it's bad, it was badly written. Most, but not all, bad movies can be traced to a bad script.[1]

If you are a young director, or wish to be, the number one thing you've got to have is a screenplay. You can't win your millions on the roulette table unless you've got a chip to put on the numbers—and your chip in the film business is a script.   MICHAEL WINNER[2]

A script is the basic building block of any dramatic project, whether in theater, radio, videotape, or film. It is a carefully devised blueprint from which actors, director, and technicians will work. Through a succession of dramatic scenes, it presents the writer's vision of a fictitious world, a world in which characters fight battles, weep, fall in love, reach for the stars, or die . . . a world that will be shaped and interpreted by a director and communicated through actors to an audience.

Because the script is of such fundamental importance to the success of any dramatic work, the serious director must understand certain classic principles that are essential to its effectiveness as well as the do's and don'ts of contemporary scriptwriting. The classic principles of drama date back to Aristotle. They will probably apply with equal force to scripts written a thousand years from now.

In this chapter, the principles of effective scriptwriting will be described in five discussions: (1) A Person with a Problem, (2) Script Progression, (3)

[1] In *Directing the Film*, ed. Eric Sherman (Boston: Little, Brown, 1976), p. 52.

[2] As quoted by John Brady in *The Craft of the Screenwriter* (New York: Simon & Schuster, 1982), p. 179.

Drama versus Real Life, (4) Conflict, and (5) Dialog. Because of its special concerns for a director, the area of character development will be covered in Chapter 5.

A PERSON WITH A PROBLEM

Basic to plot construction is an understanding of drama itself. Some texts have made the script-building process appear formidable, dealing in structural paradigms and such abstruse intellectual concepts as unity of opposites and thesis versus antithesis. I bring good news: The basis for drama is contained in a simple five-word phrase.

As a preface to our discussion of that five-word phrase, I would like you to meet two contrasting characters. The first is Wendy Curtis, a good-hearted, open-faced young woman of twenty, secretary to her junior class in college and big sister to half the women on campus. Wendy's not really pretty but she has a grin that fools you into believing she is Miss America.

You should be aware of one additional fact: Wendy has missed her period two months in a row.

Once sure that she is pregnant, she hesitantly tells her boyfriend Rick. He is delighted. Because of financial problems, the two have repeatedly postponed getting married. Now, Wendy's pregnancy will be the catalyst for the big event. How do her parents feel about the pregnancy? They too are delighted. They have been urging the marriage for over a year.

The wedding is held in the school chapel, followed by the throwing of rice, the splashing of happy tears, and a whirlwind forty-eight-hour honeymoon.

After graduation, Rick finds a high-paying job with a California computer firm, the baby is born healthy and strong, and the couple lives happily ever after. In time, their son grows up to become president of the United States.

Before commenting on Wendy's story, I want you to meet another, equally fascinating character. Sam Gutterman is a slob: about fifty, unshaven, smelling of stale perspiration, tangled hair falling to his shoulders. Regrettably, Sam sometimes lies, cheats, and steals. He lives two flights up in a disgustingly dirty flat, debris and garbage littering the floor. People tend to avoid Sam since he doesn't bathe often and his breath reeks of cheap muscatel.

Sam glances out the window of his flat to see two police cars pulling up at the curb. The cops have come to arrest him. Why? A week ago Sam beat up a frail old lady and robbed her. Last night she died.

Sam runs out of his apartment, down the back stairs, and into the alley behind the building. As he reaches a side street, he stops in shock. A grim figure strides toward him, gun in hand. It is the old lady's husband. He has come to kill Sam.

What a terrifying dilemma! If Sam runs back into the building, he will confront the police. If he remains in the alley, he faces certain death at the hands of the old lady's husband. What can poor Sam do?

Does anyone care?

These two stories may not win Emmy awards but they provide some valuable clues to the nature of drama. Let's examine them individually.

An audience will watch Wendy Curtis's story for a while because viewers like her. They can care about her. They can root for her. But gradually the audience will grow restless, then impatient, and then will turn her off. Why? Because Wendy's story simply doesn't have a *problem*. Without a problem no story in the world will hold an audience for long. Audiences love to worry. They enjoy suffering over someone else's grief. That's what dramatic story-telling is all about. For a moment we thought that Wendy's pregnancy would create a problem. Delighted, we settled back in our easy chairs to watch her wage battles against boyfriend and parents. But instead of creating difficulties, Wendy's pregnancy eliminated them. Everyone lived happily ever after and the story became boring.

In Sam Gutterman's story we witnessed the reverse situation. Sam had a major life-or-death problem: police on one side, vengeful husband on the other. Did we worry about Sam? Did we suffer over his anguish? Not for a moment. Because Sam was a noninvolving, repellent character, it became impossible to root for him. We never experienced his terror; we didn't care what happened.

By studying the contrasting inadequacies of these two stories, we may extrapolate a pattern that will define drama's most basic structure. That pattern is contained in a simple five-word phrase, *a person with a problem*, which may be used to measure the essential dramatic characteristics of most manuscripts.

The Person

What kind of person does a protagonist (hero) have to be? A person with whom we can become *emotionally* involved. (I emphasize the word *emotionally* because emotion is what drama is all about.) Such a person does not have to be a Wendy Wonderful; most human beings are far from perfect. But protagonists must exhibit qualities that either make us want to identify with them or generate other involving emotions within us.

Wendy arouses *sympathy* and therefore viewers identify, actually becoming Wendy, suffering her problems, experiencing her triumphs. Sympathy is the emotion that most often creates audience involvement. A second attitude that allows identification is *empathy*, an understanding of the emotions that drive characters, awareness of the causal factors that make them act the way they do. Characters who inspire empathy may be less than sympathetic, but if we "know where they're coming from," we can relate to them.

A third attitude also evokes audience involvement—*antipathy*. Throughout history, drama has created audience involvement with despicable villains. Shakespeare's tragedies are filled with such figures (Lady Macbeth, Richard III, Shylock). We may not identify with such characters but they certainly generate strong emotions within us. We dislike them; we hate them; we may even despise them. Such strong emotions are surely as involving as sympathy. When we hate screen characters, we yearn to see them punished, getting what they deserve. Certain stars have built careers from such audience involvement: Erich von Stroheim ("the man you love to hate"), Bela Lugosi, Vincent Price, Larry Hagman (J. R. on "Dallas"), and others.

Thus, the "person" in the five-word definition of drama must generate audience involvement through *sympathy, empathy,* or *antipathy.* The greater the degree of emotional involvement, the more the spectators will forgive any script (or other) shortcomings. Witness the many foreign art films with a minimum of plot but with captivating characters that compel us to watch.

As a director, you will discover that the audience need for personal involvement has many practical applications. For example, if a scripted protagonist performs actions or makes speeches that in any way diminish spectator involvement, those speeches or actions should be carefully examined, rewritten, or perhaps excised. Occasionally directors begin a project with a "grey" character, one weak in terms of arousing audience emotions. If such a character cannot be enriched in the script, the director has a final recourse: to cast an actor whose appearance, personal magnetism, or apparent vulnerability will capture an audience's sympathy.

The Problem

Problems arise in scripts in two different ways. In the first, a protagonist blithely attends the chores of everyday life when BLAM!—a problem descends unexpectedly from the blue. Suddenly the protagonist's life disintegrates. He or she must struggle to stay afloat, attempting to escape or to destroy the problem. A kidnapping story demonstrates this pattern perfectly.

Mary Lou Hennessy walks home from school with a friend. A black limousine screeches to a stop at the curb, two heavyset men leap out, shove the friend aside, grab Mary Lou, throw her into the vehicle, and drive off. The problem has descended from nowhere. Inevitably it will get worse before it resolves. The movies *E.T., the Extraterrestrial, Poltergeist,* and *Jaws* are examples of this kind of problem, as are most detective stories.

The second kind of problem, far more common, is created when someone in opposition (an antagonist) tries to keep the hero from attaining an important personal goal. Cinderella wants to go to the ball to meet the handsome prince. Stepmother and ugly stepsisters forbid her to go. They become Cinderella's problem, the obstacle she must overcome. In many of the old fairy tales the prince asks for the hand of the beautiful princess. If you recall, her father the king always requires him to perform some herculean task first, such as slaying the three-headed dragon: a dramatic obstacle to prevent the prince from reaching his goal.

Note that in both patterns the protagonist has a *goal*. In both patterns the protagonist must overcome inimical forces in order to reach that goal. A series of struggles ensues, a tug of war; the protagonist either achieves the goal or fails.

The nature of dramatic problems seems simple enough, yet experienced writers sometimes lose sight of the need for that simplicity. They become entangled in character relationships, complicated subplots, and parallel story threads. Somewhere during the writing process the primary thrust of a story is lost. Frequently, early drafts of screenplays become more literary than dramatic in form, wandering from episode to episode. As a result, the script loses focus; it loses clarity; it loses energy. Most importantly, it loses or diminishes the requirements of "a person with a problem."

One additional point concerning the problem: *Establish it early.* Producer-director Nat Perrin describes a funny little man with a black beard and black hat who carries in his hands one of those round, black bombs you have seen in comic strips. At some point in every show, says Perrin, the little man walks on stage carrying his bomb. He deposits it on the stage floor, lights a match, and sets the fuse spluttering. Until the fuse—your story problem—has been lighted, the audience is free to leave the theater. Once it is spluttering, the audience will remain seated, waiting apprehensively for the explosion they know will come.

Generally, motion picture audiences are more patient that those seated before a TV set. They have parked their cars and paid their admission; they will give you time to introduce your problem in a more leisurely fashion. Writer Syd Field says you have about ten minutes.[3] But in television, when viewers sit with remote controls in their hands, you'd better introduce that problem quickly, usually in the first three or four minutes, before they press the dreaded button that turns you off.

When reading a script for a directorial project, consider its *person with a*

---

[3] Syd Field, *Screenplay* (New York: Delta, 1979), pp. 8–9.

problem. Can you become emotionally involved with a major character? Deeply involved? Does that character have a clearly defined goal? If not, the writer will have to crystallize that goal. And is some person or force trying to keep your protagonist from reaching his or her goal, thereby creating a problem?

SCRIPT PROGRESSION

One reason why a specific, definable goal is so important to an effective script is that a goal implies *movement.* Movement is an integral part of drama; it keeps spectators attentive as the story grows or builds in a series of struggles. With developments favoring first the protagonist, then the adversary, the problem continually worsens.

When we try to reach the treasure at the top of a mountain, we first have to climb that mountain. Our movement is focused in a single direction: upward. When an adversary (the weather, our own fears, the abominable snowman) tries to stop us, the forward movement becomes a series of skirmishes, taking us closer to the treasure or forcing a retreat back down the mountain. That dramatic movement has traditionally been visualized as a diagram resembling a jagged fork of lightning, as shown in Figure 4.1. The ascending line (resembling our climb up the mountain) represents drama's rising action. A story builds in tension through a series of minor crises to a climax that resolves the protagonist's problem. The diagram indicates the development of three major crises: the classic three-act pattern. It's interesting to note that most feature motion pictures are constructed in three-act patterns although, of course, there is usually no curtain or other definitive separation between crises.

DRAMA VERSUS REAL LIFE

While some theorists believe that the closer a dramatic work approaches reality the more effective it becomes, the director should understand that drama and real life are significantly different. Scriptwriters try to make audiences believe that they are watching reality. In truth, spectators watch a carefully devised illusion. Dramatic re-creation is far from literal; characters and events only appear to mirror life. If writers are genuinely creative, however, their scenes will contain the essence of life.

Two major characteristics separate drama from real life: (1) *economy,*

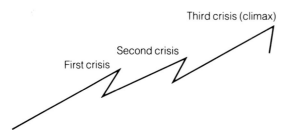

Figure 4.1   The ascending line of the lightning bolt represents drama's rising action through a series of crises.

selecting only those incidents, characters, and speeches that are significant (accentuating the positive, eliminating the negative); and (2) *logic*, which implies a kind of dramatic inevitability.

Economy

Several years ago, director Craig Gilbert took a camera and sound crew to the Santa Barbara, California, home of Pat and William Loud. His concept: to do a *cinéma vérité* study of an actual American family, filmed in their home day by day. For seven months Gilbert's camera recorded each day's most significant events, beginning at 8:30 or 9:00 in the morning and continuing sometimes until 10:00 at night.

Gilbert was lucky. While his camera was present, two extraordinary events occurred. Pat and William Loud decided to end their marriage of many years, and their son Lance, who had been living in New York, returned home to shock his family with the revelation that he was gay.

In all, Gilbert filmed 300 hours. His crew ignored the humdrum routine of everyday life, the banal details that would have little audience appeal. Instead, they turned on their camera and microphones only for those incidents that promised to be interesting, truly representative or significant. The cream.

When the program was broadcast on PBS as "An American Family," the 300 hours had been edited down to 12. The director thus had a rare opportunity to air only his most dramatic material, eliminating 288 hours or 96 percent. But the cream somehow had turned sour.

While Gilbert's exercise was hailed by some as a sociological milestone, it was generally flayed by critics. Ratings were minuscule. I personally saw only two episodes. They were so dull that I could barely sit through them. It is true that the show was never intended to be viewed as drama, but it still failed to generate any substantial degree of spectator interest, much less excitement or suspense, despite two major dramatic happenings.

Why was the material dull? Alas, real life frequently is. Because real-life incidents are sometimes *dramatic* does not make them *drama*.

Listen to conversations at your dinner table, on the bus, or in restaurants. You'll find that people repeat themselves endlessly, wander all around the subject, and bring in meaningless and unnecessary details, even when their stories are exciting ones.

A skilled scriptwriter practices dramatic economy in three areas: *dialog, characters*, and *scenes*. The writer pares away unnecessary or cluttering words of dialog, boiling speeches down to their essence. Because writers strive to create the illusion of reality, speeches retain the sound of everyday life but the excesses have carefully been deleted. The writer economizes with characters, eliminating those not essential. Examine almost any book that has been adapted into a motion picture. The film inevitably uses only a fraction of the book's characters. The award-winning film *Kramer versus Kramer* retained only one-fourth of the characters in the novel. The writer also economizes on the number of scenes. If a scene does not contribute a new plot development or reveal something new about a principal character, it probably should be deleted.

If the scriptwriter has not practiced these economies, you, as director, must. The time to eliminate excesses is before a show is photographed. Shooting a scene that will eventually be edited out of a picture wastes everyone's time and money. Unnecessary characters clutter up the show, taking attention away from central characters. Unnecessary dialog destroys the effectiveness of speeches, dissipating their energy and muddying their ideas (see examples later in the chapter). Wise directors get rid of the "fat" and use only the "lean."

Logic

The second characteristic that separates drama from real life is logic. Drama is structured logically; real life is not.

Ben Chapman urgently needs $20,000. Two weeks ago his daughter was injured in a hit-and-run accident, placing her eyesight in jeopardy. The $20,000 will fly her to Boston for needed surgery. Ben doesn't have even $1,000. The medical bills have depleted the family savings and Ben has been out of work for months. Now, on his way home from the employment office, Ben sighs at the gross impossibility of obtaining such a large sum of money. As he walks, he spots a bulging manila envelope on the pavement. He stoops and picks it up, opens the clasp, and glances inside. What do you suppose the envelope contains? How did you ever guess? It contains *money*! Almost $21,000!

Because Ben's an honest man, he reports his find to the police and advertises for the owner in newspapers. No one claims the money and so Ben is allowed to keep it. His daughter has the operation and regains her eyesight. What an incredible stroke of good fortune!

Such a human interest story might appear in a newspaper but never in a carefully crafted dramatic script. Why not? Because the solution to Ben's problem did not emerge logically from the fabric of his story. The writer conveniently handed it to him. In ancient Greek tragedy, problems sometimes were solved in the last act of a play when a golden chariot descended from the flies (area above stage). Out stepped a god who produced a miracle, instantly solving everyone's problems. Such convenient solutions, *deus ex machina* (god out of the machine), generally are rejected by audiences who regard them as cheating; the writer apparently could find no legitimate way of ending the story.

Because drama is logical, events that occur in the third act should grow out of elements established in the first two acts. Events occurring in the second act should grow out of material established in the first. The solution to a problem cannot descend conveniently from the blue sky. As with Ben's discovery of the manila envelope, such easy solutions smack of coincidence. Since coincidence defies the laws of logic, it plays a limited role in drama.

Is coincidence ever allowed? Yes, a writer may use coincidence on only two occasions in a script. First, coincidence may appear at the beginning of a story. Many of Alfred Hitchcock's most successful films began with outrageous coincidences. In *North by Northwest*, for example, the advertising executive played by Cary Grant called for a telephone in New York's Plaza Bar, mistakenly convincing foreign spies that he was a CIA agent, thus plunging him into a bizarre series of misadventures. Audiences accept such initial coincidences with the apparent rationale that had the coincidence not occurred, the story would never have taken place.

Second, coincidence is also accepted by audiences when it worsens the protagonist's problem. When a small boy fleeing through a labyrinth of caves accidentally bumps into one of his pursuers, the accident (coincidence) not only is acceptable but is savored by audiences. The writer isn't taking shortcuts to solve a protagonist's problem. On the contrary, the boy is now in deeper trouble than before and the writer must work harder to extricate him. As I indicated earlier, audiences love to worry. Coincidences that give them more to worry about are gratefully accepted.

As a director, when you encounter a script in which the writer has used coincidence unacceptably to solve a problem, you must either *eliminate it* by solving the problem in a different fashion or *set it up* in such a way that the coincidence appears logical. You can set up a coincidence by laying the groundwork for it earlier in the script.

Let's take the example of Ben Chapman's convenient discovery of an envelope containing money. How can we make that discovery appear logical, an outgrowth of what has gone before? Perhaps by revealing how the money came to be there. If, for example, the writer has woven another thread into the fabric of the story, a thread in which bank robbers from another state had lost a portion of their booty, then the audience would be prepared for Ben's discovering it on a city street. In this circumstance, the robbers might read Ben's newspaper advertisement but would be afraid to come forward, fearing a police trap. Once a coincidence grows out of earlier plot circumstances, it can no longer be labelled coincidence.

CONFLICT

We have established that one of drama's primary ingredients is a *problem*, but how should that problem be dramatized? Through a series of struggles between protagonist and antagonist, a continuing tug of war that seems to favor first one and then the other. Defining the struggle and itself part of drama's essential nature is the element of *conflict*.

While we discussed conflict in Chapter 2 as an element of entertainment and, accordingly, part of a director's bag of tricks, we discuss it here as a prime ingredient of drama. The atavistic search for conflict is certainly one of the reasons for the theater's continuing appeal century after century, whether on stage, on a TV or movie screen, or in a Punch and Judy show. Conflict lies at the core of drama: protagonist pitted against antagonist, often in a life-or-death arena, with the spectator vicariously experiencing the pains and thrills of battle.

Patterns of Conflict

Traditionally, conflict has fallen into three categories: conflict with others, conflict with the environment, and conflict with self. With the release of so many fantasy films in recent years I might add a fourth category that doesn't precisely fit the others: conflict with the supernatural.

Of the four, conflict with others appears most often on TV and movie screens. A sheriff in pursuit of a vicious desperado, a student bickering with her boyfriend, a boxer challenging a hated foe, are all variations on the theme. Most well-written drama includes more than one type of conflict.

Conflict with the environment usually is dramatized in terms of conflict with nature or conflict with society. The sheriff pursuing the desperado changes categories when the scriptwriter sends him across a parched desert, fighting the merciless sun, a dwindling water supply, and snakebite. The novel and feature film *1984* ideally demonstrate the subcategory, conflict with society.

When the sheriff captures the desperado and begins the long trek home, the desperado reveals his humanity by saving the sheriff's life. (We've all seen this one, haven't we?) Now the sheriff faces a torturing dilemma. Can he turn the desperado over to a town that will certainly lynch him? Or must he betray the town's trust by allowing the desperado to break free? The story has developed into the richest kind of conflict, in which a protagonist must wrestle with his or her conscience—conflict with self.

Conflict: A Useful Tool

When scenes don't work, when they seem pale and vapid, they frequently lack the seeds of conflict. Some of you may find it difficult to believe that every scene is richer if it contains conflict. *Every* scene? Surely not *every* scene! I promise you: Conflict can only improve a scene, provided it has honest motivation. A scene between two people who completely agree with each other about everything probably should not contain conflict. But neither should a writer devise such an empty scene.

Conflict takes many forms. It may be overt, expressing itself in shouted words and violent actions. It may lie buried beneath the surface, simmering, steaming, adding pressure—coloring the words of the players or revealed only through a concealed gesture, fingers twisting paper or fists clenching. It may emerge as gentle teasing, as banter between a boy and a girl, mocking words that still express the language of love.

A detective format often creates problems for both writer and director, problems that may be resolved by adding a judicious bit of conflict. In the early stages of most investigative shows, the protagonist must gather clues. The process usually involves confronting a number of people who may or may not shed light on the circumstances surrounding the crime. If the investigator secures answers quickly or easily, each scene is dull. A succession of such scenes would turn any show into a bowl of lukewarm jelly.

The investigator visits the murder victim's landlady. "Good afternoon, ma'am. I'm investigating the killing of Natalie Plum. Was she living here on July 7?"

"Yes, she was."

"Did you see her after that date?"

"No."

"Did she receive any visitors?"

"No. Never."

"Thank you very much."

End of scene. The investigator gets in his European sports car and drives off. An exciting scene? Suspenseful? About as suspenseful as watching whiskers grow.

If we make the investigator's job more difficult, the scene suddenly becomes interesting. Let's assume that the youthful landlady is attracted to the investigator and wants him to come inside and have a drink with her. But he's in a hurry. He doesn't have time for a drink. When he tries to obtain information, the landlady has trouble remembering. She invites him again to have a beer. The businesslike investigator refuses, hammering away with his questions. When the landlady continues to hem and haw, he finally realizes (he's a little slow!) that the only way he will get straight answers is to indulge this lady. Inside, over a beer and popcorn, he secures the information he needs; the landlady gets the companionship she needs, and they make a date to see each other again.

The detective then goes to a seventy-year-old inventor, seeking information. But the inventor doesn't have time for foolish questions. He must finish his invention today. He tries to shoo the investigator away. Our hero keeps pressing, humoring the flaky old man, admiring his invention, and eventually gets the information he needs.

He talks to a child of three or four who has a vivid imagination. The boy has trouble separating reality from fantasy. Now the investigator must labor to find the truth, perhaps bribing the youngster with an ice cream cone.

Any of these scenes could be played in a dull question-and-answer pattern. Instead, they spark our interest through the addition of entertainment elements and colorful characters—and something more. Something far more significant than colorful characters. In each of the above situations I have devised a way for *conflict* to enter the scene. When the protagonist found his answers easily, the scenes were boring. When the going became *difficult*, the scenes became entertaining.

There's a major lesson here about drama and about life. Things easily obtained seem to have little value. Goals that we must struggle diligently to achieve, clawing our way past formidable obstacles, take on increased value. In any dramatic situation, make life difficult for your protagonist by keeping the goal elusive. Allow your audience the luxury of worrying. They'll love you for it!

Character Contrast

Characters with an identical point of view, the same ethnic, cultural, and political backgrounds, rarely argue. When they play scenes together, they agree with smiles on almost every issue. Such scenes inevitably are dull because they lack conflict. Both writers and directors should search for contrasting characters whenever possible because contrast tends to create richer scenes than similarity. Contrasting characters create texture through varying points of view. They create tension by making the scene's outcome problematic. They create entertainment through the sparks of conflict.

A marked contrast between leading characters brings such strength to any dramatic concept that it has formed the spine of countless stage plays and feature films as well as entire television series. Neil Simon's *The Odd Couple* is the prototype: the effete, meticulous, sensitive Felix Unger sharing an apartment with heavy-drinking, cigar-smoking Oscar Madison, a man of sloppy personal habits and animal appetites. No matter what situation a writer devised for the TV series, the odd couple faced it and struggled to solve it with conflicting attitudes. No matter what the plot progression, their opposing points of view placed them on a collision course and stories inevitably erupted into open warfare.

Realizing that contrasting characters create dramatic tension, wise directors search for ways to build differing attitudes into characters in scripts and, whenever possible, to reinforce those contrasts in casting.

DIALOG

Since dialog is the most apparent of a script's elements, it generally receives more scrutiny than any of the others. Yet surprisingly, in spite of meticulous examination by writers, producers, directors, and actors, speeches in most motion pictures and TV programs are less than excellent. Such lack of quality undermines the illusion of reality that a production team works so hard to establish. It undermines spectator involvement with characters. If sufficiently off the mark, poor dialog can even invite embarrassed laughter from the audience.

Because dialog is such an overt expression of a character, aware directors give early attention to its effectiveness. If dissatisfied, they call for script rewrites prior to production, rather than wait to find out whether the words will fit comfortably into actors' mouths. Such directors understand the following critical dialog factors: economy, simplicity, characteristic speech, and invisibility.

ECONOMY

In examining the differences between drama and real life, we noted earlier that economy is an essential dramatic principle. Nowhere is it more necessary than in the writing of dialog. When thoughts are restated, audiences become bored. When unnecessary words clutter a speech, ideas appear muddled. Experienced professionals examine dialog meticulously, stripping each speech to its essentials.

The fact that good dialog is spare, however, doesn't mean that you should remove words simply because they don't contribute to the plot. Often dialog helps create an understanding of a character or establish a mood. Such dialog, obviously, should not be amputated in the name of economy.

Many television shows contain excessive dialog. Their writers probably have discovered that telling a story through dialog takes less effort than searching for visual ways to dramatize an idea. Such writers fall into the stage-play pattern in which characters tend to talk about offstage events. In the theater such descriptive dialog is necessary because limited stage space doesn't allow the proper dramatization of large-scale, physical events. In television and film, however, no such limitations exist. Good writers know that it's vastly more effective to show a piece of action than to talk about it. Dramatizing an action is vivid. For the viewer, seeing an event provides far greater impact than merely hearing someone describe it.

Occasionally, an event's effect upon a character becomes more significant than the event itself. In such circumstances, the character's description should certainly be dramatized. For example, when a newlywed's husband is killed in an automobile accident, she is devastated. Her broken description provides greater impact—certainly far more emotion—than a dramatization of the accident itself. Such a circumstance, however, is an exception. Generally, it makes good dramatic sense to show the event rather than talk about it.

Chapter 6 discusses the fact that dialog is often unreliable, that actions frequently are more revealing—and more trustworthy—than the words characters speak.

Simplicity

If you're like me, when you were writing essays in high school you tried to impress your English teachers by using as many big words as you knew—and perhaps a few you didn't know. (My particular favorites were *omnipotent* and *omniscient.* I managed to work them into every essay I wrote.) While big words inevitably appear in high school essays and term papers, they don't occur often in everyday speech.

Listen to the conversations of your family and friends. How often do the words *omnipotent* or *omniscient* crop up? Not often. The words most of us use in everyday speech are short, simple, easy to say. They convey our thoughts easily, without getting in the way of meaning or calling attention to themselves.

Good writers are aware of this simplicity of speech. The characters they create generally speak in short, declarative sentences with one- and two-syllable words. If you have access to motion picture or television scripts (many have been anthologized), read them carefully. Note how simple the words are. Note that even the most profound thoughts can be expressed in everyday one-syllable words.

As a director, if you are unsure of speeches, if they seem false or manufactured, *read them out loud*. There is a great difference between dialog in novels and dialog in well-written scripts. The acid test is that the speeches must be capable of being spoken aloud. They must sound spontaneous, as if the thoughts they express had just occurred to the character. Stilted speech patterns, complex sentences, or difficult words will be immediately apparent when you read the words aloud. The solution to "unspeakable" dialog usually is to simplify it.

Most of us know people who delight in using long words. Some doctors, research scientists, and college professors use erudite or esoteric words as a badge of their professions. When these characters appear in a script, they may become valid exceptions to the rule of simplicity. They may. Among my acquaintances are about thirty college professors and half a dozen doctors. How do they speak? Mostly in one-syllable words. Pass a college professor on the street and he'll say, "Hi! How you doin'?" just like everyone else. Face it: Most people, most of the time, speak in short, simple sentences of short, simple words. Even doctors, scientists, and college professors.

Characteristic Speech

Speech patterns vary, depending on where the speakers come from and the socioeconomic world they live in. Most of us as we grow up tend to echo the speech patterns of our parents. If we live in the South or the East or the Midwest, our speech reflects the phrases and patterns and intonations of the area. When we move away to college, our speech is affected and partially transformed by our new friends and the speech patterns of the college area. When we enter the business community, our speech changes again, its vocabulary enlarging and absorbing the technical jargon of our new professions.

Each person has a way of speaking that is unique. One person watching a touchdown on television will exclaim, "Dynamite!" Another will say, "Awesome!" A third might mutter a four-letter word. Members of each subculture create their own speech fads, invent words, and change meanings. Many of these fads eventually drift into the mainstream of our language.

In a well-written speech, each character has a distinctive speech pattern, consistent from scene to scene. Scripts in which speeches can be interchanged between characters usually reflect an inept or insensitive writer.

When you read a script dealing with racetrack touts or oil well drillers or bacteriologists and their dialog seems drab and colorless, lacking the pungent smell of reality, what can you as a director do? First, you can prevail upon the producer to hire another writer who either understands the characters or is willing to research them. Second, you can enter that world yourself, absorbing its color and flavor, talking at length with its inhabitants, studying their attitudes, listening to their speech patterns and vocabulary, familiarizing yourself with their lifestyle. Take along a tape recorder. Bring back conversations that will be helpful to your actors. Such research contributes far more than dialog accuracy. It provides you with the ambience of your character's world, helping you to re-create that world with a vividness possible only from firsthand observation.

Lacking the time to conduct in-person research, you can visit the public library and read about the world your characters live in. Books and magazines often provide valuable insights. If you find particularly revealing material, make photocopies that you can give to cast members.

Invisibility

Directors, writers, and actors labor to make audiences believe that they are watching an actual event, to make them become emotionally involved in that event. The moment spectators become conscious of contrivance, either from intrusive music or a flashy directorial fillip or overacting, the illusion promptly disappears. Writing that calls attention to itself similarly shatters the illusion of reality. A writer showing off through use of "clever" dialog simply reminds the audience that the words are not the spontaneous, honest expressions of a character but speeches contrived by a writer.

What about the comedies of Mel Brooks and Woody Allen? What about such flashy comedy-adventure films as the James Bond series? The humorous, clever, or bizarre dialog in those films certainly calls attention to itself. Of course. Those shows seldom try to convince audiences that they are watching reality. Spectators usually remain aware that what they are watching is an exercise in theatricality, fun and games. Reality has been abandoned. In comedy, anything that gets a laugh is justified. In shows that seek genuine audience involvement, however, the production elements must remain invisible.

Bad Dialog: What to Do With It

The word *corny* is often used to describe bad dialog. It's an all-inclusive term that generally indicates artificial, melodramatic, or old-fashioned speeches. Usually there is a specific, definable reason why a line sounds corny. Directors working with writers have an obligation to define for them as specifically as possible why a scene doesn't work or what is wrong with its dialog.

The following short scene is guaranteed to win prizes at any film festival for "Most Disastrous Dialog of the Year." See if you can determine the reason why each of the following lines seems so corny.

INT. APARTMENT - FULL SHOT - DAY

Greg watches a soap opera on television, sipping occasionally from a bottle of beer. Suddenly the door swings open and Lorna strides in angrily. Greg rises in surprise.

> GREG
>
> Lorna! What are you doing home from work two and a half hours early?

> LORNA
>
> I'm leaving you, Greg. I'm through, finished. I've had it up to here.

> GREG
>
> What do you mean, leaving?

> LORNA
>
> Did you think I didn't know about Julia Murphy? About the apartment over on North Elm Street that you two have been sharing for thirteen months?

She snaps off the television set angrily.

> LORNA
> (continuing)
> How long did you think you could pull the wool over my eyes? All those weekends you said you were visiting your mother! Well, your mother has been in Europe for months, Greg, so you couldn't have been visiting her!

> GREG
>
> Lorna, *listen* to me . . .

> LORNA
>
> What for? So you can lie to me again? Don't you understand, Greg? I hate you. I can't stand the sight of you.

She takes a gun from her purse.

> GREG
>
> Where did you get that gun?

> LORNA
>
> I'm going to kill you, Greg. I'm going to shoot you. I'm going to put a bullet through your heart. You're just so much excess baggage now.

> GREG
>
> Lorna, in the name of God. . . .

> LORNA
>
> Goodbye, Greg.

> GREG
>
> Lorna. . . .

She fires the gun and Greg collapses to the floor.

An incredibly bad scene with incredibly bad dialog. Why is it so bad? Let's examine the scene line by line and determine the reasons—if you think you can stomach it again.

First line: "Lorna, what are you doing home from work two and a half hours early?" Why does the line seem artificial? Because the writer has added unnecessary words just for the audience's benefit, to feed information. While it may be significant that Lorna is home early, the two and a half hours are totally gratuitous. Would Greg (or anyone) honestly say that? Never.

In any script there is always certain information that an audience requires in order to understand what the story is all about. Such information is called *exposition*. A skilled writer works it into dialog unobtrusively; spectators never become aware that they are being spoon-fed. Indifferent writers dump exposition on spectators heavy-handedly. The worst offenses are scenes in which two characters state facts that both already know, facts that appear in dialog solely because the author needs to explain them to the audience. That's why Greg asks, "What are you doing home from work two and a half hours early?" Wouldn't the line be more honest if he simply said, "Hi, you're home early."

Next line: "I'm leaving you, Greg. I'm through, finished. I've had it up to here." One of the major lapses in any kind of writing (of course) is the use of hackneyed figures of speech. This scene contains three or four of them. "I've had it up to here" is a particularly stomach-wrenching example. Others include "How long did you think you could pull the wool over my eyes?" and "You're just so much excess baggage." All of those lines are excess baggage. Clichés.

Lorna's speech contains other problems. As we have discussed, effective dialog is usually *economical*. In this speech Lorna expresses the same thought in four different ways. The line would be vastly improved if she stated it only once: "I'm leaving you, Greg." Also, just as drama builds from scene to scene and act to act, so does healthy dialog build from the least important thought in a speech to the most important. (For example: A few of the soldiers had been wounded. A few had lost limbs. A few were becoming dust on some forgotten battlefield.) Lorna's speech does not build at all. It merely states and restates a single idea.

In another Lorna speech later in the scene, her lines actually diminish in importance. "I'm going to kill you, Greg. I'm going to shoot you. I'm going to put a bullet in your heart. You're just so much excess baggage now." Such a reverse progression—building downward—sometimes triggers audience laughter. Lajos Egri recalls a classic line that warns against murder because it may lead to drinking which may lead to smoking which may lead to nonobservance of the Sabbath![4] Reversing the normal dramatic growth makes excellent humor—but dreadful dialog!

Next line: "What do you mean, leaving?" Poor Greg doesn't have a single meaty speech in the entire scene; they are all *feed lines*, relatively meaningless words that have been inserted for the sole purpose of breaking up Lorna's speeches. We could erase almost all of Greg's lines and the scene would lose nothing. Occasionally every writer must invent words in order to keep a character "alive" in a scene, to prevent the dominant character's speeches from becoming a monolog. But "What do you mean" lines are a most tired and feeble invention.

Next: "Did you think I didn't know about Julia Murphy? About the apartment over on North Elm Street that you two have been sharing for thirteen months?" More dishonest exposition, words inserted solely for the audience's benefit. All Lorna has to say is, "I know about Julia."

Do you notice a pattern emerging? To improve each of these speeches the writer must prune, make the lines simpler and more honest, apply the first rule for writing dialog: economize.

As you read the scene, you may become conscious of a pattern that many inexperienced writers fall into—using character names too frequently. Do

---

[4]*The Art of Dramatic Writing* (New York: Simon & Schuster, 1946), p. 242.

you repeat the names of friends each time you address them? Of course not. It would sound ludicrous. Yet in the above scene, Lorna and Greg call each other by name in almost every speech.

"I'm going to kill you, Greg."

"Lorna, in the game of God. . . ."

"Goodbye, Greg."

"Lorna!"

There is one place where names are essential and that is when a character is first introduced. The audience needs help. Who is this new character? What is his or her relationship to characters we've already met? Viewers are grateful when someone pins a label on the new character by calling him or her by name. Clues to the character's identity—"Bob, I want you to meet my mother" or "Mom, this is my boyfriend, Tim"—will orient the audience.

Two final points may be helpful. The first concerns Greg's line, "Where did you get that gun?" Aside from being rather stupid (who cares where she got the gun?), the line is significant because it is a throwback to an earlier era. Today's TV viewers are generally too young to recall radio plays in which dialog had to describe what was happening because audiences couldn't see it. Radio drama was one-dimensional: sound only. It forced audiences to use their imaginations; they created dramatic action, scenery, characters' faces, and costumes in their minds. But the writer had to give the audience clues. Therefore, the characters in radio plays used to utter lines such as "What's that on the floor? Good Lord, it's a body!" And "Darling, your face is all bruised. Have you been in a fight?" And "Where did you get that gun?"

Radio lines, of course, are unnecessary in a visual medium. Yet, surprisingly, they creep into scripts again and again. When they do, use your blue pencil.

Finally, much of the scene's phony melodrama arises from the fact that its dialog is "on the nose." *On the nose* is a phrase used by industry professionals to indicate dialog (or other dramatic aspects) that is blunt and heavy-handed. When a line is stated in the most obvious way, allowing the viewer no room for interpretation or participation, it's on the nose.

When a scene is as melodramatic as the Lorna–Greg confrontation, you can bring a greater degree of reality to it—and avoid being on the nose—by "playing against" the melodrama. The concept of *playing against* something simply means taking a different dramatic tack, going to the opposite extreme. For example, keeping the dialog simple and honest would undercut the potential melodrama in the above confrontation, making it more believable. So would the addition of wry or sardonic humor.

As a director, you can play against the thrust of a tragic scene merely by changing the attitudes of the players. If you allow your characters to wear mournful faces, feeling sorry for themselves, your scene will instantly turn to soap. If you play against the tragedy, if your characters pretend that the sadness doesn't exist, if they play it lightly, making jokes to cover their inner pain, then your scene will become enormously moving.

A DIRECTOR'S CHECKLIST

In examining a script for any directorial project, ask yourself these questions:

1. Is the concept original and fresh or is it clichéd? A genuinely fresh concept compensates for a dozen problems. An original concept justifies all of the work necessary to study, discuss, rewrite, and polish otherwise second-rate material. Stated another way, is the story worth telling?

2. Does the script contain a protagonist you can care about, root for, become emotionally involved with? Can you find a way to increase the depth of spectator involvement?

3. Does the protagonist face a single, major problem? Does the problem emerge from a powerful, perhaps frightening antagonist?

4. Is the element of conflict present in each of the scenes and as an undercurrent (tension) throughout the script?

5. Does the story (and tension) continually develop, build, progress? Does the script contain unnecessary scenes that simply restate plot or character points? If so, they must be deleted.

6. Does the dialog meet the chapter's standards of economy, simplicity, vernacularism, and spontaneity? Does it fall into any of the traps described in the bad dialog scene?

CHAPTER HIGHLIGHTS

- Since the success of any dramatic project depends in large part on the effectiveness of its script, aware directors understand the classic principles of dramatic construction as well as the specific do's and don'ts of successful scriptwriting.

- *A person with a problem:* This convenient five-word phrase contains the essence of what drama is. The person must involve audiences emotionally. The stronger the involvement, the more the viewers will care about a protagonist's (hero's) goals or problems. Audience involvement may emerge from feelings of sympathy, empathy, or antipathy.

- The problem comes into a drama in two ways: (1) it descends from the blue unexpectedly, creating havoc in the hero's life, or (2) it results from someone's attempt to keep the hero from reaching a worthwhile goal. Note that in both patterns the problem is goal related. In the first instance, the hero's goal is simply to escape from the calamity that has befallen him or her.

- Drama traditionally builds in tension. The hero's problem worsens from act to act and audience apprehension grows. This fundamental climbing, building, growing action is central to drama.

- Drama is not reality; it is the *illusion* of reality. Skilled writers and directors are able to convince audiences that the illusion is real. Two basic factors separate drama from real life: economy and logic. Real life is frequently boring, filled with repetition, irrelevance, and meaningless detail. Drama prevents boredom by selecting the meat of a story and trimming away the unnecessary fat. Real life is frequently illogical, filled with coincidence and happenstance. Drama, in contrast, is almost mathematically logical, building into its structure the elements necessary to its growth and resolution.

- Fundamental to drama, conflict is the natural manifestation of the hero's problem. When some antagonistic force tries to prevent the hero from achieving a goal, conflict is inevitable. Such struggles take one of four forms: conflict with others (one or more personal antagonists), conflict with the environment (usually nature or society), conflict with the supernatural, and conflict with self. Most well-written drama contains more than one form of conflict. By building contrasts into characters—contrasts in race, background, or point of view—directors can assure themselves that conflict will inevitably emerge.

- Good dialog generally is *simple*. Regardless of their professions or lifestyles, most people speak in short, declarative sentences of one- and two-syllable words. Good dialog is *economical*; it is not repetitious; it contains no unnecessary or irrelevant detail. Good dialog is in the *vernacular* of the character who speaks it. Good dialog does not call attention to itself.

- Dialog does not replace action. Skilled writers dramatize events rather than allow their characters to talk about them. For audiences, witnessing an action carries far more impact than descriptive words.

- Bad or corny dialog results from clichés; awkward or inept exposition (giving information to audience); "on the nose" lines that are blunt, obvious, and heavy-handed; "radio lines" that describe what viewers can see; and a failure to build speeches effectively.

- Good writers try to "play against" melodrama or tragedy to keep scenes from becoming corny or soapy. They take a different approach to dialog than the expected, playing light or humorous dialog in a tragic scene and simple, honest dialog in a melodramatic scene.

C H A P T E R 5

Finding the characters

*T*he director's concept of a character begins with skeletal clues provided by the writer. In time, as that concept is discussed, evaluated, reshaped, and enriched by director and actor, the skeleton acquires muscle and sinew, flesh and blood. On the soundstage, before video or film cameras, it acquires life.

Where do directors find the characteristics that transform skeletal clues into a dimensional human being? In the same place that actors do: the reservoir of their entire background of experience. When a director reads a script, its characters stir vague memories, perhaps consciously, perhaps un-consciously—memories of everyone in the director's past life, real or imag-ined, who might somehow relate to the character in question: family, friends, casual acquaintances, characters in books or magazines or from the stage or screen. Sometimes only fragmentary characteristics spring to mind: a way of walking, a gesture, a facial expression, a childhood trauma. Imagination will synthesize both characters and characteristics, rearranging them into possible prototypes of the scripted character.

In this chapter we will discuss ways in which directors build upon those imagined prototypes, giving them shape through comprehensive personal notes. From these notes, directors fashion a detailed character background that they share and explore with the actor chosen to play each role. We will examine methods of revealing that character to an audience and the concept of characters wearing masks. We will study some psychological factors in fashioning a dimensional character, and finally, we will examine some of the subtleties of capturing that character on film or videotape.

You imagine yourself the person that the author has written, and you sink yourself into that. Then out of your throat comes, perhaps, quite a different voice.   LYNN FONTANNE[1]

A DIRECTOR'S NOTES

Before studying characters, a director logically must study the script, determining the role of each character in relation to the play's theme or central meaning. Serious directors often prepare pages of notes for themselves, attempting to define the writer's overall purpose and the goals or drives of each primary character. To the best of my knowledge, directorial notes for a film production have never been published. But excellent notes for stage plays have been published occasionally and offer the student a rare opportunity to gain insights into the thought patterns and preparational procedures of topflight theatrical directors.[2]

The Story Spine

The central meaning of a play often is called its *spine*, a term popularized by director Harold Clurman. He adapted the word from a term used by acting

---

[1]*Actors Talk About Acting*, ed. Lewis Funke and John E. Booth (New York: Avon Books, 1963), p. 27.

[2]See *Directors on Directing*, ed. Toby Cole and Helen Krich Chinoy (Indianapolis: Bobbs-Merrill, 1963).

teacher Constantin Stanislavski—*super-objective*. In defining a play's spine, a director must ask:

> What fundamental desire does the plot of his play symbolize, what deep struggle gives it shape and direction? What is the play's CORE?[3]

A story spine succinctly expresses a play's theme or root idea. Thus, the spine of *Amadeus* might be "Envy withers the soul." The spine of *Places in the Heart*: "Great determination overcomes all obstacles." The spine of *Star Wars*: "Good destroys evil" or "Youth achieves maturity through the performance of heroic deeds." Note that a story spine is not absolute; it may vary from director to director depending upon individual interpretation. In every case, the story spine approximates the spines/goals of the major characters. Thus, in *Star Wars* Luke Skywalker's character spine could be "to rescue the princess" (thereby overcoming evil) or "to achieve maturity" (by performing a heroic deed).

The Character Spine

Writer-director Robert Towne (*Chinatown*) once stated that you can understand a character if you know what he or she fears most. Directors trained in the Stanislavski method take another tack (and the two are directly related), believing that understanding grows from awareness of a character's basic needs or goals or drives. They express such needs as *character spines*, defining them with verbs that suggest action or movement. It is possible that Towne's definition expresses the same concept in reverse. That is, characters fear most that their goals will be frustrated or defeated.

Many of the best dramatic directors were once actors. Because of this practical, behind-the-footlights experience, these directors understand an actor's needs, the sudden panic when a line is forgotten, the hunger for approval, what it feels like to be directed. Such experience makes it easy for directors to reread a script from the perspective of the characters, as if they were playing each of the parts themselves. Such carefully focused reading can be enormously helpful in finding the spine for each character. The spine emerges inevitably from the character's actions and dialog and expresses that character's personal viewpoint.

---

[3]Harold Clurman in John Gassner, *Producing the Play* (New York: The Dryden Press, 1953), p. 277.

We have all seen snarling "bad guys" in television melodrama and won-dered why they appeared so corny, so unbelievable. The reason is simply that the actors were playing the audience reaction rather than legitimate charac-ters with strong personal views and with goals that are positive and praise-worthy! Audiences identify with a protagonist. Any character opposing the protagonist for less than praiseworthy reasons automatically becomes a villain. If an actor thinks of himself as a bad guy, curling his lip and sneering, he is playing the audience reaction.

> Very few people who behave badly consider themselves "wicked."
> They justify themselves, and the director who plans their theatrical
> embodiment must "justify" them too. The actor who plays a villain
> as such (with negative intent) is usually a bad actor: obvious, stagey
> and often involuntarily laughable.[4]

The more specific the spine, the easier it is for an actor to absorb and use in fashioning a character. Thus, "to find an unselfish mate" is more valuable than "to find happiness." "To win her husband's love" is more helpful than "to build an enduring home life."

Dramatic Actions

During the course of a film or television show, characters undertake a number of specific dramatic actions. If the script has been well constructed, each of these actions relates, directly or indirectly, to achieving a specific character goal. For example, if a protagonist wants to reach the pot of gold at the end of a rainbow, he or she might have to deceive others who also are searching for the gold, to cross a raging river, to plead with the guardian of the gold, and so forth. In the theater, each of these dramatic actions is broken down into individual *beats*, each beat representing the specific steps necessary to com-plete the action.

In helping actors to find the proper approach to actions or beats, direc-tors must select (again) the proper verb. Strong or active verbs challenge and stimulate; inactive or passive verbs offer little help. Thus, words such as *gloating* or *mocking* or *provoking* are more valuable than such words as *question-ing* or *arguing*.

Sometimes imagery totally foreign to the dramatic situation awakens empathetic responses in an actor, enabling that actor to find an appropriate

---

[4]Harold Clurman, *On Directing* (Macmillan, 1972), p. 74.

approach. For example, in a situation in which one actor must dominate another, engendering fear or panic, a director might suggest the mental imagery of a jungle encounter: a lion dominating a deer—the lion staring hypnotically, the deer transfixed, paralyzed in fear.

Animal imagery has long been used by both actors and directors as a way of evoking a character concept and stimulating emotional response. An actress given the role of a seductress, for example, might imagine herself a cat, with a feline walk, a catlike manner of stretching and moving, an inner feeling of purring when happy or hissing with arched back when angry.

While directors cannot unilaterally create characters—actors must ultimately fashion their own—they can be enormously helpful in stimulating an actor's imagination, in awakening sense memory, in goading or guiding the creative actor into effective characterizations.

Creating Character Background

Skilled writers usually prepare a few pages of *back story*, an in-depth history of each character, before commencing a script. This exploratory material provides a comfortable familiarity with characters, an understanding of their basic fears, hungers, and goals that will help bring them to life. A skilled director should do likewise for the same reason.

In his seminal *Art of Dramatic Writing*, Lajos Egri discusses a dialectic approach to characterization in which characters change and grow because of contradictions in their nature or environment. Egri divides the study of a character's background into three categories: physiology, sociology, and psychology.[5] In preparing notes on character backgrounds, directors might do well to use those same convenient, all-embracing categories. *Physiology*: a character's physical appearance. *Sociology*: a character's place in society and in the family. *Psychology*: such internal values as temperament, moral code, personality, fears, drives, sense of humor, and imagination (or lack of it).

From detailed notes you can develop a comfortable familiarity with each of your characters. About a female character ask such questions as: What kind of childhood did she have? What were her earliest fears? Was she obedient? Rebellious? How did she get along with brothers and sisters? Was she ever abused? Was she successful in school? What were her best subjects? How much schooling did she have? Did she go to church? As a teenager, did she have many friends or was she a loner? When did she first have sex?

---

[5]Lajos Egri, *The Art of Dramatic Writing* (New York: Simon & Schuster, 1946), pp. 49–59.

By answering such questions, you can develop dimension for each major character. A conscientious actress also will explore the character, discovering personal answers from her own reservoir of experience. Her answers will necessarily differ from yours, yet surprisingly often, major background elements will coincide. Of course, it is not important that they do. The actress will test you (perhaps not consciously) to find out how thoroughly you understand the character. You will win her respect once she realizes you have done your homework.

> The more detailed the background the director imagines for the play's characters, the richer the performances become—with good actors! The antecedent life histories are only helpful to the actor if they lead him to kindred material wrought from his own imagination.
>
> The director's intentions, howsoever interesting, may leave the actor untouched. In either case, what is imagined should stem from certain elements in the playwright's script. "My" characterizations derive from three sources—the script, the actor's imagination, my own nature.[6]

Usually it is wise for a director to meet each star individually before the start of a project. Such a meeting over lunch or coffee gives each a chance to learn what ideas the other has about the character. If their concepts are miles apart, there is still time to discuss and rethink. Such a discovery on the first day of shooting could be disastrous, with the resulting conflict consuming hours of valuable production time.

Experienced directors are seldom arbitrary about their character concepts. They respect good actors and welcome their input. Sometimes unexpected concepts are so rich, so creative, so exciting, that directors discard their own ideas, changing scenes and dialog to accommodate the new direction. But if an actor's concept is misconceived, based on incorrect or insufficient thought, then the director must make that clear. Without being arbitrary or abrasive, the director can suggest a rereading of the material and perhaps some alternative ways of developing the character.

Inflexible or defensive actors sometimes are unwilling to commit themselves too early to a characterization, requiring time to let a role simmer in the subconscious. The theatrical practice of cast readings (also used occasionally in film and videotape) is an excellent way to allow characters to emerge

---

[6]Clurman, p. 77.

naturally and unforced; it is a process of trial and error, tentative exploration, and happy discovery. Such readings by an entire cast—seated around a table with director, writer, and producer—also provide an early opportunity for cuts and script changes. When scenes don't work, the writer can take them home and fix them, avoiding frantic last-minute changes on the set.

Inexperienced directors sometimes panic at first cast readings since the characterizations they expect seldom appear. Many actors are insecure and refrain from committing themselves too early; they "hide" behind quiet, underplayed readings. As they become comfortable with the dialog and other cast members, they gain confidence and their characters gradually emerge.

HOW CHARACTER IS REVEALED

Once director and actor have settled upon a character concept—or at least its rudimentary outline—they must consider how that character will reveal itself to an audience. Realistically, much of this character revelation happens almost automatically. It springs from an awareness in the actor's mind, a sense of *being* that character, experiencing that character's thoughts and emotions. Audiences form impressions of characters from the following overt information:

1. The character's entire physical aspect
2. The character's traits and mannerisms
3. What the character does or does not do
4. What the character says or does not say
5. How other characters react

Physical Aspect

In their scripts writers rarely provide more than a phrase or two describing characters. Frequently such descriptions are limited to name, age, and general appearance (for example, Elaine Garibaldi, 22, thin, painfully shy). Sometimes writers throw in clues to the essential nature of a character, but not often. Why not a more complete character analysis? Because writers correctly prefer to let a character's *behavior* provide that information. Moreover, minimum descriptive data allows considerable creative freedom for producer and director in casting and in delineating the character. The fact that writers haven't described every pore and wrinkle by no means implies that they haven't done their homework. The best ones prepare pages of detailed notes on each major character before beginning a script.

From the script's spare beginning point, the director adds coloration based on his or her examination of the character. Such coloration might concern the character's appearance, posture, dress, manner of walking, personal history, moral code, personality, hairstyle, thought processes, speech patterns, and so on. These factors are affected by the physical appearance of the actor chosen to portray the character and by that actor's creative input. Eventually, actor and character will merge: The actor will take on the qualities and traits of the character; the character will subtly change to accommodate the style, manner, and appearance of the actor.

From repeated script readings and creative imaginings, the director forms mental pictures of all major characters, in considerable detail and covering wide-ranging aspects of their lives. While such minutiae may appear ludicrous here, it will prove enormously helpful in talks with the art director, the set dresser, and those in charge of makeup, hairstyling, wardrobe, transportation, and so forth.

Are the characters fat? Sloppily fat or just nicely padded? Are they thin? Hungry thin or elegantly slim? If a male character, is he bald? Is his hair neat or shaggy, long or short? Does he wear an afro? Does he have a beard or a mustache? If either, is it neat and trim or long and bushy? Does he wear spectacles? A hearing aid?

What kind of clothing does he wear? High fashion or old-fashioned? New or old, clean or dirty, freshly pressed or rumpled? Are his shoes scuffed or are they shined? Wing tipped or moccasins? Are there holes in the soles? Does he wear a necktie? If so, is it wide or narrow, conservatively striped or covered with gaudy flowers?

What kind of car does the character drive? New or old? If old, has it been meticulously maintained or has it gone to seed? Is there a bumper sticker? What does it say? Is there a good luck charm hanging from the mirror?

What kind of commentary would the character's bedroom provide? Is the room tidy or are clothes thrown on the floor in disarray? Is the bed made? Are there stuffed animals on it? What kind of pictures hang on the wall: Picasso prints, *Playboy* centerfolds, or rock posters? Are there textbooks or magazines on the nightstand? What magazines: *National Geographic* or *Penthouse*? Are there pipes or cigarettes on the dresser? Ashtrays filled with cigarette butts? Is there stereo equipment? What kind of music: acid rock, easy rock, big bands, or classical? What color is the room painted? Are there lace curtains?

Answers to such questions provide definitive clues to the nature of a character. Audiences cannot read the script. There is no godlike narrator to describe or define the qualities of a show's characters. Instead, audiences must play detective and interpret the characters from the information they are given. Piecing the clues together will form a composite picture, a mosaic that the director-actor team has carefully contrived.

Traits and Mannerisms

Traits and mannerisms acquire significance because they often reveal inner feelings or thought processes not always explained in dialog. In many cases, such feelings are actually *concealed* by dialog. (You will find an elaboration of such actions in Chapter 6 under the heading "Business.") Society has taught us that displaying our feelings is a sign of weakness. We therefore go to elaborate lengths to remain "cool," covering our emotions with a smile or a glib phrase. But inevitably we reveal ourselves, sometimes overtly, sometimes through small, virtually undetectable actions.

By studying the actions of people around you, you will become sensitive to the meanings of many of their mannerisms. What does it signify when people constantly polish their glasses? What do they reveal when they keep glancing at themselves in mirrors or combing and recombing their hair? Veteran film director Richard Fleischer recently pointed to *awareness* as a key characteristic of successful directors.

> A director is basically an observer and has to be aware of everything that's going on around him, mostly in terms of human behavior. You have to be an observer of the current scene and watch people: how they behave in certain situations. You must be aware that there is a body language, that there are awkward pauses (in conversations).
>
> I think you can develop this awareness if you don't become too involved with yourself. In a social situation you can watch the byplay between people in a room, see the little subtle changes that happen when people suddenly become hurt . . . or what makes them laugh . . . or who goes through a door first. Sooner or later, in some script, you're going to be reproducing that situation.

As you become a habitual people watcher, you will discover the foot tappers, the fingernail biters, the teeth grinders, the frightened few who hide behind their hands or dark glasses, the lip chewers, the hair twirlers, the blinkers, and others. While many of these mannerisms indicate some form of tension, others imply more significant mental states. Photographs taken during production of a TV movie in Utah show me repeatedly standing with my arms crossed protectively in front of my chest, hands resting on shoulders. The pose, totally uncharacteristic, revealed that I was unconsciously shielding myself from the world, from the harrowing pressures of an extremely difficult and problem-filled project.

Become aware of the way people walk. Tired people walk differently than excited people do; old people usually walk differently than young people. Become aware of how people talk. Do they stammer? Do they speak quickly, words rushing out in a torrent? Do they speak carefully, examining the texture of each syllable? Do they speak loudly, as if to intimidate? Or do they speak quietly, timidly, afraid someone might take offense?

Action or Inaction

It is obvious that we learn much about characters from the actions they perform. As we will learn in Chapter 6, such actions are often a more accurate barometer of feelings than words are. It is somewhat less obvious that a lack of action can be equally revealing.

When a man desperately running for his life stops to help someone, at great risk to himself, we recognize that here is a character worthy of our respect. If he encounters children urgently needing help and walks on by, pretending not to see them, we regard him with contempt because he obviously thinks only of himself. If he encounters the children and hesitates, torn, aware of his own vulnerability, starts to help them and then suddenly hurries off, that indecision also creates a picture of the man and the pressures that weigh on him. Newspapers in recent years have recited countless stories of women being attacked, screaming for help from passersby who refuse to acknowledge them. Such lack of action eloquently describes the nature of such passersby.

Speech or Silence

Equally obvious as a criterion for evaluating characters is their dialog: what they say, or what they don't say. Is a teenage boy quick to tell a girl that he loves her or is he unable to share his emotions? Does a housewife report a murder to the police or does she remain silent for fear of reprisal? Does a newlywed yell at his wife for ignoring household chores or does he remain quiet? And does he remain quiet out of timidity or out of love? Does an old lady confess that she was responsible for a fire in the retirement home or does she clamp her mouth shut, allowing someone else to take the blame?

In dramatic terms, unspoken words can be louder than spoken ones.

Reactions of Others

A final clue enabling audiences to assess the nature of a dramatic character is how other characters in the play react to him or her. Their attitudes, however, may not be immediately definitive. If the women in a small town despise a sexy young widow, does that mean that the widow is a bad person? Perhaps. But not necessarily. It is also possible that the small-town women are jealous and mean minded. If such is the case, then the widow may actually merit our sympathy. We cannot gauge the validity of such a clue until we understand the nature of the peripheral characters.

In the early stages of a play, reactions of other cast members provide only tentative information, subject to change without notice. When a sympathetic protagonist violently dislikes a character, we automatically accept that hostility as our own—until a plot development redeems the character and proves our hostility unjustified.

WEARING MASKS

In 1925 Eugene O'Neill wrote *The Great God Brown*, a play in which characters wore masks. In most cases, the masks depicted youth or strength or cynical sophistication, concealing (and protecting) the characters' vulnerability. Characters fell in love, not with other characters but with the masks they wore.

O'Neill recognized, of course, that we all wear masks, presenting one face to our parents, another to our enemies, another to our mates. Which is the real us? In today's stressed society, most of us wear "cool" masks, hiding and protecting our anxieties. Sometimes, with loved ones whom we consider no threat, we take off our masks. But consider this: When you take off your mask, is there another underneath?

When an actor assumes a role, he or she fashions a multilayered, multidimensional person, wearing protective masks that conceal either vulnerability or some other emotion (or affliction) inappropriate to the occasion. Such layers (masks beneath masks) bring richness to a characterization; lack of them usually creates a character that is paper thin and that audiences quickly tire of. Audience awareness of such hidden layers increases interest in a scene.

Sensitive directors concern themselves with the emotional stirrings beneath surface dialog or actions: the fear beneath the bravado, the shame beneath the smile, the guilt beneath the show of love. It is the face we cannot see that attracts and holds us, fascinating because it acquires richness in our imaginations.

The director's search for a dimensional character is really a search for the many characters who inhabit a single body, some in conflict with others, all adding texture and coloration.

TRANSFERRING THE CHARACTER TO TAPE OR FILM

Unfortunately (and understandably), many actors are insecure. It is they who must stand in the spotlight. It is they who must expose themselves to the scrutiny (perhaps ridicule) of critics and audiences. It is they who must cry, scream, or laugh on cue, convincingly, in character, sometimes over and over again.

As a director, you can help to alleviate actors' anxieties in a number of ways. Initially, you can discuss their characterizations with them, encouraging their input, reaching agreement on each character's background, style of dress, personality, moral code, traits and mannerisms, even the type of car he or she drives. You demonstrate at this early meeting that you have done your homework, just as you expect them to do theirs. Lack of agreement or confusion on a characterization creates disquiet. Early agreement allows actors to begin digging deeper, enriching the character.

Because of the tremendous volume of dramatic programs aired on television, character clichés abound. In searching for a characterization, actors sometimes fall into stereotypical patterns, unaware that the character they have selected is a too familiar one. The director must convince them that their feelings of security come from recognition. New directions are frightening; familiar ones (like old shoes) are comfortable. A good director encourages capable actors to be adventuresome, to try new directions, to take a chance. Such a director protects them from failure, applauding their efforts, encouraging and steering them into a fresh and viable character pattern.

Some directors—especially those with a background in theater—help actors find a characterization through improvisation. They place the actor in a variety of dramatic or everyday situations: defending a client in court, proposing marriage, asking for a raise. The actor behaves and reacts in character, becoming comfortable and secure in the new characterization.

Directors can encourage security in yet another way. In early discussions and rehearsal, the director must earn the actors' confidence. Specifically, actors must feel that the director understands their characters as well as (or better than) they do. They must know that the director understands *them* as actors, that he or she has seen them perform previously and is acutely aware of their strengths and weaknesses. Because of this personal insight, actors can feel confident that the director will never allow them to "look bad." Once actors know that their director refuses to settle for mediocrity—demanding that they perform at the very peak of their abilities—anxiety frequently becomes anticipation, even excitement.

At the beginning of a project, facing a new crew, new cast members, and commitment to a new role, other apprehensions sometimes arise. A director can provide support on the set by protecting actors from intrusions into their privacy, allow them the space to develop their characters and to find a rapport with other cast members.

Some directors (Richard Fleischer, Delbert Mann, and others) actually ask all crew members and guests to leave the stage when preparing to rehearse significant scenes. In the privacy of an empty stage, released from the scrutiny of outsiders, actors lose any feelings of self-consciousness. Now, guided by the director, they may explore offbeat stagings or adventuresome character developments without feeling that they are making fools of themselves.

The "film method" (also used for videotape) of shooting out of sequence poses a number of problems for actors and can be disruptive to characterizations. Shooting all of the scenes that occur in a single set (no matter when they appear in the script) provides tremendous financial advantages to a production company, but the pattern creates mental and emotional hazards for both actor and director.

In the theater an actor has time to "get into" a role, building a performance smoothly from scene to scene in continuous action. When shooting out of sequence, director and actor have no such luxury; they frequently face the problem of re-creating the emotional intensity, mood, or energy of a scene that was taped or filmed weeks ago. In the script, the previously photographed scene (scene A) occurs immediately before the one taped or filmed later (scene B). When the scenes are later spliced together, any lapse on the actor's (or the director's) part will be instantly discernible. The emotional level at the beginning of scene B must exactly coincide with the level at the end of scene A.

Such a recapturing of mood is even more difficult when scene B is photographed first. Now director and actor must calculate the emotional intensity to be reached when scene A will be photographed, perhaps weeks later. From this rough calculation, they must now begin scene B, hoping that when they later stage scene A, they will have perfect recall and that its climax will match the previously recorded scene B.

Such character and performance problems are more the director's concern than the actor's. Before any scene is photographed, usually while the crew is lighting the set, the director spends time with actors rehearsing dialog, discussing the scene's mood, character relationships, tempo, potential staging problems—and ironing out any wrinkles. Usually at this time the director describes the emotional level of adjacent scenes, attempting to match those levels in the scene being rehearsed. If the matching is critical, the wise director will have screened the adjacent scene, perhaps a few hours earlier, familiarizing himself or herself with its emotional intensity. Sometimes directors ask that a moviola or videotape player be brought to the stage so that the earlier scene may actually be shown to cast members. In this way the director and cast may plant the previous scene's mood or emotional level firmly in their minds only moments before the new scene is photographed.

Despite the director's thoroughness in talking through a scene, some actors need additional time and space to prepare on their own. They sometimes retreat from the set, taking a few quiet moments to re-create the character. Like other creative artists, actors often have individual needs and very personal methods of preparation. Removing themselves from the real world, each actor enters his or her character's world, finding the character's mental and emotional state for the upcoming scene.

Just as individual actors prepare differently, so do they differ in the length of time necessary to achieve emotional depth. Directors must be vigilant to prevent them from reaching such depth too early. Occasionally actors try to play a scene with full intensity during rehearsal. Vigilant directors usually stop them, advising them just to walk it through, fearful that they may achieve a performance of such depth that they will be unable to achieve it again when cameras are rolling. In the days of live televised drama, I watched directors deliberately break up their dress rehearsals, pretending to criticize lighting or sound, in order to prevent the cast from expending their emotions, to keep them from going "dry" on the air.

Director Delbert Mann tells of an experience with Sophia Loren in which she played the part of a mother who had lost a child. Because the role paralleled a tragic, real-life experience, the actress began getting misty-eyed during the scene's first walk-through. Mann understood the reasons for her sudden emotion and asked her just to walk through the scene casually without any attempt at acting. Even that was difficult for her, although she tried valiantly to do as the director had requested.

When it came time to film the master (wide) angle, Mann again cautioned her not to "act" the scene, advising her to play it coolly, with only minimal emotion. He understood the depths of which she was capable and wanted her to save her "performance" for closer angles. Moments later he rolled the cameras. The scene played beautifully until, about halfway through, the actress began sobbing. She had become the character, participating deeply in the scene's emotional content. It was a stunning, enormously moving moment—but it had played only in a very full shot, where the audience impact would be slight.

Later, when the director shot closeups, Loren summoned up as much emotion as she was capable of. But the moment had passed. While her closeup performance was technically flawless, it never quite reached the heart-tugging poignancy that she had achieved in the master angle.

Interestingly, Mann was confronted with a similar situation some years later. A sensitive young actress was so filled with emotion that the director sensed she would spill her tears in the master angle. He secretly directed his cinematographer to put a long lens on the camera so that he could photograph her in closeup throughout the scene. As expected, the actress gave a tear-filled, deeply moving performance. And this time Mann had photographed it in a closeup!

While some actors find a character's emotional depth easily, others have tremendous difficulty experiencing inner pain. We have all heard stories of how directors "trick" certain actors into giving performances above their emotional capabilities, by abusing or shocking them, by relating untrue stories, by driving them to emotional exhaustion. While such gimmicks seem less reliable than emotion reached through an honest characterization, if they manage to create the necessary tears or anger or fear—and all other methods fail—then perhaps they are justified.

Although some directors obtain effective characterizations from harsh, authoritarian methods, most do not. Most contemporary directors understand the frailty of the human ego; they achieve their best results through support and encouragement. When, in the shooting of a scene, directors need to make corrections or improvements, they usually offer some positive comment before discussing the questionable action or line reading. When such directors make corrections, they do so in privacy, taking the actor off the set.

CHAPTER HIGHLIGHTS

- Directors find the nature of characters much as actors do: first from the script and then from their own background experience, synthesizing bits and pieces of people they have known. They share their concepts of each character with the actor chosen to play the role; together they fashion a final character concept.

- When directors study a script, they determine its *story spine* and its *character spines*. The word *spine* usually refers to a personal goal, need, or desire. A story spine defines the play's theme or root idea. Usually the spines of major characters are closely related to the story spine. Spine concepts vary from director to director, according to the personal vision of each.

- In creating character backgrounds, some directors use three convenient categories: physiology (describing physical characteristics), sociology (a character's place in society), and psychology (internal values such as moral code, fears, personality, sense of humor). By examining character backgrounds in detail, directors may stimulate good actors to dig into their own imaginations. Directors usually arrange personal meetings with each major cast member prior to production to discuss, and find agreement, on character concepts.

- Once a character has been defined by the director and the actor, that character is revealed to audiences by the character's entire physical aspect, the character's traits and mannerisms, what the character does or does not do, what the character says or does not say, and how other characters react to him or her. Good directors are keen observers; their observations help to enrich each of these categories.

- Most people wear "masks." That is, they conceal their vulnerabilities beneath protective masks that they present to the world. Sensitive directors and actors use the concept of masks to achieve multi-dimensional characterizations: the fear beneath the bravado, the shame beneath the smile.

- For understandable reasons, many actors are insecure. Part of a director's function is to support and protect them, providing an atmosphere that will simultaneously challenge and stimulate. Sensitive directors understand when an actor reaches optimum performance and refuse to accept less. They prevent actors from reaching their optimum during rehearsal.

C H A P T E R 6

Staging the actor

Elia Kazan's words (at the top of the next page) establish the theme for this chapter dealing with the behavior of actors in front of a camera. A part of the process of turning psychology into behavior, translating thoughts and emotions into dramatic action, is called *blocking*. Directors block the positions and movements of both actors and cameras. We will discuss camera blocking in the next chapter.

In drama, actors are one of a director's key creative elements, the door through which spectators enter a story. Their physical movements, gestures, and positions in relation to other actors are governed by specific dramatic principles, many of them as old as the theater. This chapter will examine those principles in the following discussions:

- WHERE STAGING ORIGINATES: the director's role in planning and preparing scenes for rehearsal

- EXTERNALIZING THOUGHTS OR EMOTIONS: the relative validity of dialog and action

- BUSINESS: specific character actions, traditionally called *business*; their dramatic purpose and function

- REVEALING INNER THOUGHTS: how directors provide insights into hidden thoughts or emotions

A thought—directing finally consists of turning Psychology into Behavior.   ELIA KAZAN[1]

- INTERNAL MOTIVATIONS: three fundamental emotional states that impel character action

- EXTERNAL MOTIVATIONS: usually arising from the script or a need for emphasis; a comparison with stage techniques for achieving emphasis

- SYMBOLIC RELATIONSHIPS: physical positioning of characters is often a key to their relationships

- BLOCKING CAMERA TO ACTORS: the importance of the viewer-actor relationship and the need for honesty in performance

- BLOCKING ACTORS TO CAMERA: the occasions when camera needs take precedence over performance needs

- PREPARATION: the steps in preproduction and production necessary to turn "Psychology into Behavior"

---

[1]*Directors on Directing*, ed. Toby Cole and Helen Chinoy (Indianapolis: Bobbs-Merrill, 1979), p. 364.

WHERE STAGING ORIGINATES

We're watching a scene on television. Todd, an earnest, balding man of forty, pleads with his wife to send her mother to a home for the aged. The wife, Debbie, angrily refuses, moving to the window. Todd pursues her, taking her arm. He's fed up. The old lady allows them no privacy. She's destroying their marriage.

Through the partially open doorway we can see Debbie's mother in the next room listening, hand trembling as she grips the back of a chair.

Debbie breaks away from her husband and sinks onto the couch, close to camera. She stares at her mother's crochet work on the couch. She picks it up almost tenderly. The camera tilts up from the crochet work to Debbie's face, her eyes glistening now. After a moment, she nods. All right, she will make the arrangements.

Camera pans to the doorway. The old lady's shoulders slump and she moves away.

If they stopped to think about it, most viewers would assume that actors' movements in such scenes are spontaneous, growing naturally out of the dramatic moment. Why does Debbie break away from Todd when he takes her arm? Spectators accept the action at face value: because Debbie's deep emotions at that instant impel her to move. Professionals familiar with dramatic staging understand that such action was adapted by a director from a script, rehearsed with actors, adjusted and refined and refined again. The finished product appears simple, natural, inevitable: art that conceals art.

Generally, the only time that audiences become aware of dramatic contrivance is when actors' movements seem false, in apparent disharmony with their characters' thoughts or emotions. Then audiences are disquieted only in a general sense, aware that "something's wrong," not that a director or actor has miscalculated. Such awareness creates a rupture in audience attention, causing spectators to disengage themselves from the magic world in which they are participating, to step back through the proscenium arch of their television sets or movie screens and again become dispassionate viewers.

EXTERNALIZING THOUGHTS OR EMOTIONS

How does an audience recognize honest emotion? By what characters say? Or by what they do?

The timeworn phrase, "Actions speak louder than words," applies forcibly in any visual dramatic medium. While dialog usually provides reliable insights into a character's thoughts or emotions, there are occasions when words simply cannot be trusted. An obvious example: People lie about their weaknesses. A coward will stoutly deny his fear. A woman who is tense in a new job situation will pretend composure. Ask a dozen people how they feel. Some will exaggerate; others will understate; others, looking for sympathy, will baldly invent physical problems.

A shy boy and a timid girl in the moonlight may speak of a hundred casual matters that have nothing whatsoever to do with what they are thinking or feeling. But their thoughts and feelings are the significant content of such a scene. Therefore, the director's goal must be to *externalize* those feelings, somehow making the audience aware of their depth and nature.

The Validity of Dialog

A basic dramatic truth understood by experienced directors: *Dialog often has little relationship to the essential thrust of a scene.* Sometimes it is merely an accompaniment. I recall a scene from an episode of the TV series "The Fugitive" in which director Billy Graham panned his camera with a small, folded note as it was passed surreptitiously from one character to another, totally ignoring the faces of the characters. Yes, we heard their dialog. Yes, we got occasional glimpses of them. But the note represented the heart of the scene. Dialog merely provided a background.

Husband and wife at a party exchange casual dialog with friends. As they talk, the husband's eyes seek out a handsome dark-eyed woman across the room. The woman across the room becomes aware of his glance and stares back at him curiously. The husband smiles at her, unseen by his wife. The woman across the room lifts her champagne glass slightly, as if toasting him, then turns away. As in the previous example, the dialog provided nothing more than an accompaniment to the scene's significant content: the eye contact between the husband and the dark-eyed woman.

A more extreme example may be one in which characters say one thing but mean something entirely different. A mother attends her daughter's open house at junior high school. While visiting an art class, she's shocked to discover that the teacher is a man she had an affair with only a year before. They instantly recognize each other but because of the daughter's presence can only comment on the array of student sketches and watercolors. Their dialog is meaningless. But beneath the banal words a second, more significant conversation takes place. The exchanged glances, the handshake held a moment too long, the veiled references, and innuendo are what the scene is all about. A spectator aware of the earlier love affair will focus attention on the subtext, dramatized not *by* the dialog but *in spite of it*, vastly more compelling because it is hidden beneath an apparently innocent teacher-parent encounter.

The Validity of Actions

Just as dialog is not totally trustworthy in revealing thoughts or emotions, neither are actions. Timid characters may strut. Lovesick characters may pretend disinterest. Most of us act casual in order to conceal our anxieties or fears. (See the discussion on wearing masks in Chapter 5.)

While actions sometimes distort the truth, however, they still provide a far more accurate barometer than words do. Thus, Mr. Jones plays it flip and unperturbed when his boss fires him. But we see his fingers tearing at the eraser on the end of his pencil. Lucy Ann pretends fondness for her date, yet she constantly moves away from him, glancing furtively at her watch.

In the short scene that began the chapter, we understood Debbie's agitation as much from her actions as from what she said. We understood her mother's anxiety from her trembling hands and realized her disappointment from the sudden slumping of her shoulders.

As kids we all played "Show and Tell." As directors, we should realize that showing usually proves superior to telling. It's more visual. It's more honest. Most importantly, it's stronger. Why stronger? Because showing requires some degree of spectator *participation*. Audiences must interpret actions. They must draw conclusions as to their significance.

If Debbie overtly states, "I love my mother," the information is dumped in our laps. There's little interaction between Debbie and the audience. But when Debbie picks up her mother's crochet work and holds it to her cheek, eyes glistening, we immediately participate. We have witnessed earlier scenes in which the mother continually crocheted. The delicate handwork thus becomes a symbol of the older woman. When Debbie holds the half-finished sweater to her cheek, she is holding her mother. Her tears complete the unspoken thought: an expression of grief that the old woman will be sent to a home.

While reciting the steps of such a sequence seems obvious and unnecessary, it nevertheless enables us to appreciate the contrast between the action, simple as it is, and Debbie's overt statement, which allows no spectator participation at all. Actions require the audience to contribute from remembered experience. By contributing, viewers automatically become more deeply involved.

BUSINESS

Debbie's action with the crochet work is called *business*, a term inherited from the theater. Business really means "busy-ness" and refers to character actions within a scene, such as sewing, reading a newspaper, polishing fingernails, cleaning a gun, or washing a car. Ideally, business should make a statement either about the character who performs it or about the scene itself. A man who continually combs his hair, for example, offers insights to his character. A woman who sculpts probably has different instincts than one who practices witchcraft or one who mud wrestles in a neighborhood nightclub. What characters *do* suggests what they *are!*

Russian director and theorist, V. I. Pudovkin, used the term *plastic material* to indicate visually expressive actions that help audiences to define a character. He described a sequence of shots from the silent film, *Tol'able David*, to illustrate his concept:

1. The tramp—a degenerate brute, his face overgrown with unshaven bristles—is about to enter a house, but stops, his attention caught by something.

2. Closeup of the face of the watching tramp.

3. Showing what he sees—a tiny, fluffy kitten asleep in the sun.

4. The tramp again. He raises a heavy stone with the transparent intention of using it to obliterate the sleeping little beast, and only the casual push of a fellow, just then carrying objects into the house, hinders him from carrying out his cruel intention.

Thus (using Pudovkin's words) "the heavy stone in the hands of the huge man immediately becomes the symbol of absurd and senseless cruelty," providing viewers with an obvious insight into the tramp's nature.[2]

Business may also contribute to the dynamics of a scene. The action of cleaning a gun adds an unspoken threat to a scene in which one man makes sinister demands on another. A woman's declaration of love for her husband is contradicted when she ignores him to apply fingernail polish. Rubbing suntan oil on a girlfriend's back adds sensuality and innuendo to a young man's suggestion that they live together.

Probably the most obvious reason for creating business is that it contributes to the illusion of reality. In real life people seldom stand in the center of a room and make speeches to one another. Instead, they busy themselves with the thousand necessary tasks that clutter their lives. A woman in her office may write notes, straighten papers on her desk, or make telephone calls while playing a scene with a business associate. If those actions heighten the dramatic thrust of the scene, so much the better. A man at home may trim hedges, mow, or water his lawn while playing a scene with a neighbor. Those

---

[2]V. I. Pudovkin, *Film Technique and Film Acting* (London: Vision Press, 1958), p. 56. (First published in English in 1929.)

actions contribute to the illusion of reality but they also comment on the nature of the man. He obviously cares about his home and its appearance. A different character might say the same dialog while swilling beer and watching a porno film on cable TV.

Writers too seldom describe business in their scripts. It thus becomes a major directorial contribution. Business should always appear as a natural and legitimate part of any dramatic scene and should be appropriate to (and define) the character who performs it.

For years, both on the stage and in film, whenever directors needed a piece of business they would instruct a character to light a cigarette. Cigarette business became a directorial cliché. Today the business of preparing or sipping drinks has fallen into that same odious category; it has been overworked so much that the action becomes almost meaningless.

REVEALING INNER THOUGHTS

Debbie's picking up her mother's crochet work, beyond constituting a simple piece of business, also demonstrates another directorial technique. How can a director convey to an audience what a character is thinking about? In a novel or a short story, such communication is easy: The author simply *tells* the reader what's happening inside a character's mind. For a director, the problem becomes somewhat more difficult.

One effective solution is to select a symbol whose significance the spectator will understand. Our lives are filled with such symbols: a funny T-shirt given to us by someone we love, a high school baseball trophy, a bundle of yellowing letters, a worn teddy bear from our youth. The manner in which characters then relate to those symbols provides the audience with insights into the characters' thoughts and feelings. For example, when a former heavyweight boxer looks wistfully at his gloves hanging on the wall, viewers know what thoughts are filling his mind. When a woman cleans and polishes the bicycle that once belonged to her dead son, the audience can understand her emotions.

Audiences are brighter than show business cynics seem to believe. Viewers seize upon any clue the director gives them, eager to understand and contribute. But they need a beginning point—a symbol of a place, an event, or a person—that the director must provide.

INTERNAL MOTIVATIONS

When I was handed my first dramatic directorial assignment, I experienced a few hours of panic. My knowledge of the art was minimal. Few books on the subject existed and I was reluctant to confess to colleagues that I needed advice. One experienced professional understood my anxiety and volunteered a rule of thumb: Every scene is a chase. A man pursues a woman around a kitchen, he catches up with her, and they face each other for a showdown. Then, perhaps, the man begins to retreat and the woman pursues. What a simple solution to my problems! I was home free!

Well, it took me fewer than twenty-four hours to realize that this so-called rule of thumb is far from infallible. It does work—but only on occasion. The Debbie-Todd scene is one of those occasions. Todd pursues Debbie, driven by anger and his need to save their marriage. Debbie retreats from Todd and from her own fears until, finally, backed into a corner, she makes a decision.

The fact that a chase works sometimes and not others set me to thinking. What dynamics are involved that make a character a pursuer in one scene and a retreater in another? Study of a number of different scenes in different dramatic modes revealed that movement is most often triggered *within* a character. Such internal motivation—thoughts, feelings, emotions—is generally one of three types: involvement, disinvolvement, or emotional turbulence.

Involvement

Movement *toward* another character, seeking involvement, may be motivated by a wide variety of emotions: rage, anger or annoyance, sadism, lust, desire, love or affection. Also, one character moves to another out of need: for understanding, for information (or to impart information), for forgiveness, for love's favors, or to acquire a physical object. Generally speaking, the more urgent the emotion, the more intense will be the action it generates. When greed or rage become psychotic, for example, the forward movement may become an attack, inflicting bodily injury or death.

This list of aggressive or seeking motivations (as with those that follow) is far from complete, but it provides aspiring directors with a beginning point in understanding the motivations for character movement. By studying well-directed television or feature films, the student director will undoubtedly discover other emotions that impel one character toward another.

Disinvolvement

Moves of avoidance, rejection, or retreat—movement *away from* another character—generally are triggered by emotions of fear, shame, guilt, or timidity; hatred, dislike, disgust, or disinterest; rage, anger, annoyance, coquettishness, or teasing (entrapment). Notice that the emotions of rage, anger, and annoyance appear as motivations for both advancing and retreating moves.

In any chase situation, the pursuer will frequently (but not always) be driven by an emotion of involvement and the retreater by an emotion of disinvolvement. In the earlier scene, Todd is driven by anger and frustration, Debbie by guilt. Such labels are simplistic, of course. In any dimensional dramatic work, motivations inevitably become a complex blending of emotions with individual character traits created by the specific actor for a specific role in a specific script. A timid character generally tends to retreat; an aggressive character tends to advance. Thus, built-in character values must be superimposed on values generated by scene content. When modified in such a way, the labels may change slightly or enormously or not at all. A tense, highly neurotic character, for example, may act atypically, attacking someone when afraid rather than retreating. In directing as in other creative crafts, rules cannot remain inflexible. All I can suggest is that most character moves are triggered by the listed emotions most of the time.

It frequently happens that characters retreat into *business*. When Ellen doesn't want to hear her husband's angry complaints, she escapes by paying close attention to her cooking. When Michael wants to escape from the clamoring of his kids, he immerses himself in the evening newspaper. Sometimes characters retreat by withdrawing mentally from a boring or uncomfortable situation, escaping into the snug harbor of private fantasy. Students in my classes (alas) occasionally lapse into a glassy, alpha wave state. Although they are physically present in the classroom, their minds have taken them back to last night's date or forward to Saturday's basketball game.

Emotional Turbulence

Moves that are *nondirected*, that have no relationship to other characters, frequently emerge from emotional turbulence or agitation. Such anxiety motivations as guilt, worry, apprehension, anger, loss of love or other security may trigger the movement. But positive emotional states such as ecstasy, joy, excitement, eagerness, or exhilaration may also create nondirected movement. Disorientation or disequilibrium—as from alcohol, drugs, or psychosis—can also cause nondirected movement. Sometimes, as with aggressive and retreating behavior, nondirected movement is built into a character. We all know people who by their very nature are restless, constantly in motion.

Professional directors understand internal motivations—but not always on a conscious level. Frequently they suggest movement to an actor simply because it "feels right." Such intuitive feelings usually derive from long experience, from observation and study, from discipline, from well-honed dramatic instincts, from projects that failed and projects that soared. While most professional directors may not be able to articulate in so many words the nature of the motivations described here, they will demonstrate those principles inevitably in every scene of every project they ever direct.

EXTERNAL MOTIVATIONS

While some character movements are triggered by thoughts or emotions—by internal motivations—others are generated by considerations *outside* the character.

Script

The most common external motivations arise directly from the script. A major part of a director's job is simply to tell the story. The staging of scenes, the manner in which characters move, their business, gestures, facial expressions, all serve that primary goal: to act out the plot points as defined by the writer. Thus, characters kiss, kill, fight, drink poison, dress, undress, enter and exit scenes, all as part of the basic requirement of telling a story. When the script calls for a ringing telephone, a protagonist is obliged to answer it; the move to the phone is thus dictated by script, although the director has a number of options: where to place the phone, where to position the protagonist prior to the ring, and so forth.

While the writer may suggest blockings for a scene, usually very roughly, sometimes in enormous detail, the director has the freedom either to use suggested blockings or to modify them. Since staging is acknowledged to be primarily a directorial skill, the director is frequently able to improve on a writer's suggestions. The writer and the director work together as a collaborating team.[3] The director constructs a building from a blueprint provided by the writer. If both have performed their jobs well, the skyscraper will emerge not only structurally strong but aesthetically satisfying.

Emphasis

A major directorial function is to steer spectators' attention to subject matter that carries the greatest dramatic impact at each moment in the story progression. Primarily through blocking of actors and camera, directors maximize elements they consider significant and minimize those of lesser importance: accentuating the positive, eliminating the negative. Additionally, through a variety of techniques, they are able to control how much impact their material will have upon a spectator.

---

[3]A concept articulated by Wolf Rilla in *The Writer and the Screen* (New York: William Morrow, 1974).

Stage Techniques.   In order to define how a television or film director accentuates significant elements, let us begin with an examination of traditional stage techniques for creating emphasis. There are a surprisingly large number of them.

- AREA OF STAGE: When actors stand downstage center, they attract the greatest degree of audience attention. As they move to the side or upstage, their impact gradually diminishes. (Note: downstage is nearest the audience, upstage farthest away.)

- POSITION OF ACTOR'S BODY: When actors *face* the audience, they achieve the greatest emphasis. As they turn away, they gradually lose impact until, finally, with their backs to the audience, they attract the least audience attention. (Exception: If an actor is the only cast member facing upstage, he or she may attract some degree of attention.)

- DIRECTION OF ACTORS' LOOKS: The actor at whom other actors focus their attention receives major emphasis.

- SEPARATION FROM GROUP: An actor isolated from others usually gains audience attention.

- MOVEMENT: An actor in movement attracts more attention than actors who are stationary.

- LEVELS: An actor on a different stage level than others gains emphasis. Similarly, a standing actor attracts more attention than seated actors. If all stand, then the seated actor may have the greatest emphasis.

- LIGHTING: An actor more brilliantly lighted or an unlighted actor in silhouette attracts more attention than those normally lighted.

- COSTUME: An actor costumed differently than others inevitably attracts attention.

- PICTORIAL COMPOSITION: Elements of scenery may direct the spectator's eye to a key actor. The diagonal line of a staircase, for example, directs attention to an actor on a landing. Arches, doorways, and windows tend to frame (and therefore emphasize) actors.

Notice that in a number of these categories, emphasis is achieved through *difference*—that is, when one character somehow is separated or distinguished from the others by costume, lighting, positioning, and so on.

Through use of these stage techniques, a director can emphasize certain actors at certain key moments, then divert that attention to others as the dramatic focus of a scene changes.

Stage versus TV and Film

Most of the stage techniques just listed can be directly transferred to videotape or film. When three actors in a film scene direct their attention to a fourth, for example, viewers will focus on that fourth actor. An actor standing in profile has less emphasis than one facing the camera. The primary difference between stage and screen, of course, is that a camera replaces the live audience. Thus, in TV or film, actors' relationship with their audience is in direct proportion to their relationship with the camera. Generally speaking, the closer they are to the camera, the more impact the actors will have, the more powerful will be their actions, reactions, and words they utter. (See Figure 6.1.)

If, for reasons of staging, it becomes awkward to bring an actor to the camera, the director may take the camera to the actor. A camera dollying in on an actor is similar (in the degree of emphasis only) to an actor in a theatrical presentation moving downstage (toward the audience). By moving closer, the actor achieves greater impact. A director may achieve emphasis instantaneously by cutting to a closer angle (for example, from a medium shot to a closeup).

Emphasis can also be gained through the relationship between dialog and business or between dialog and movement. An old theatrical rule of thumb states: Action before dialog points (emphasizes) the dialog; dialog before action points the action. In the scene that began this chapter, if Debbie rises from the couch, crosses slowly to Todd, sighs, and states, "I'll have her out of here by Friday," her *line* receives the impact. However, if she first tells him, "I'll have her out of here by Friday," and then crosses to the window, presses her forehead to the cold glass, and fights back tears, it is her *action* that achieves the greater impact.

Consider:

BLAISDELL
Why am I going to kill you?

He stares at his knife, tests the sharpness of its blade.

Greatest Impact

(Extreme Closeup)

Diminishing Impact

(Closeup)

Diminishing Impact

(Medium Shot)

Least Impact

(Full Shot)

Figure 6.1   In TV and film, as on the stage, the closer performers get to their audience, the greater the impact they create.

> BLAISDELL
> (continuing)
> Because you bore me.

Compare that relationship between line and business with:

> BLAISDELL
> Why am I going to kill you?
> Because you bore me.

He stares at his knife, deliberately, tauntingly tests the sharpness of its blade.

In the first example, Blaisdell's line "Because you bore me" gained impact because it had been set up by his knife business. The business whetted the viewers' appetite, built apprehension. In the second example, the knife business gained greater impact; the dialog had set it up.

Determining Significance

In order to achieve appropriate emphasis, directors must be aware of which moments in a play are significant and which are not—and the *degree* of significance generated by plot and characters. While such awareness equates with an understanding of drama itself and is largely subjective, varying from director to director, a few clues here may be helpful.

It should be obvious that any drama cannot be continuously intense; audiences need periods of relaxation in which to recover from moments of dramatic stress. Without those contrasting moments, tensions would lose much of their impact. Shakespeare's use of farce in many of his tragedies demonstrates the effectiveness of such contrast.

The growth of tension usually begins in the script. As indicated in Chapter 4, each act generally starts on a quiet note. Then gradually, from scene to scene (and within each scene), emotions build to higher and higher levels of intensity, peaking in a moment of genuine crisis at the act's end. As emotions build, so does emphasis. In moments of emotional pressure, cameras usually are close. In moments of *extreme* pressure, cameras are *extremely* close. Thus, a director's first requirement: Emphasis should match the degree of dramatic tension generated by a scene. Let's examine a few other requirements for emphasis.

Pain.   Pain is closely related to dramatic tension but is significant enough to warrant a category of its own. The degree of emphasis always should reflect the anguish generated within the characters. As the intensity of pain builds, the need for impact increases. Thus, in most scenes, the anguished character usually warrants greater emphasis than the others. This principle will be directly affected or modified by the degree of the spectators' emotional involvement with that character. If they care more, his or her anguish becomes significant. When they don't care, it becomes relatively meaningless.

Decisions.   Many scenes build to a moment in which a character must make a key decision. The moment *before* that decision is made becomes the scene's climax and should therefore be emphasized, often through attenuation. Major character decisions, however, do not always occur at the end of a scene. Whenever characters make decisions serious enough to alter their purpose, direction, or goals in a play, such moments merit emphasis.

As mentioned earlier, labels tend to become arbitrary. They oversimplify. We must realize that making a key decision is necessarily a pressured moment. Such a moment generates emotional tension and perhaps engenders mental anguish. Thus, all of the categories listed here for determining emphasis necessarily overlap, reinforcing and supporting one another.

Revelations.   Directors generally emphasize major revelations in plot or character. Such revelations often become turning points for a plot (reversals) or change the audience's concept of a character. In the motion picture *The Third Man*, for example, Harry Lime (played by Orson Welles) is "killed" prior to the film's opening. Later, when the director reveals that Lime is alive and well, the moment warrants special emphasis.

Revelations sometimes give viewers special privilege, providing them with greater knowledge than the film's characters have. When a grieving son attends his mother's funeral, for example, and we see him try to conceal a smile, that moment requires emphasis since (1) it reveals a significant aspect of his character and (2) it gives us special, privileged information denied those inside the drama. D. W. Griffith's extreme closeup of Mae Marsh's hands in *Intolerance*, fingers twisting nervously, revealed the depth of her feelings at her husband's murder trial.

Directors often must walk the narrow line between emphasis and overemphasis, especially in situations that border on melodrama. When we discover that a loving wife is actually plotting her husband's demise, for example, or that a timid bank teller is really a psychotic assassin, the director must be careful to avoid the overstatement that cheapens and blunts such insights.

The next chapter will discuss emphasis at greater length, specifically in its relationship with the camera.

SYMBOLIC RELATIONSHIPS

Have you ever watched an airline movie without earphones? Or studied a TV soap opera with the sound off? Chances are, if the show was well directed, you were able to make some fairly shrewd inferences about the relationships between characters—not so much from their gestures or facial expressions as from their movements and physical positioning in relation to one another.

Let's return to the Todd-Debbie scene one last time. We'll turn off the volume and pretend to know nothing of their story. We see a balding man pursuing an attractive, middle-aged woman. She breaks away from him and sits on a couch. He towers over her, staring down at her. She says something and starts to cry. Maybe he's accusing her of unfaithfulness, maybe of squandering their money. We don't know, of course, without hearing the words. But the visual image provides clues to their *relationship*.

Clearly the balding man is the aggressor, the dominant person making angry demands, and she is troubled, retreating, unable to face him. The picture alone provides insights. Ideally, the behavior and physical positioning of characters in every dramatic scene should provide that same kind of dramatic context, should create a recognizable representation of the characters' emotional or symbolic relationship.

Let's examine a typical soap opera situation and see how the physical positioning of characters might symbolize or reflect their emotional relationship. Larry's employer-mistress pays a visit to his wife. Her purpose: to convince the wife to divorce Larry so that he will be free to marry her. Larry's wife is shocked; this is the first she has known of her husband's affair with his attractive boss. More than shocked, she is blazing angry. At that moment, Larry enters, home early from work.

As director, where do you position Larry in this scene? Initially, probably in the middle, employer-mistress on one side, wife on the other, pulled in two directions by the women who love him. How does Larry feel about these women? If he truly loves his wife, he will go to her, trying to explain his actions, seeking forgiveness. Will she remain beside him, permitting this closeness? Probably not. Motivated by anger and resentment, she will move away. She has distanced herself from her husband emotionally and now she will distance herself from him physically. The external mirrors the internal. What of the mistress? If she loves Larry, she will go to him. Perhaps he moves away, rejecting her. Perhaps the mistress will place herself between husband and wife, physically as well as symbolically the divisive force in their marriage.

Presented in such naked terms, with unidimensional characters, such staging appears simplistic, old-fashioned, melodramatic, and arbitrary. With the complexities offered by more mature characters and the introduction of plot subtleties, however, the scene achieves some degree of dimension and believability.

When blocking a scene, begin with questions. What are the emotions that drive your characters? Are they angry with each other, emotionally far apart? Then perhaps your staging should place them far apart. If the scene's progression allows them gradually to rediscover their love, to become emotionally closer and closer, then perhaps your blocking should parallel that pattern, bringing them physically closer and closer, creating in the scene's final moments an atmosphere of delicious intimacy.

Examine your scene as written. Try to visualize the movement of characters in your mind. Let their emotions create your mental imagery. Let their relationship determine their relative positioning. Draw a quick diagram of the scene, just as you saw it in your mind. Then apply this test: Would an audience be able to deduce the relationships of your characters just from your staging?

Watch dramatic programs on TV. Turn off the volume. If the programs have been skillfully directed, the silent pictures will speak loudly.

BLOCKING CAMERA TO ACTORS

Most experienced directors begin the taping or filming of a scene by blocking their actors. Once satisfied that movement and business are comfortable, honest, and dramatically effective, they then block their camera(s) to cover the action. Why not the other way around? Why not start with dynamic camera angles and then block actors to camera? Because, as indicated earlier, audiences become involved with *people*. So close and sensitive is this relationship that, for the duration of the program, the spectator *becomes* the protagonist. Dishonesty in staging or performance creates obstacles to that rapport.

While the director and crew remain acutely aware of the camera's important, extremely creative functions, the average spectator notes them only as part of the production mosaic, aware of angles and camera movement on a subconscious rather than conscious level. Surprisingly, even production veterans tend to get lost in drama, temporarily oblivious to its technological aspects, submerged in a fantasy world until some extraordinary camera movement or editorial fillip snaps them out of it.

When a director begins blocking with camera rather than with actors, staging can appear manufactured. An actor's movement, forced into precircumscribed patterns, then must accommodate the needs of the glass-eyed monster instead of emerging honestly from thoughts or emotions.

The director's hand should remain invisible. Action that appears contrived or arbitrary makes it difficult for an audience to forget that those people on the screen are actors wearing costumes and makeup, speaking scripted words in front of painted sets.

Occasionally, inexperienced directors loudly proclaim their presence with flashy camera angles and attention-getting gimmicks. Every overstated shot shouts, "Look at me! I'm directing!" They are showing off; they are also destroying the show, making the audience aware of contrivance and artifice by calling attention to themselves.

Sensitive acting, well directed, can make a show succeed in spite of mediocre camera work. Mediocre acting and staging, however, usually condemn a show to failure despite the most brilliant camera work in the world.

Actors first, then camera.

BLOCKING ACTORS TO CAMERA

Are there ever occasions when it is appropriate to think of camera first? Yes, dozens of situations require that directors begin their planning with the camera's perspective.

At the start of a show or sequence, *orientation* frequently becomes a concern. Where is the action taking place? On another planet? In an apartment building? In a submarine? When orientation is more important than human values, select an angle that will clearly establish the locale for your audience. Such footage, often appearing under opening titles, also establishes the mood or atmosphere of the show, much as the overture in a Broadway play prepares the audience emotionally for the action to follow.

On occasion, the camera must make a *plot point*. Perhaps an angle past the leading lady must include a closet in which the villain hides. Perhaps you must begin a scene on a cigar butt in an ashtray to establish that the villain has been here. Perhaps, when the villain is present in a scene, his identity must be kept secret. Then the camera can shoot from a special angle that reveals only his shadow or his legs or his hand wearing a distinctive ring.

In shows where believability is not a factor, where honesty of performance is irrelevant, you may begin anywhere you choose. In farce, for instance, the director's only goal is to get laughs. If that means phony action, dishonest line readings, and distortion lenses, so be it. As comedy moves away from farce, however, and approaches reality (such as the situation comedy), honesty of performance becomes a more critical factor.

Sometimes camera location is determined by a scene's mood or atmosphere, as when a camera begins on a window or on a screen door banging restlessly in the wind to establish stormy weather.

Occasionally camera position is determined by optical effects (*EFX*) or animation. Perhaps a factory on fire will be *matted* (optically printed) into your scene after you have photographed it. In order not to dislocate geographies, you must lock your camera down in one master angle. Then, as in the previous circumstances, the blocking of actors cannot be the primary consideration.

Once a scene has been blocked, rehearsed, and lighted, actors frequently must make adjustments in the blocking so that camera angles will be clean and effective and will make the dramatic statement required by the director. Sometimes one actor will obstruct another while crossing downstage or will throw a disruptive shadow. Any professional actor can comfortably make simple adjustments that will not affect the integrity of his or her actions. When actors' positions are critical, be sure that they are clearly marked on the stage floor with chalk or tape.

PREPARATION

Most directors plan their blocking ahead of time, the night before shooting or even earlier. As I have indicated and will certainly indicate again, meticulous preparation is a hallmark of the successful director.

During the always-too-short preparation period, the director has selected locations, discussed the script and a succession of rewrites with producer and writer, examined props, met with the cinematographer or technical director to debate the style and "look" of the project, selected stars and supporting cast, examined and approved sets and discussed their dressing, studied and reorganized the production schedule, sweated over script deletions required by budget, approved the cast's wardrobe, makeup, and hairdressing, plus a hundred other tasks that overflowed each preparation day and made it appear that the project would never get off the ground.

By the time directors begin production, they know each scene practically by heart. They understand their characters in depth. They have explored their characters' childhoods; their manner of speaking, walking, and dressing; their fears; the kind of cars they drive; their relationships with other characters; perhaps even their sexual proclivities.

Before the project begins, the art director gives the director floor plans of all major sets plus photographs or sketches of key locations that the director will use in blocking the action. Inevitably, during preparation, the director begins to visualize how many key scenes will play. That visualization will change in some degree as shooting begins and the characters acquire dimension.

The final blocking of a day's work (or reexamination of an earlier blocking) usually is accomplished the night before shooting. With floor plans and script rewrites in hand, the director sets out to define the actions and business of characters in each scene. Directors, particularly those who are inexperienced, should ask themselves such questions as:

1. Do I clearly understand the writer's intentions? Reexamine the scene in terms of its place in the plot progression. What scene precedes it, what scene follows? What will be the transitions? Is this a key scene or one of relative unimportance?

2. When was the last time these characters were together? What happened then? What was their relationship then? Has anything happened since then that might affect their relationship?

3. What were these characters doing immediately before the scene begins? Will their prior activities affect this scene?

4. What normal activities would the characters be engaged in at this time of day in this setting? (You are searching for logical *business* for the scene.)

5. What will be the characters' emotional state? Will it change during the scene? How will their emotional states affect their movements and business during the scene?

6. Where will the focus of interest (emphasis) lie at each moment? How will I direct audience attention there, with appropriate impact?

7. What will be the audience position in this scene? How can I generate suspense (tension) and build it to a climax?

8. Will the scene create any special camera or lighting problems? Have I discussed them with my cinematographer or technical director? Generally, what kind of camera coverage will the scene require?

9. Will the dialog fit comfortably into the mouths of the actors? (While dialog should have been polished earlier, television's last-minute urgency often makes such questioning necessary.) Will the dialog need to be adjusted?

10. How much time should I allow myself for the shooting of this scene? Shooting time varies in direct proportion to a scene's importance in the script. Other factors include night shooting on location and such physical problems as stunts, helicopters, and animals.

Once the tentative blocking has been worked out, the director then makes a rough sketch, usually on the blank (left) script page facing the dialog. Examples of such sketches appear in Figure 6.2. Some directors prepare simple, crude diagrams; others draw detailed sketches coded with one specific color for each actor, tracing his or her movement through the scene, another color for the camera, and still another enumerating properties and other physical requirements.

Because the day's work has been carefully prepared, the director walks onto the stage with confidence. While rehearsal procedures vary enormously, the following pattern is used most frequently in film.

While the crew watches, the director walks through a scene with the actors, trying out blockings tentatively, making sure that the pattern is comfortable for the cast and that it makes the necessary dramatic statement. Because a director has blocked a scene in a certain way on paper doesn't mean it will necessarily end up that way on film. Sometimes homework provides the perfect blocking for a scene; sometimes the blocking requires adjustment; sometimes it goes out the window. Actors often come up with excellent ideas that will change or modify a scene's movement or business. Secure with preblocked concepts, the director can remain flexible, objectively assessing suggested variations rather than clinging defensively to a fixed blocking. If proposed changes are not appropriate, the director must be firm, following original instincts and returning to the original blocking.

Onstage blocking usually begins with a brief discussion of a scene's content followed by tentative explorations of its staging. Actors walk through

Figure 6.2   These notes and sketches from Walter Grauman's shooting script of an episode of "Streets of San Francisco" demonstrate a director's attention to detail and the complexities of staging. The sketches on page 147 were drawn on the back of the first page of script. (From "A Room with a View" written by Del Reisman and Cliff Gould. © 1973 QM Productions. Used with permission of The Taft Entertainment Company and Walter E. Grauman.)

various patterns, feeling their way, allowing the scene's emotional thrust to guide them, responding to suggestions from the director.

Director Walter Grauman notes that when actors follow their instincts, working out movement and business for themselves, their blocking frequently turns out almost identical to the blocking he had devised at home the previous

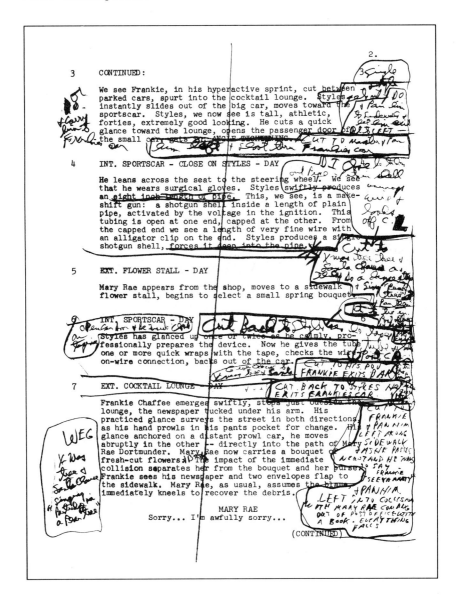

night. Some actors feel more secure working out a blocking for themselves; others are delighted to have a director guide them. *All* actors need the security of a director who has studied the scene and is ready with answers should problems develop. Additional notes on rehearsal techniques can be found in Chapter 5.

Once everyone has agreed on the pattern of movement, the actors' positions are marked on the floor and the director discusses coverage with the cinematographer. Experienced directors are seldom arbitrary; they encourage input from their cinematographers, who often make major contributions to a scene's visual effectiveness.

Now director and actors leave the set, getting out of the way of the camera crew and electricians. For lighting purposes, stand-ins take the place of the principal cast. Off in a corner, the director and cast go over the scene's dialog. They discuss the dramatic spine of the scene, reexamining relationships and the emotions of the characters, rewriting words or phrases that seem awkward.

On some videotaped shows (rarely in film), the director schedules cast readings prior to the start of production. Seated around a table with the producer and the writer, the cast tentatively reads through the material, exploring its content. Sometimes several days are devoted to such readings. When scenes don't work, they are returned to the writer for reexamination. When speeches seem uncomfortable, the writer fixes them. Problems concerning characters and relationships are ironed out now, removing pressure from the production schedule.

Once the set has been lighted, the director and cast begin final rehearsal—with camera. Now the director must decide when the actors are "into" a scene, when optimum performance has been reached as well as perfect coordination between camera crew and cast. Traditionally, directors do not ask actors to give their top performance in rehearsal; most actors would refrain anyway, because they try to save their best efforts for tape or film. They dislike reaching a dramatic peak too early, fearing that they will be unable to achieve it again. Some camera-wise professionals are notorious for saving their best performances for closeups, thereby hoping to ensure that those closeups will be included in the final cut.

An experienced director who notices a problem with a performance or a line reading does not embarrass the actor by making a correction in front of the cast and crew. Instead, the director takes the actor aside and quietly discusses the problem. Likewise, if the director is unhappy with a member of the camera crew—a dolly has been too fast or a pan too slow—the director takes it up quietly with the cinematographer who then discusses it with the crew member.

Once everyone is ready for a "take," final lighting adjustments are made. Makeup people and hairdressers hurry into the set to make certain that the cast's appearance is camera perfect.

The assistant director rolls film. When sound is up to speed, the director calls, "Action," and the filming begins. There may be several takes before the director feels the scene is acceptable and advises the camera assistant to print it. Usually, the director then repositions the camera for editorial coverage, breaking the master angle into two-shots, closeups, or whatever angles may be necessary for appropriate dramatic emphasis.

CHAPTER HIGHLIGHTS

- Director Elia Kazan's words, "Directing finally consists of turning Psychology into Behavior," establish the theme for this chapter concerning the staging of actors. While audiences generally believe that actors' movements in a scene arise spontaneously, professionals recognize that such actions grow from a script, from a director's vision, and from repeated and painstaking rehearsal. The director's manipulation of actors on a stage is called *blocking*.

- In general, actions are more revealing of character thoughts or emotions than is dialog. In many scenes, dialog provides a meaningless accompaniment to the more significant content, revealed through actions. Action also demands greater spectator participation since its meaning must be interpreted.

- Specific character activities such as combing hair or mixing drinks are called *business*. While business contributes significantly to the reality of scenes, it should also reveal facets of the character who performs it or contribute to the dynamics of a scene.

- Part of a director's job is to reveal characters' thoughts or emotions through actions. Symbols often provide an answer. For example, the actions of a young woman in relation to a stuffed animal given her by her boyfriend will reveal her feelings about him. Thus, when she trashes the animal, she is, in a sense, trashing him.

- When characters move in a scene, usually there is some *internal motivation*. Such motivations fall into three categories: involvement, disinvolvement, and emotional turbulence. *Involvement* moves a character toward another; it is either an aggressive or a seeking action, motivated by such emotions as anger, lust, affection, and love. Its forward moves sometimes arise out of need for an object or information. *Disinvolvement* suggests retreat, movement away from another character, and generally is triggered by such emotions as shame, fear, hatred, or anger. Characters often retreat into business. *Emotional turbulence* suggests nondirected movement and is triggered by anxiety or nervousness and by such positive emotions as ecstasy and exhilaration. Nondirected movement also is motivated by drugs, alcohol, or psychosis. These simplistic labels are often modified by the nature of the character or the content of the scene.

- Some character moves are generated by considerations *outside* the character. First, the script accounts for most such moves, requiring actors to answer telephones, kiss, kill, dress, undress, and so forth. These are movements necessary to the simple telling of a story. The second external reason for character movement is to provide dramatic emphasis. Part of a director's job is to focus viewer attention on subject matter that carries the greatest significance from moment to moment.

- The theater provides effective patterns for emphasis through staging. Stage directors emphasize actors by moving them downstage, center-stage, or facing the audience, or by contrasting them with other actors through costume, lighting, or stage position. Many of these stage techniques may be adapted to videotape or film with the camera replacing the live audience.

- Emphasis can also be achieved through the relationship between business or movement and dialog. Whichever comes first sets up the importance of the second.

- The relative positions of characters within a frame often symbolize their emotional relationships. By watching a TV drama without sound, for example, we may make shrewd inferences about the relationships of its characters. Characters far apart emotionally often are staged apart, the external mirroring the internal.

- In staging a scene, directors usually block actors before they block camera. The reason: what happens *in front of* the camera is more significant to audiences than the camera work.

- Sometimes directors place camera considerations first, such as when the director needs to orient the audience, usually at the start of a show or sequence; to use the camera to make a plot point; to establish a mood or atmosphere; and to let the camera provide the photographic basis for animation or optical effects.

- Meticulous preparation is a hallmark of a successful director. Preparation culminates on the night before shooting. The director finalizes each scene in the schedule, blocking (or reblocking) the action, examining dialog and all other aspects of the day's work.

- On the soundstage, the director may suggest a pattern of movement or the actors may prefer to find their own blocking, allowing the scene's emotional thrust to steer them. In either event, the director should be prepared.

C   H   A   P   T   E   R   7

Staging the camera

The camera has three basic functions. The first seems obvious: *Camera covers the action*. It tells the story, revealing to the spectator what is happening. If this function is ineffective, the audience won't stay around to watch the other two.

The second function echoes a major discussion from the last chapter. Camera calls attention to the significant; it minimizes or eliminates the unimportant. And it creates various degrees of impact for significant elements. Thus, *camera creates appropriate emphasis*. The discussion of camera emphasis complements the last chapter's examination of actor emphasis.

Less obvious than the first two functions is that *camera contributes to mood and atmosphere*. Every aspect of a camera's use makes some definable dramatic statement, obvious or subtle, that helps to shape an audience's emotional response.

It should be remembered that the following discussion will not attempt any comprehensive examination of the mechanics of camera operation. As indicated in the preface, this is no production manual. Were we to discuss production aspects of television and film, this volume would double or treble its present size. This chapter explores primarily camera's three dramatic functions:

1. Covering the action
2. Creating appropriate emphasis
3. Creating mood and atmosphere

One must compose images as the old masters did their canvases, with the same preoccupation with effect and expression.   MARCEL CARNÉ[1]

COVERING THE ACTION

The simplest method of photographing a dramatic scene would be to place a camera some distance from the cast and record all of the action in a fixed wide angle. This was how pioneer directors first photographed silent films. It was as if the camera were recording a stage play, anchored to a seat in the fourth or fifth row and photographing dramatic action through a proscenium arch. Actors moved laterally across the frame, seldom if ever upstage or downstage; inevitably they were framed head to toe or wider. When David Wark Griffith tried to move his camera closer, the producer screamed. Audiences would never be satisfied with half an actor![2]

Creativity prevailed. Griffith discovered that closer angles not only reveal more of facial expressions and detail, but they also carry far greater impact. Additionally, by moving the camera from the fourth row and placing it "on the stage," within the scene itself, actions immediately became more dynamic and camera angles more interesting. The audience became *part* of the unfolding drama rather than merely a spectator.

[1]Quoted by Louis Giannetti in *Understanding Movies* (Englewood Cliffs, N.J.: Prentice-Hall, 1976), p. 48.

[2]As cited by Arthur Knight in *The Liveliest Art* (New York: New American Library, 1979), p. 24.

During this century's first two decades, pioneers developed most of the techniques that still provide the basis for film and video dramatic structures: closeups, over-the-shoulder shots, dolly and panning shots, dissolves, split screen, and all the rest. As Hollywood grew to become the world's film capital, its production techniques became oriented to mass production. As yearly output grew, certain filmic patterns became standard. Most scenes began with a wide shot for orientation: If the producer had spent $10,000 for a set, by thunder, he wanted to make certain that audiences would see it! Orientation also revealed who was in the scene and what they were doing. Gradually, as tensions built, camera angles would move closer until, at the scene's climax, action usually played in closeups.

This was Hollywood's pattern for covering dramatic action in the teens, twenties, and thirties; it is still valid for most scenes today.

Camera Progression

The next time you attend a stage play, become aware of what happens to your attention. As you take a seat and begin to leaf through your program, you note that the man next to you has a terrible cough. Involuntarily, you draw away from him. The woman in front of you wears a bouffant hairstyle, almost obscuring the stage. You lean to your left so as to see better. A young couple two rows down is cuddling and kissing. You try not to watch them. Moments later the lights dim, the curtain rises, and the play begins.

Gradually, as the actors establish their characters and their problems, your interest grows. You ignore the man with the cough, the bouffant hairdo, and the couple cuddling and kissing. While a small part of your consciousness remains in the audience, aware that you are watching a performance, the larger part is moving closer to the stage ("camera dollying in"). At first you're absorbing the stage setting and figuring out character identities as well as the nature of their relationships. As you become more deeply involved, you fasten your attention first on one actor and then another. As concentration heightens, you lock your attention more closely onto faces. In a sense, your attention has moved from a full shot to a medium shot to individual closeups. When the curtain descends at the end of the act, you reluctantly "dolly back" to your seat in the audience. As the house lights come up, you again become aware of the coughing man and the others. You had totally forgotten them.

By studying your own reactions to stage plays and other dramatic forms, you can recognize the psychological validity of the camera pattern established by Hollywood so long ago. By creating a progression of increasingly closer angles, the director parallels the consciousness of the attentive viewer.

Are there exceptions to the "start wide and move closer" theory? Of course. Frequently it becomes dramatically effective to begin a scene on the face of an actor as he or she utters a trenchant line or on a close shot of a prop or a significant piece of business. One overused beginning to a scene is a ringing telephone. As a hand enters the shot, the camera pulls back to reveal the person answering. Beginning a scene on hands pouring a drink, a phonograph needle in a dead groove, or a close reflection shot in a mirror are all patterns we have seen repeatedly on television. Close opening shots are frequently effective following a scene that ends wide, the contrast in angles providing a change that is visually refreshing.

Even when a scene begins in a close angle, the director needs to orientate the audience soon, especially if the scene lasts more than a minute or two. Such orientation may be achieved either by dropping back to a wide shot or by panning an actor across the set, thereby allowing viewers to discover where the action is taking place.

Style of Coverage

Photographing the action, telling a story with a camera, may be achieved in an endless variety of ways, depending on the director's individual style and the dramatic requirements of the scene. Some directors, especially those who learned their craft in the early days of live television, avoid frequent cutting to new angles. They prefer a fluid, moving camera that follows actors about the set. Such directors carefully interrelate movements of cast and camera so that the most significant moments play in close angles. Often such staging is beautiful to watch, a carefully choreographed ballet of actors and camera.

Other directors prefer to shoot a single *master angle,* that is, a comprehensive shot, usually wide, that covers the action of an entire scene. Then they "break up" the scene into closer angles: medium shots, over-the-shoulder shots, and closeups. The editor then builds a progressive structure that follows the scene's dramatic growth. The additional angles are called *coverage.* In network television where time strictures are necessary, some coverage is essential, allowing the editor to trim final footage to the exact time required.

Camera coverage also provides editorial flexibility in dealing with dramatic values. It permits an editor to tighten scenes that play too slowly or to stretch moments that play magnificently; to eliminate bad line readings or unnecessary dialog; to favor an excellent actor and minimize a bad one. Such coverage is primarily used, however, for purposes of dramatic emphasis, which we discussed in the last chapter and which we will return to in a moment.

The Set-up

Each time the director moves a camera to a new position in order to photograph the action from a different angle, the new position is called a *camera set-up* or, simply, a *set-up*. Each new camera set-up requires a new lighting set-up. Since lighting can consume a considerable amount of time, varying with the size of the set and the complexity of the staging—and each minute of production time costs hundreds of dollars—each set-up is expensive. Unnecessary set-ups are fiscally irresponsible. For feature films with extravagant budgets, economy in numbers of set-ups is not a major consideration. But for many television programs where dollars are limited, the number of set-ups per day becomes a significant directorial concern.

Can a scene be covered in two set-ups? Three set-ups? Four? In planning a day's work, television directors must think in such terms. Sometimes by eliminating set-ups in unimportant scenes, a director will gain the luxury of additional coverage for a major scene or the time needed to shoot an additional location, giving the show a handsomer look.

In staging scenes, then, the director should consider two factors: how to make it good (dramatically effective) and how to make it "cheap," that is, within the anticipated budget. While the budget is primarily the unit manager's (and the producer's) concern, any director who wants to work again must respect its limitations.

Staging a Scene

Let's stage a simple, two-person scene and consider some of the ways in which a director might use a camera to cover the action.

> *The Plot:* David McKenna's girlfriend, Eileen, announces that she is leaving him. She has been promoted to an executive-level job in another city and has decided to go there alone. As she packs, David reminds her of the good times they've shared, asking her to reconsider. She coldly refuses. David's anger flares and he tells her to get out of his house. She starts to pack a photograph of David and herself but he takes it, tears it in half, and gives her back the half in which only she appears. He grins wryly as she slams shut the suitcase and storms from the room.

Simplicity in Staging.   The most economical way of covering the action of this scene (though probably not the most effective) is in a single camera angle. Examine Figure 7.1, which arbitrarily places the bed in the center of the set with Eileen on one side packing and David facing her from the other side.

What are the positive aspects of such a staging? Well, the physical separation of David and Eileen symbolizes their emotional separation. Perhaps at one point he walks around the bed to her as he asks her to stay. But she pulls

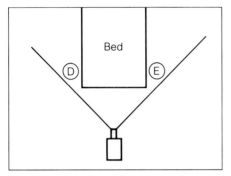

Figure 7.1   The camera photographs David and Eileen in profile, from a static side angle, with minimum impact.

Figure 7.2   What the camera in Figure 7.1 would see: Separated by a bed, the figures would probably be smaller (with less impact) than indicated here.

away, takes her suitcase, and leaves. Now the separation is complete. Camera dollies in to a closeup of David to register his reaction.

What are the negative aspects of such a staging? First, the camera shoots both actors in profile for most of the scene, which provides little impact. Second, the separation requires a wide angle, which (again) diminishes the impact. Third, the angle presents a balanced, symmetrical, static composition, lacking in visual dynamics. Glance at Figure 7.2. Not very exciting, is it?

Suppose I change things around and place the bed in the *foreground.* Eileen enters through a door in the upstage wall, takes a suitcase from under the bed, and begins packing. David comes up behind her. Now both actors *face the camera* (see Figure 7.3). Eileen ignores his pleas, continues to pack hurriedly, crossing to dresser from time to time, camera panning with her, the motion helping to keep the picture visually interesting. The audience sees both characters in full face and in depth for most of the scene, which makes the picture dynamic.

Some directors use this kind of simplified staging when they need to gain time. It's functional, especially if a scene is short or not of great dramatic significance.

If time permits, a director might expand the camera coverage slightly by allowing Eileen to turn upstage at a critical point to face David. Now the scene will require one additional angle, a complementary over-the-shoulder shot, camera facing Eileen (see Figure 7.4). With this added angle, the film or tape editor will be able to cut back and forth between the two shots, favoring first David and then Eileen, as dramatic emphasis changes.

Figure 7.3   With David behind Eileen, both facing camera, impact would be vastly increased. Dotted lines indicate a closer shot, achieved when the camera zooms or dollies closer.

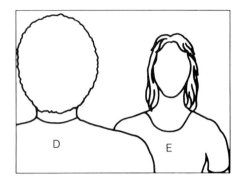

Figure 7.4   The reverse of the closer shot shown in Figure 7.3: what the camera would photograph when Eileen turns to face David.

A Typical Staging.   If given more time and if the scene is critically important to the script, a director might attempt a slightly more ambitious staging that requires additional camera coverage. Examine Figure 7.5.

The letter *D* indicates David's position as the scene begins; *E* indicates Eileen's entrance and her initial move to David who is repairing a cabinet. The camera is positioned in a master angle that will photograph the entire scene. Note that from this basic camera position a director could either start the scene close on David and widen to include the door as Eileen enters, or start close on the door (adjusting David's opening position slightly) as Eileen enters and dolly back to include David when she moves to him. Each of these shots carries implications. Beginning on David implies faintly that it's "his" scene, played from his general perspective. Beginning on Eileen's entrance implies the reverse.

A director could play the first confrontation in the master angle, but in order to see David's reaction to Eileen's announcement, he or she would need a second set-up, a reverse of the master angle, as indicated in Figure 7.6. The master angle plus the reverse provide loose over-the-shoulder shots as indicated in Figures 7.7 and 7.8.

Crossing the Line.   Notice that in Figures 7.7 and 7.8 David is positioned on the left side of the frame and Eileen is on the right. If after photographing the

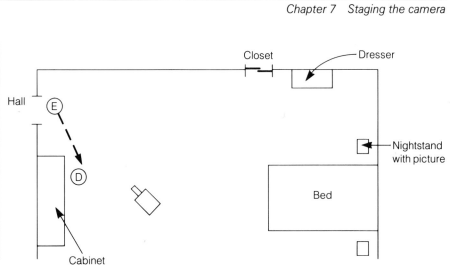

Figure 7.5   David and Eileen's bedroom. The diagram indicates camera's position as Eileen enters and moves to David.

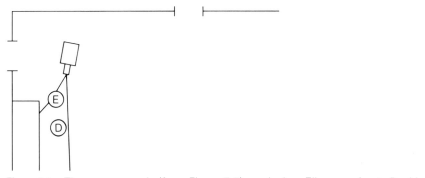

Figure 7.6   The reverse angle (from Figure 7.5) used when Eileen confronts David.

Figure 7.7   What the camera photographs in Figure 7.5: an over-the-shoulder shot favoring Eileen.

Figure 7.8   The reverse of Figure 7.7: an over-the-shoulder shot favoring David.

first set-up, a director accidentally moves the camera across the invisible line that bisects the two actors (that is, if the camera in Figure 7.6 were located in the doorway) and photographs the second set-up from that camera position, there would be a disconcerting *jump* when the two angles were edited together. David would abruptly switch position from the left to the right side of the frame, and Eileen would do the reverse. Such mismatching of images, *crossing the line*, is awkward and disorienting—the mark of an amateur director. So long as the camera angles remain on the same side of that magic line running through the two players, their positions will remain constant from cut to cut.

Developing the Scene.   Let's assume that after a few lines of dialog Eileen impatiently crosses to the closet and pulls out a small suitcase that she places on the bed. During the remaining action, she repeatedly crosses to the dresser, taking clothing from drawers and arranging it hurriedly in the suitcase. Picture the action in your mind as the camera in its master angle (as shown in Figure 7.5) pans with Eileen as she crosses first to the closet and then to the bed. When she moves to the dresser to get her clothing, she moves upstage in the shot. (See Figure 7.9.)

When David pursues her, moving to the bed, he enters the master angle, which had panned away from him and stayed with Eileen when she crossed to the closet. The camera now holds another two-shot, and again David is positioned on the left side of the frame. The camera operator may have to

Figure 7.9   Camera pans right as Eileen crosses to the closet, takes out the suitcase, and carries it to the bed. She moves back and forth from closet to bed, carrying and packing articles of clothing.

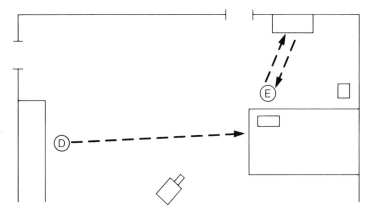

Figure 7.10   David crosses from his original position and enters the camera's master angle, a loose over-the-shoulder shot.

adjust slightly in order to accommodate a clean over-the-shoulder shot. (See Figure 7.10.)

In this position, as in the initial angle by the cabinet, the camera is angled past David toward Eileen who packs busily, almost ignoring him. We need one final angle, one which favors David as he stands at the corner of the bed. It will be the reverse of the master angle, shooting past Eileen toward David. We begin this last set-up with David still in his position by the cabinet and bring him into the two-shot. The editor may be able to use this extra coverage, intercutting it with Eileen's action. This third camera position is shown in Figure 7.11. The camera shoots past Eileen in profile toward David who now faces almost directly into camera as he pleads with her.

Finally, when Eileen picks up the picture from the nightstand beside the bed, her movement can be photographed from the master angle (Figure 7.10), panning her to the nightstand and back to the suitcase.

If a director wants to play the final confrontation between Eileen and David in closeups rather than complementary over-the-shoulder shots, he or she may do so "merely" by changing lenses. This gives the scene the feeling of five set-ups rather than three, with relatively little loss of time. I placed the word *merely* in quotation marks since the lighting director may want to make a few adjustments in order to accommodate the closer angles.

The staging of this scene, while relatively simple, was arbitrary. It could be blocked in a hundred different ways, with dozens of camera variations of each. The set was designed specifically to accommodate the action and to permit effective but economical camera coverage. Similarly, action can be tailored to accommodate a set. When production companies work in actual locations, a phenomenon happening more and more frequently in both television and feature films, directors must adapt their staging to whatever settings they encounter. In most productions, directors and art directors work closely together, shaping both the set and its dressing to specific staging requirements.

Creative Planning.   It might be helpful to describe the thought processes that went into designing the set for the Eileen-David scene so that you can understand the integration necessary between scenery, properties, and physical action.

In a sense, the tail wagged the dog. The action of packing a suitcase seemed essential to the thrust of the scene; it added immediacy and urgency. Therefore the closet (location for the suitcase), dresser, and bed had to be relatively near one another in order to keep the action from becoming unwieldy. I needed to find some occupation for David (business) at the top of the scene. Yes, he could have been reading a newspaper or watching television, but both are passive occupations. Either would have created the impression

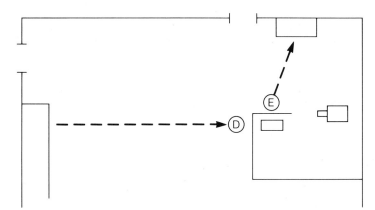

Figure 7.11   Camera is now in a reverse position, shooting toward David as he crosses from the cabinet to the bed.

that Eileen was out working while David lounged lazily at home. Better by far to put him to work painting or repairing a cabinet.

Because of the need to be economical in terms of set-ups, I placed the door in a spot where Eileen could enter and walk immediately into an over-the-shoulder shot. Had a director been shooting in an actual location, he or she would have placed David wherever necessary to achieve that same camera position. Similarly, the closet and bed were placed in proximity so that a camera could conveniently pan Eileen into her second, packing position, maintaining the economy of one master angle.

Three-Shots

Camera coverage of three characters requires more care in planning than coverage of two since the possibility of disorientation becomes more likely. Recall that the director of a two-shot creates an imaginary line that bisects the characters. So long as the camera remains on one side of that invisible line, the characters maintain their same relative positions in the frame, from cut to cut.

The same principle applies to camera coverage of three characters. Figure 7.12 shows how the camera in its master angle would view the positions of three characters. When a director breaks a three-shot into two-shots or singles, he or she must again respect the invisible lines that bisect the characters.

Figure 7.12 A triangular three-shot. Additional angles, two-shots, would maintain same relative positions of performers: Terry remaining on the left, Vanessa on the right. Tim, who stands at the apex of the triangle in the three-shot, now faces left to Terry and right to Vanessa.

Note that three characters will always form some kind of triangle—unless you place them in a line which is visually static and therefore generally undesirable.

If you were the director, how would you cover the actors in Figure 7.12? (That is, how would you break the three shot into two-shots?) In order to avoid audience confusion, the characters in each leg of the triangle must maintain their same relative positions (see Figures 7.13–7.16). Note that Terry always remains on screen left when facing Tim or Vanessa. Vanessa always remains on screen right when facing Tim or Terry. But Tim, who

Figure 7.13   In an over-the-shoulder angle, Tim faces left to Terry.

stands at the apex of the triangle, will always face *right* when playing to Vanessa and *left* when playing to Terry.

In closeups, the directions of characters' *looks* conform to these patterns. Thus, Tim will look right to Vanessa and left to Terry. In actual practice you will find that characters' looks may be cheated toward the camera in order to give the audience a more frontal view without disorientation.

If the characters change positions relative to one another or if the camera changes position relative to the three characters, an entirely new triangle is established—with new physical relationships. Then the director must care-

Figure 7.14   In a reverse of Figure 7.13, Terry faces right to Tim.

fully reexamine the camera coverage and adjust it to the new positions in order to avoid disorienting the audience.

Direction of Movement

Audience expectancy grows from simple logic. When the cavalry chases Indians over a hill, both (of course) head in the same direction. When directors divide their camera coverage into separate shots—as they necessarily must when cavalry and Indians are separated by considerable distance—audience expectancy logically remains the same. Both will be heading in the same screen direction: right to left or left to right (see Figure 7.17).

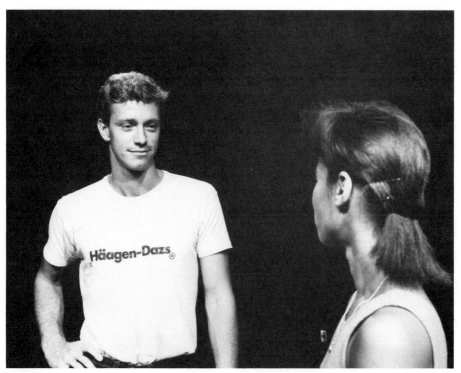

Figure 7.15   In over-the-shoulder angles between Tim and Vanessa, Tim faces right, Vanessa faces left, maintaining the same relative positions as in the original triangular three-shot.

Removed from any story context, such intercut shots carry no implications regarding who is chasing whom. Indians could be chasing cavalry; cavalry could be chasing Indians. But the very fact that the shots are intercut unmistakably implies *relationship*. The two elements somehow are acting upon each other. Visual clues such as the Indians repeatedly glancing backward or the cavalry firing their guns in a forward direction would, of course, clarify their relative positions.

Examine the implications if just one of the elements changes directions. Suppose that the cavalry races from left to right and the Indians from right to left. What would be your assumption? It would, of course, depend on story context, but generally there are two possibilities. The cavalry and Indians are

Figure 7.16   In a reverse of Figure 7.15, Vanessa faces left to Tim.

either running *away* from each other (perhaps after a confrontation) or heading *toward* each other (the confrontation still to come).

Practical Applications.   Writers and directors frequently use the implications in the direction of character movement in order to build suspense. It is late at night. A young secretary has been working late. She locks the office and begins walking home, left to right. On another street, a psychotic killer moves along in the shadows. He walks *right to left*! Clearly, the implication of these intercut camera angles is that the killer will intercept the secretary. Instantly the audience begins to worry.

Figure 7.17   When the cavalry charges, its screen direction must remain constant from shot to shot (left to right or right to left); otherwise, audiences may become disoriented. (From *Stagecoach*. Used with permission of Caidin Film Company.)

Patterns of screen direction create geographies in the spectator's mind. If the young secretary has repeatedly left her office to go home and each time has walked from left to right, viewers create a mental picture of her home located somewhere to the right of her office. If after establishing such a geographical relationship, the director then violates it, allowing the girl to walk toward her home in a right-to-left progression, the audience would certainly become disoriented.

A similar principle governs the flight of airplanes or the direction of travel of buses or trains. Audiences tend to superimpose a subconscious map of the United States (or whatever country) over the action. Thus, planes flying from

Los Angeles to New York should travel from left to right; trains travelling from Washington, D.C., to Denver should travel from right to left. When they travel north or south, you're on your own!

Changing Directions.   If the cavalry has been pursuing Indians in a right-to-left progression and the director for good reason needs to change directions, the pursuit cannot be arbitrarily reversed without creating audience confusion.

The director's problem may be solved in two ways. The director can *change the progression within a shot*. If, for example, the Indians have been riding left to right and suddenly confront a sheer cliff wall, they must stop, wheel their horses and take off on another tangent, right to left. In another cut, the cavalry riders also reach the cliff, spot the hoofprints in the soft earth, and change directions, following the new progression taken by the Indians. Also, when the camera changes position, crossing the line of progression, the cavalry or Indians change direction within the shot. Such a transition is easily accomplished when the camera is mounted in a helicopter that flies from one side of the racing cavalry to the other.

The director can also change the direction of movement by *placing a directionless shot between the two progressions*. If the Indians ride from left to right in cut A and then ride directly *into camera* in cut B, they may ride from right to left in cut C without causing confusion in the audience.

It must be recognized that certain directors (such as John Ford) have occasionally violated these "rules" with no great degree of audience confusion, proving again that in any creative medium principles cannot be arbitrary.

Complementary Shots

Another of the conventions that audiences have accepted as a normal and necessary part of camera treatment is the use of complementary shots. When David and Eileen confronted each other earlier, camera coverage consisted of two matching over-the-shoulder shots, one favoring David, one favoring Eileen. Later in the scene, camera coverage consisted of closeups: one of David, one of Eileen.

Since close shots are used primarily for emphasis—to give special impact to an action, reaction, or line of dialog—isn't it possible to highlight a moment without the necessity of playing closeups on *both* characters? Yes, of course it is possible. We see such coverage occasionally in both television and motion pictures. But directors use matching shots for three reasons: audience expectancy, dramatic progression, and balance.

Audience Expectancy.   Since the 1920s, movie scenes usually have been photographed in complementary angles. When live television gained popularity in the late 1940s, it adopted some of Hollywood's film techniques. When TV drama made the transition to film a few years later, it completed the pattern, embracing the tools, facilities, and techniques that the film industry had developed.

"It has always been done that way" is not a valid reason for continuing any practice. Yet, for television directors working within narrow budgets, with little time for experimentation, there is a certain security in the crisp, professional, symmetrical look afforded by complementary coverage. They know that they are providing audiences with a visually dramatic pattern they will feel comfortable with. Yet symmetry is the least important of reasons for using complementary angles.

Dramatic Progression.   As we discussed in Chapter 4, most well-written scenes grow through increasing levels of conflict and audience arousal. Such growth usually results from an interplay between characters, each feeding the other, emotion building on emotion. With more than one character in a scene, it's seldom possible to play a big moment for one without involving big moments for others. Ted tells his father that he's quitting college. When his father tries to reason with him, Ted's jaw tightens. His father becomes angry. Ted forces down his own anger, finally explodes. His father threatens financial reprisal. Ted storms out, slamming the door. Such dramatic peaks are seldom one-sided. Their growth can effectively be recorded through increasingly close complementary angles.

Balance.   Every camera angle carries implications. When in a two-person scene the angles are close on one and medium on the other, audiences infer that the scene is played from the general perspective of the closeup character. It would become his or her scene. In the dramatic confrontation between Ted and his father, the director could play Ted in close angles and his father in wider shots. This would suggest that Ted's dialog, actions, and reactions are more significant than his father's. Shots of his father would become (almost literally) Ted's point of view.

Such unequal coverage, were it to remain consistent throughout a scene, would have a second—and necessarily negative—effect. It would create far greater impact for the closeup character than was possible for the distant character. Thus, if Ted's father made a jarring pronouncement, its impact would be diminished simply because it wasn't played in a close angle. As indicated before, scenes usually build in tension between characters; both contribute. If the buildup appears one-sided, unequal in intensity, the scene limps along on one strong leg and one weak one. Thus, for a scene to build to a powerful climax, most directors fashion a complementary camera pattern with characters assuming approximately equal size and occupying similar (complementary) screen positions. To complete the pattern, focal length of lenses in both angles should be the same.

However, rules cannot be inflexible. There are occasions when—for reasons of mood, character, or style—some directors deliberately elect not to utilize complementary angles. But for most directors most of the time in most dramatic situations, such angles facilitate the buildup of dramatic intensity.

CREATING APPROPRIATE EMPHASIS

It should be obvious that in any dramatic scene certain moments are more significant than others. At those moments, certain characters or actions require the audience's concentrated attention as well as the greatest degree of impact that a director can provide.

We will examine six methods by which the camera can direct audience attention and create varying degrees of emphasis: closeness, separation, positioning, duration, variation, and visual composition.

Closeness

The last chapter examined stage directors' techniques by which they called audience attention to specific characters or actions at specific moments. In one such technique, as characters moved downstage, that is, closer to the audience, they gained importance. In film and television, when a camera replaces the audience, its distance from the actors (or size of the image) will, to a great extent, determine the degree of impact. A closeup provides greater impact than a medium shot, a medium show more impact than a full shot. (See Figure 6.1.)

What if the director cuts to a close shot of an unimportant character, a mere spectator to the action? Would such a cut create enormous impact? Of course not. It would simply bring that character to the audience's attention. Impact is inextricably related to a character's dramatic significance at any particular moment. Mere closeness is not sufficient. If the moment has created dramatic tension and a character directly contributes to that tension, then a closeup will effectively heighten its impact. Thus, closeups tend to *increase* or *intensify* whatever dramatic values already exist.

Close angles serve additional dramatic functions. They *clarify* in that they reveal detail that could not be seen in wider angles. A tear in the corner of an eye would be lost in a medium shot. Knuckles tightly clenched or an ingenue nervously biting her lip might go unseen in a full shot. Closeups may reveal thoughts or feelings, internal values, or such emotional subtleties as darkening despair in a character's eyes.

Part of the fascination of drama is the degree to which spectators contribute to such emotions. A classic example of such involvement is the famous Lev Kuleshov experiment in the 1920s with film footage of the actor Ivan Mozhukin. Kuleshov snipped a neutral, expressionless closeup of Mozhukin from one of his feature films and broke it arbitrarily into three pieces. He carefully spliced three other shots between the closeups: a steaming bowl of soup, a little girl playing with a teddy bear, and the corpse of an old woman lying in her coffin. Remember, the actor's expression remained unchanging throughout the sequence. When audiences viewed the strip of film, they applauded Mozhukin's virtuosity as an actor, remarking how hungry he looked when viewing the bowl of soup, how gentle and loving he appeared when watching his daughter at play, how sad he looked at the death of his mother. While such was not his purpose, Kuleshov vividly demonstrated an audience's ability to project their own thoughts or emotions into what they watch. (Would a spectator who despised soup have read Mozhukin's expression as repugnance when he viewed the steaming bowl?)

Many film and tape editors, aware of such audience projection and lacking necessary footage, sometimes "steal" closeups of an actor from one scene in a picture and insert it into another. Such deceptions are rarely detected; viewers see in the actor's face the emotions or reactions they expect.

Close shots also tend to *create empathy* between an audience and a character. Repeated closeups create the illusion that the story is being told from that character's essential point of view. They create a feeling of physical closeness, of relationship, so that the spectator may more easily identify with a character.

Separation

Camera emphasis utilizes another principle adapted from the theater whenever it separates one character from a group, thereby focusing attention on that character. Earlier we discussed breaking a triangular staging—three characters facing one another—into over-the-shoulder shots. In such a pattern, each character assumes a degree of impact exactly equal to that of the other characters. But what would be the implication if the director divided that triangle into a single shot and a two-shot? Note (in Figure 7.18a) that the isolated character suddenly becomes important. Whether in the theater or in film or TV, separating one character from a group implies that that character is special. The director can heighten the degree of that specialness by moving the camera closer.

Whenever characters share a frame, the emphasis, logically, is divided. In the two-shot in Figure 7.18b, the character nearer the camera, being larger,

Figure 7.18   When three actors are covered in a two-shot and a single, the performer in the single shot gains emphasis.

assumes more importance than the background character. Thus, in a scene between three characters, the one occupying a frame alone assumes primary importance, the figure in the foreground in the two-shot assumes secondary importance, and the background figure assumes the least importance.

When four characters appear in a scene, the director can photograph them in a pair of two-shots without giving emphasis to any specific character. But when the director divides camera coverage into a three-shot and a single, the character in the single instantly becomes significant.

Positioning

In another parallel from the theater, whenever a character presents full face to camera, impact is greater than if that character appears in profile. In film and TV, profile shots are generally unsatisfactory. They rob us of the chance to look into a character's eyes. Occasionally, students in my directing class cut to a closeup of an actor in profile and then wonder why the shot doesn't have the power usually associated with closeups. To be sure, closeness provides impact—but only if the actor faces camera. Thus, my students achieve a degree of impact by using a close camera angle, and then dissipate the energy of the closeup by playing the actor in profile.

When two characters share a frame, assuming both are identical in screen size, the one more nearly facing the camera draws the greater degree of attention. When two characters share a frame in profile, emphasis is divided equally; one will have the same impact as the other (see Figure 7.19).

As the camera arcs (moves in a curved path) around to favor one charac-

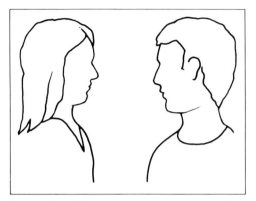

Figure 7.19   When two characters share a frame equally, each assumes the same degree of emphasis as the other.

ter, that character gradually assumes more impact while the second character's impact simultaneously diminishes. Once the camera has moved to a position where it completely favors one character, the shot becomes the traditional over-the-shoulder shot.

Over-the-shoulder angles are often used when directors want to convey a sense of relationship between characters. Visualize a love scene played entirely in closeups. True, closeups increase impact, but consider that each character is separated from the other, isolated, confined within a frame. Such fragmentation of images is sterile. Visualize the same scene in tight over-the-shoulder angles in which viewers see the physical as well as emotional closeness of the two lovers, together within a single frame. The difference is unmistakable. Over-the-shoulder shots also place the favored character in the Golden Mean of the frame, that spot believed by some to be the aesthetically perfect focus of attention.

Duration

It's a common experience: Moments with a loved one at an exhilarating party fly by quickly. Other moments, boring or distasteful, drag on for hours. Time seems to be elastic, changing with the event, stretching in anguish, contracting in pleasure.

Film or video time, like real time, distorts to fit the quality of the moment. While in real life such distortions are primarily psychological, in television and film they become tools of the sensitive director. While in real life such distortions relate to criteria of pleasure, boredom, or pain, in TV and film they depend primarily on the significance of the dramatic event and its need for emphasis.

One of Russia's great director-theorists, Sergei Eisenstein, in the making of *The Battleship Potemkin,* discovered that it is possible to gain greater emphasis for a dramatic moment simply by *prolonging* it. In a sequence in which a rebellious sailor smashes a dinner plate, Eisenstein photographed the action from a number of different angles. Then, in editing those angles together, he overlapped a few frames of film at each splice, thus stretching the duration of the action by actually repeating moments within the action.

Although Eisenstein's technique of overlapping frames is seldom employed today, modern directors have other methods for achieving emphasis through duration. Among these are *slow motion* and *editing.* The latter may be used to stretch significant moments or to diminish or eliminate unimportant ones.

Slow Motion.   The most easily recognized method of prolonging a dramatic moment is to play it in slow motion. In film, *slow motion* is achieved by photographing action at speeds greater than the normal sound speed of twenty-four frames per second. When the film is later projected at the normal rate, actions are slowed proportionately; moments are prolonged, usually achieving greater dramatic weight. In video, slow motion may be achieved simply by slowing the replay of tape upon which an action has been recorded, an effect seen most frequently in sports broadcasts.

In drama this type of emphasis plays most effectively with broad or violent action: a criminal leaping to his death from a twelfth-story window in an explosion of shattered glass; the final scene of *Bonnie and Clyde,* prolonging the shocking moment when the two criminals are stitched with machine gun bullets.

Slow motion also adds an emotional factor to its emphasis: a sense of grace, an almost poetic fluidity. Terrifying as it was, *Bonnie and Clyde's* final moment conveyed a feeling of *pas de deux,* a grotesque ballet choreographed by the devil. In the film *The World of Henry Orient,* director George Roy Hill used slow motion primarily for its balletic qualities, transforming a romp through the streets by two teenage girls leaping over fire hydrants and swinging on lampposts into visual poetry.

Editing to Prolong.   Significant moments may be expanded simply by adding reaction cuts. Ideally, such a technique heightens dramatic tension rather than merely stretching time. Returning to Eileen's departure from David, let's change circumstances and suggest that the scene builds to a confession that Eileen is carrying David's child. The director or the editor decides that such a momentous revelation must play in extreme closeup for maximum impact.

David's reaction must also play in a tight closeup since his reaction may be more evocative than the announcement itself. Because of the moment's significance, many directors and editors would cut to Eileen as she tries to repress her deep emotions and again to David as he stares unbelievingly. In real life such a moment might take a second or less. Television and film are able to enrich the drama by prolonging the tension. On tape or film, such a moment might last three or four seconds.

Of course we have all seen such editorial techniques abused. Directors and editors sometimes try to build a moment that simply isn't there, to extract drama from a scene where little drama exists. They prolong; they do not enrich. The result frequently becomes laughable.

David's initial reaction to Eileen's announcement should be noted well. A reaction can be far more powerful in evoking spectator emotion than the action or statement that motivates it. Reaction from a character becomes a catalyst for the spectator.

In the early days of television I produced an NBC series that showcased young professional actors. My partners and I had written a scene in which a psychotic French artist threatened to kill his young model. As we began rehearsal, the actress cast as the model came to us in tears. Her partner in the scene had most of the dialog; she had little. It wasn't fair!

We assured her that it was really her scene. She had most of the reactions, and reactions are far more important than dialog. She nodded, accepting but disbelieving. When she saw the completed show, she was ecstatic. The NBC director, a veteran, had recognized instantly that the scene's drama was on her face, in her growing hysteria. And that's where he focused his cameras for most of the scene.

In most dramatic situations, characters and spectators echo and reflect each other. Both react to the same stimulus. Through identification, we as the viewers *become* the reactor. In the model's scene, her tears evoked our own. Her fear sparked our own—and *magnified* our own.

Prolonging a dramatic moment is frequently used for purposes of building suspense. In a small Western town a robber casually enters a bank. In individual cuts the robber notes each of his cohorts, who have timed their arrival to coincide with his. One is at the counter filling out a deposit slip. Another stands in line at a teller's window. A third has been hired as a janitor; he sweeps the floor near the vault. The last waits outside the bank, holding the horses at the hitching rail.

The leader's eyes flick around the room. Again director or editor cuts to each as the gang members exchange glances with their leader. Now each moves into position in their well-rehearsed robbery scheme. *Again* director or editor cuts to each of them, setting the stage, delaying the moment when violence will erupt, stretching seconds into minutes in order to build anticipation and apprehension.

While moments may be prolonged in order to achieve greater dramatic emphasis, the reverse is also true. Moments of little or no dramatic weight may be shortened or eliminated.

Editing to Diminish.   One of the discoveries made by pioneer director D. W. Griffith was that a scene didn't always have to play from beginning to end. Frequently beginnings of scenes are littered with meaningless niceties. Griffith often found it effective to jump into the middle of a scene, getting right to the heart of a dramatic situation. Similarly, he discovered that concluding moments may sometimes be amputated to achieve dramatic economy, dispensing with cluttering handshakes and goodbyes.

Modern directors borrow from Griffith's concept, cutting away the fat, eliminating the dispensable or the boring in order to quicken pace and build spectator interest. A director named Jack English introduced me to the concept of a *timing cut* on Twentieth Century Fox's very first television series, "My Friend, Flicka." The script called for the boy, Ken, to receive a tongue lashing from his father on the porch of their ranch house. Then Ken was to walk to the barn and pour out his woes to his horse, Flicka. The barn was located about two hundred feet from the house. To watch the boy traverse that distance would consume thirty seconds of dull film. How did English handle it? At the conclusion of the tongue lashing, Ken exited the two-shot and the camera held on his father who stared regretfully after him. The next shot began inside the barn on a closeup of the horse and then panned to the barn door as Ken entered. Audiences never missed what certainly would have been tedious footage. Without an opportunity to study the distances involved, they accepted the timing. Timing cuts eliminate dull footage by cutting around it, jumping ahead to the next shot in a dramatic sequence, thus propelling a story forward. In commercials where every second must contribute, timing cuts are a way of life.

Variations of the timing cut are used repeatedly by TV and film directors. Dramatic time is elastic. It expands to enhance the significant or the entertaining. It contracts to eliminate or minimize the boring. Wouldn't it be exhilarating to transfer such techniques to everyday life?

Variation

We have discussed four ways to increase dramatic emphasis on a character or an action. We have not yet considered the fact that emphasis necessarily changes during the progression of a scene.

Editing.   The editing of videotape or film seems the most obvious technique for changing emphasis within a scene. Yet surprisingly, many within the entertainment industry never fully understand why directors or editors cut from actor to actor. When Eileen tells her boyfriend that she is leaving him, most editors would automatically play the announcement in her closeup so that we will receive the full impact. Then most editors would immediately change emphasis, cutting to David's face as he registers shock. "Being on the right face at the right time" is the way some editors phrase it, directing audience attention to where the maximum drama is, as it changes from moment to moment. It might appear that editors are manipulating the audience for dramatic effect. While this is true to some degree, they are also paralleling the direction of spectator interest. If they were physically present to watch the two actors play the scene, their eyes would flick back and forth from face to face as their interest changed. Editing merely reproduces those changes in spectator attention.

Selective Focus.   One frequently seen device for changing emphasis is *racking focus* (also known as *pulling focus*), that is, changing the camera focus from foreground objects or characters to background objects or characters. Viewer attention understandably follows the focus, attracted to what is most easily distinguished. Such changes in focus parallel the action of our eyes in everyday life; as we focus on a single person in a room, all others (without our being aware of it) automatically go out of focus.

Through the years a few motion pictures have been photographed with *depth of field,* that is, with both foreground and background sharp. Such overall sharpness is achieved through use of an extremely small aperture in the camera lens and correspondingly higher levels of light. *Citizen Kane* and *The Magnificent Ambersons,* both directed by Orson Welles and photographed by Gregg Toland, are celebrated examples (see Figure 7.20).

Deep focus photography has been heralded by some critics as contributing significantly to a film's reality.[3] In real life no one tells us where to look; we fasten our attention wherever we like. There are no cuts from face to face or predesigned changes of focus from one friend to another. Similarly, claim these critics, deep focus photography allows a spectator the freedom to direct attention without manipulation.

In most pictures, whether tape or film, camera focus tends to be needle sharp on some characters and fuzzy on others. This selective focus remains a time-honored device for directing and controlling emphasis. As shown in Figure 7.21a, when focus is sharp on the man, viewers direct their attention

---

[3]Specifically, André Bazin in *What Is Cinema?* volume I (Berkeley: University of California Press, 1967), pp. 33–37.

Figure 7.20   In *Citizen Kane,* director Orson Welles used deep focus photography, presenting both foreground and background in needle-sharp focus. (Used with permission of RKO Pictures, Inc.)

to him. When focus changes to the woman (Figure 7.21b), viewers transfer attention to her, usually without any awareness that they are being manipulated.

Visual Composition

Just as theater directors use elements of their sets to create emphasis for characters (see Chapter 6), TV and film directors use elements of visual composition to achieve the same goal. The intersecting lines of doorways and windows attract and focus audience attention on the character within the structural frame (see Figures 3.16 and 3.21). In Figure 7.20, the strong vertical lines of two columns drive the viewer's attention downward to the figure of Citizen Kane. Notice two other compositional forces at work here: The rapt attention of the character at camera left creates a line that directs

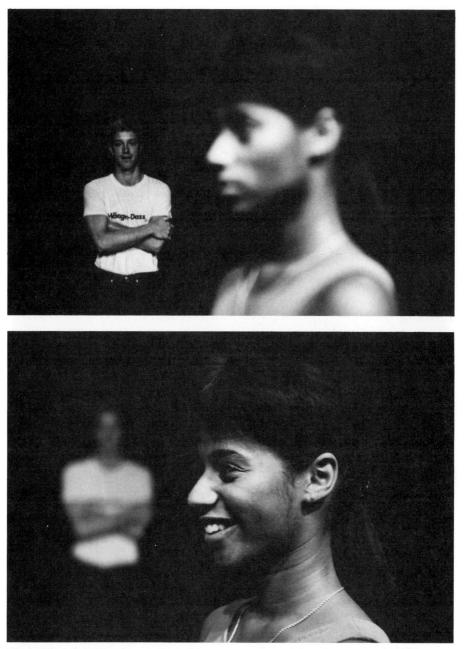

Figure 7.21   Selective focus offers directors a method of directing emphasis. With two actors, audience attention goes to the actor in focus. Attention shifts as the focus changes.

our gaze to Kane. Finally, Kane stands in strong contrast to his background, a composition that also compels audience attention.

In Figure 7.22, director John Schlesinger has used his New York location to create a framing that surrounds and confines Jon Voight and Dustin Hoffman, locking our attention within the frame. The powerful diagonal line of the wooden beam also drives attention inward. Notice that the setting does more than compel our attention; it creates dramatic tension; it compresses the characters within its claustrophobic walls; it contributes significantly to the scene's mood and atmosphere.

CREATING MOOD AND ATMOSPHERE

Every story has its own flavor, personality, style, ambience. When reading a script, a director becomes aware of such characteristics often from the very first scene. They will color all major creative choices: selection of actors, music, editing, scenery, locations, wardrobe, properties, and hairstyles. They will also color the style of acting and even the nature of character relationships. They will shape the way in which the director uses a camera.

Is it a hard-hitting contemporary yarn played in the back alleys of a large city, calling for a gritty, grainy, naturalistic texture? Is it a nineteenth-century love story suggesting sepia tones and the soft, shimmery image created by fog filters? During preparation, most directors develop an image in their minds, a "look" that they feel is appropriate for the project. The intelligent director discusses that look in preproduction with the cinematographer or technical director, seeking their creative input.

The camera contributes to the creation of mood and atmosphere through *position, movement,* and *lenses and filters.*

Camera Position

Where a camera is placed in relation to actors creates certain inferences in the spectator. Many directors position their cameras instinctively. That "instinct" is based on knowledge accumulated through study and experience, knowledge overtly concerned with the mechanics of telling a story. But other factors are also at work. The relationship between camera and characters in a scene creates emotional overtones, making subtle, almost subliminal statements about the characters' relationships with one another and with their environment, about their states of mind and their emotional stances.

Usually a camera is placed at eye level since that is our normal way of looking at the world. When we look at our friends, we look them in the face, eye to eye. But there are many occasions when a director intentionally places a camera above or below eye level.

Figure 7.22   Directors often use lines created by the environment to bring emphasis to characters, as in this scene from *Midnight Cowboy*. (A UA release © 1969 Jerome Hellman Productions, Inc. Used with permission.)

High Angle Shots.   When we look down on someone, figuratively as well as literally, we place him or her in an inferior position. He or she becomes subordinate, recessive, smaller than we. An insecure teacher has a violent argument with a girl in his class. In protest, all of the students get up and leave. The teacher sinks down in his chair, stunned, ashamed, sick at what he has brought about. A director photographing that scene might play the final moment in a wide, high angle shot, aware that the high angle would make the teacher appear diminished, a small, pitiful figure surrounded by empty chairs, alone in an empty room. The angle does more than cover the action. It makes a comment. It instills emotion.

A little boy breaks a valuable antique and his mother threatens to punish him. A high camera position provides a down angle on the boy, diminishing him, showing the spectator how small and insignificant he feels, evoking sympathy.

High angle shots are ideal for establishing a locale. They orient the viewer to a scene's geography and the physical relationship of its elements. They provide an overview.

A seldom used variation of the high angle shot is the *overhead shot* in which a camera is positioned directly above the actors rather than angling down at them. Now the camera assumes a detached, godlike role, watching impersonally from high above as actors move through their paces. The overhead shot gained attention in the early 1930s when director Busby Berkeley used it to photograph elaborate dance numbers. The high camera emphasized patterns rather than people as dancers performed intricately choreographed maneuvers.

The overhead shot is occasionally used for startling or shocking effect. Director Walter Grauman devised such a shot in a television movie starring Edward G. Robinson. The camera began close on the actor's face in what appeared to be a normal closeup. Then the camera suddenly zoomed back to an overhead position, revealing that Robinson was strapped to a bed in a mental hospital.

Low Angle Shots.   We look up to people we respect, who occupy a higher position in society, who tower above us intellectually or professionally. Similarly, when a director places the camera below eye level, looking up at a character, that character assumes a position of dominance, of strength, of importance. Perhaps such feelings originated when we were children staring up at the gigantic adult figures who dominated our world.

In the classroom scene earlier, another director might play the argument between teacher and student in two angles: a high shot angling down on the student to make her appear diminutive and a low angle on the teacher to make him dominant. At the scene's conclusion, a low angle shot on the teacher would make a totally opposite statement from the one described earlier, leaving him in a power position.

Since some characters are dominant and others recessive in almost every scene, a few directors believe that a camera should almost never be placed at eye level. Others, a misguided minority, prefer to shoot scene after scene from a low camera position, claiming that such shots are more "dynamic," that low angles automatically add theatricality. Realistically, such low angles seem striking because all characters tower above the camera, creating a melodramatic world of diagonal lines and dominating fantasy figures. Theatricality works in scenes that require it. Scenes of horror or terror, a chase sequence, a gunfight, and any action that leans toward melodrama can all be enhanced through occasional use of low or bizarre camera angles. But such theatricality in normal, honest dramatic scenes becomes an overstatement that renders serious dramatic values absurd.

When photographing dance numbers, directors often use low angles since they tend to accentuate and exaggerate legs and feet. Such shots feature skillful footwork and at the same time convey a certain sensual appeal.

Subjective Shots.   In most cases, the camera serves as a recorder of action, a neutral, objective, dispassionate observer. Occasionally, however, the camera becomes a participant; its angle becomes the perspective of a character. The most usual form of such participation is known as a *POV (point of view) shot.* Frequently, such a shot is preceded by a closeup as a character stares at some off-camera action. The subsequent angle then becomes that character's point of view, the camera looking at the world through that character's eyes.

An entire motion picture once used subjective camera treatment. The 1946 film *Lady in the Lake* played its story from the literal point of view of its protagonist, actor Robert Montgomery. The only time the audience saw him was when he glanced in a mirror.

Usually, POV shots depict a character's actual angle of vision. If a character glances up at a tower, the POV shot necessarily becomes an up angle. Often, however, because of directorial or audience needs, POV shots are cheated. If specific visual information is needed, for example, the POV shot may be cheated closer so that viewers can read the headline of a newspaper. During the chase sequence in *The French Connection,* director William Friedkin cheated the driver's forward POV, attaching his camera to the car's bumper. The lower angle gave a far greater sensation of speed as the pavement whizzed by only inches below, yet audiences accepted the shot as the driver's perspective.

The POV shot represents the most easily understood as well as the most commonly practiced example of subjective camera. In a broader sense, however, the entire stylistic treatment of a film or videotape can represent and reflect a character's emotional state. The most celebrated example is the German expressionistic film *The Cabinet of Dr. Caligari,* in which the distorted sets and grotesque actions represented the perspective of the story's narrator, a madman.

We have seen examples of this broader concept of subjective camera dozens of times. When a central character becomes depressed, the entire ambience changes. The sky becomes grey. Accompanying music sours. Colors seem muted. The lighting key is low. When characters become elated, the film's atmosphere echoes and enhances that elation through blue skies and brilliant sunshine, sparkling music, upbeat settings, and a smiling world. How many burial scenes have you watched on television or in the movies in which mourners held umbrellas to protect them from the rain?

Film theorists use the term *pathetic fallacy* (from *pathos*) when the external world, usually the elements of nature, reflect the inner state of a character.

Thus, in burial scenes, the darkening skies reflect the characters' depression; the rain externalizes the tears they are shedding or withholding.

Note the difference between the two types of subjective camera. When a man becomes drunk, his world distorts tipsily. On the one hand, if the editor cuts to the character's literal POV, viewers watch his room tilt or grow fuzzy *through his eyes, as he sees it.* If, on the other hand, the audience watches him stagger down a street (objective camera) and the entire picture tilts or blurs or weaves, the picture is *suggesting* his mental condition rather than depicting his point of view literally. Viewers infer his mental state through the entire stylistic treatment, including camera work, music, sound, special effects, and whatever the directorial imagination may invent.

Tilted or Canted Angles.   You stand on the front porch of your home staring at the horizon, reassured by its implications of serenity, stability, security. But what if the horizon suddenly tilted? What would be your feelings? Shock? Panic? Disequilibrium?

To make their camera angles effective, directors frequently rely on basic human emotions and psychological responses. The tilted shot is a prime example, suggesting a world that has gone awry, in which normal standards of security have disappeared.

Directors search for appropriate ways to suggest a character's mental or emotional state. A tilted angle, suggesting disequilibrium, might be appropriate for the drunken gentleman described above, for a madman whose world has come unhinged, or for someone on an LSD trip. It fits comfortably with "tangerine trees and marmalade skies."[4] Such an angle might even comment appropriately on a love scene if the lovers' emotions swell to the bursting point, so ecstatic that the horizon itself stands on end.

Tilted or canted shots work effectively in montage sequences, image superimposed on image, composing a kaleidoscope of visual concepts. Most of the time, however, they simply call attention to themselves. They are bizarre and unnerving. Use them sparingly.

Hand-held Shots.   Often without realizing it, our minds make associations. When a character in a script is named Ethel, that character takes on resonances of everyone we have ever known, seen, or read about named Ethel. We automatically transfer feelings from those earlier associations. Similarly, when a television or movie program is tinted sepia, we recall yellowing tintypes; the

---

[4]From the Beatles' song "Lucy in the Sky with Diamonds," said to suggest the LSD experience.

program connotes the nineteenth century, which is exactly what its director anticipated.

Hand-held shots are associated in the public's mind with news and special events coverage. When network or local TV station personnel carry minicams to the scene of a fire, they grab shots as best they can, camera moving awkwardly, unevenly, jostled by passersby. When a director selects a hand-held camera for a sequence, it is with the knowledge that such coverage will create such associations in the viewers' minds. A hand-held camera creates a feeling of participation in exciting action, of shots taken on the run. It provides a gritty, documentary look as opposed to the conventional "slick and glossy" appearance often associated with Hollywood filmmaking.

Camera Movement

You should understand by now that in well-directed drama, little happens without a reason. Each element in a script exists to serve a plot or a character goal. Every move or piece of business performed by actors ideally is motivated by a thought or emotion.

In a similar fashion, movement by the camera should be neither arbitrary nor capricious. Each time a director pans, tilts, dollies, or trucks a camera, there should be a definable dramatic reason. In some cases, those reasons will touch on concepts we discussed earlier.

The Dolly. As interest in a scene increases, the audience fastens its attention more and more closely on the faces of the players. In early Hollywood films, such growing involvement was paralleled by a series of editorial cuts, each angle closer to the action than the last.

The forward dolly accomplishes the identical purpose but in a more fluid way. While dramatically motivated cuts (those that follow viewer interest) are almost undetectable, the slow forward dolly is still less apparent. It is almost invisible because in most scenes it exactly mirrors the action of the viewer's mind. Conversely, dollying out represents a disengaging of attention, detaching the viewer from the scene.

As the camera dollies toward characters, their impact increases with their screen size. *Increasing emphasis* constitutes the primary reason for most dollying in. If the dollying camera is in a low position, its approach will gradually increase the degree of the up angle so that a character will simultaneously gain *impact* and become more *dominant.*

Although a scene's increasing tension is the primary reason for dollying in, such a move may also be physically motivated. When a dolly accompanies a character (or other physical action), the character seems to propel the camera's forward movement. Such a dolly appears both graceful and motivated.

By definition, dolly shots move forward and backward. *Zoom lenses* also move forward or backward within a lens field. While a dolly physically travels within a setting, changing perspectives as it moves, the zoom changes the focal length of its lens, foreshortening space, moving within a single plane. Zoom lenses provide great convenience for directors, but they have been overused in recent years.

Trucking and Tracking Shots. When a camera *trucks*, the movement is usually lateral (sideways) and almost always accompanies the movement of characters. The traditional trucking shot is a raking side angle, moving with characters as they walk down a path. Inventive directors often allow lampposts, passersby, or other atmospheric elements to pass between camera and characters, thus contributing to the ambience.

When a camera precedes characters, retreating as they advance, such a variation is labelled a tracking shot. Sometimes a tracking shot follows characters from behind, accentuating their destination or the direction in which they are heading. In actual practice, the terms *trucking* and *tracking* are often used interchangeably. In script language, a camera *tracks* a character but *trucks with* a character. Since both trucking and tracking shots are propelled by the movement of characters, there is dramatic motivation behind them.

For many directors, the moving camera does more than merely follow the movements of principal characters, mechanically covering the action. The concept, "style reflects content," is recognized in the work of sophisticated professionals, and the moving camera frequently contributes to the style of each. For Germany's Max Ophuls (*La Ronde, Lola Montes*), it became a poetic expression of a romantic world. Long, languorous trucking shots up stairs, down corridors, through opera house lobbies, commented on his characters and the mood they generated, underscoring and embellishing that mood. Contrast such graceful camera movement with a different directorial treatment, a staccato series of quick cuts from room to room as a character moves through them. Note the difference in mood generated by each treatment.

Crane Shots. When a camera is mounted on the end of a long steel arm, it suddenly becomes capable of vast, sweeping moves, usually up or down. Recall the opening shot of many Westerns, with camera high in the air, angling down on a small Western town, effectively orienting the audience. A lone rider appears at the far end of the street. As he approaches, the camera *cranes* slowly down so that, as he directs his horse to the hitching rail in the foreground, the camera is low, close to the ground, looking up at this mythic hero, emphasizing his strength.

The high camera is objective, dispassionate, godlike. It makes little comment. As it descends, quickly or slowly, it becomes part of the unfolding drama, a participant, creating greater audience involvement. There is drama, even theatricality, in the great, majestic sweeping movement of the boom arm. At the conclusion of the Western, the hero rides off into the desert. The camera cranes upward, making him appear a small, lonely figure and exaggerating the vastness of the desert that surrounds him.

Panning and Tilting.   Previous examples of camera moves (trucking, dollying, craning) all involved the physical movement of both the camera and its base or pedestal. The camera changed position in relation to either actors or scenery. In panning and tilting, the camera base remains stationary and only the head moves. In *panning*, the camera head rotates from side to side, its field travelling horizontally, from right to left or from left to right. In *tilting*, the head moves upward or downward, the camera field travelling vertically.

Directors use panning and tilting most frequently to follow character movement. The camera pans with characters as they cross a room. It tilts upward as a character climbs a ladder. Sometimes directors use a pan as an orientation shot. Imagine an opening sequence, perhaps under titles, as the camera pans slowly across acres of farmland (a panorama, from which the word *pan* derives), ultimately picking up a sports car speeding along a dusty road.

Another reason for panning is to follow the direction of a character's glance, replacing the more conventional POV shot. For instance, a teenage girl looks at a window and screams. The camera slowly pans to the window to reveal a monstrous face leering at her. The slowness of the pan deliberately teases the audience, building apprehension, delaying the revelation. The director would probably cut rather than pan back to the girl since a second pan might seem labored.

A quick pan offers shock value. In the example, the trauma would have been increased if the camera had unexpectedly *whipped* to the window in a sudden, stunning moment. The director of *Poltergeist* occasionally used such quick pans for their nerve-scraping effect.

Lenses and Filters

Lenses and filters affect the quality of an image as it is focused on film or videotape. *Lenses* control the optical properties of an image; *filters* modify that image either by making aesthetic corrections or refinements, by affecting the color balance, or by changing the exposure.

Lenses.   Lenses may be divided into three categories: *normal, wide angle,* and *long.* Since normal (middle range) lenses are relatively distortion free, they are used most often by most directors for most scenes. Their angle approximates the angle of the human eye.

Both wide angle and long lenses distort the photographic image; the wider or longer the lens, the greater the degree of distortion. Directors intentionally use such distortion to meet aesthetic or practical requirements of a dramatic situation.

Since by definition a wide angle lens provides a comprehensive view, it is often used for orientation shots. Such orientation should not include panning, however, since extremely wide angle lenses spherically distort the field of vision, making the field appear to bend at the center. Wide angles are ideal for dollying since they tend to minimize camera vibration and seem to provide great depth of focus.

Directors frequently face situations where sets or locations are not as large as desired. One property of the wide angle lens is that it enlarges objects in the immediate foreground and reduces background objects, distorting space, creating the illusion of greater distance than actually exists. Thus, a corridor actually twenty feet long might appear double or triple that length when photographed with a wide angle lens. Should characters walk down the corridor toward camera, the director must exercise care to prevent them from coming too close, since objects in the immediate foreground will appear distorted and grotesque. If a director wants facial distortion for comedic or horrific effect, however, then such a lens is appropriate. Also, since wide angle lenses make distances appear greater than they actually are, movement toward or away from camera appears faster than normal.

The reverse is true of long lenses, which appear to compress space, to diminish distance. Characters moving toward camera seem to make little progress. Director Mike Nichols effectively used such a lens in *The Graduate* when Dustin Hoffman raced to stop a wedding, to prevent his loved one from marrying another. The long lens created the effect of a nightmare since he ran and ran but appeared to get nowhere.

Long lenses, like binoculars or a telescope, enlarge images; the longer the lens, the greater the degree of magnification. They are used for obtaining close shots from a distance. Since long lenses have a narrow depth of field, they lend themselves to selective focus. When directors want a character sharply defined but with foreground and background indistinct, they will inevitably select a long lens.

Filters.   The normal, properly focused, properly exposed picture is crisp and sharp and renders color or black and white values in relatively realistic fashion. The quality of the image may be intentionally altered by special gelatin or glass filters, which fall into two categories: technical and aesthetic. In the *technical* category are *neutral density* (ND) filters, which reduce the quantity of light transmitted through a lens, and *polarizing* filters, which control reflections or glare or darken skies for night effects.

In the *aesthetic* category lies a spectrum of filters that diffuse, distort, or otherwise change the image in order to achieve a visual effect that will influence the audience's emotional response.

Star filters have been used extensively in commercials as well as in some television and motion picture drama. The star filter transforms highlights into star-shaped lens flares or halations, creating an effect that is bright, glamorous, upbeat, glittery. Such an effect might enrich a wedding day, a posh Bel Air party, or a romp through wet streets by a couple in love.

Diffusion filters soften an image. They have been used since Hollywood's earliest days to add beauty to glamor queens, simultaneously concealing lines, wrinkles, or other skin imperfections. Early cameramen placed a scrap of silk stocking over their lenses to achieve the same gauzy effect. Diffusion filters have been used in outdoor locations to create a pastoral mood of tranquility, transforming the sometimes harsh lines of nature into the shimmery ambience of Impressionist paintings. Diffusion filters have partially given way to fog filters.

Fog filters were originally used to create the effect of—guess what? That's right, *fog*! Such shots usually were enhanced by a few wisps of smoke from a smoke pot just off camera. If you watch television, you have seen fog filters used many, many times. They create a soft, hazy brightness in a scene, especially noticeable when the camera is directed at a light source such as a window. The picture becomes idealized—misty and luminous and vastly flattering to the doe-eyed ladies who inhabit television commercials.

Although commercials were first to expand the uses of fog filters, television programming quickly followed suit. Fog filters seem appropriate for flashback sequences. The noticeable difference in picture quality places such sequences apart from scenes happening in the present. Fog filters seem appropriate for fantasy. The hazy quality seems to suggest another dimension. They seem appropriate for dream sequences. Some directors use them recklessly in comedies and in action adventure shows. One of their most effective uses was in the motion picture *All That Jazz*. Director Bob Fosse used fog filters for a number of stylized hallucinatory sequences in which protagonist Roy Scheider conversed with a glamorous woman later to be revealed as Death.

Polarizing filters reduce glare and reflective flare. Usually they are paired in a lens mount so that one may be rotated for varying degrees of effectiveness. Polarizing filters tend to darken skies, rendering them a deeper blue, and are sometimes used to approximate a night effect. They also seem to intensify colors.

Color correction filters are used occasionally to alter the color values in a scene, usually very subtly. Since color is one of a director's most valuable tools in eliciting emotional response from an audience, correction filters can prove extremely useful, especially in the hands of a sensitive cinematographer. In nightmare sequences, for example, a saturation of color might contribute to the sense of unreality; it would make proceedings seem strange, bizarre, tinged with insanity. In more realistic photography, a subtle addition of blue (of which audiences would be consciously unaware) might contribute to feelings of serenity. It should be noted that with film a shifting of color values can also be accomplished in postproduction by the processing laboratory.

In addition to color correction filters, there are many areas of color control available throughout the production process: in scenery, lighting, wardrobe, set dressing, and so on. Discussion of color motifs with a production designer or an art director during preparation can prove enormously helpful to the director.

While it is not the purpose of this book to examine audience response to color, I suggest that you not overlook such a significant area. Many art books discuss the subject in depth.

> Color can be selected equally for dramatic effects and subtle ones, to convey a feeling of conflict, of tranquility, evil or well-being, happiness or sadness, intimacy or remoteness, warmth or coolness, masculinity or femininity, and so on. It is close to music in its effects upon the sensibilities of the audience.[5]

CHAPTER HIGHLIGHTS

- A director's use of the camera falls into three major categories: (1) *covering the action* (revealing what is happening, telling the story), (2) *creating emphasis* (providing impact for significant elements), (3) contributing to a drama's *mood and atmosphere*.

- The most accepted pattern of covering the action emerged in early Hollywood films with the camera starting wide and moving closer. Beginning a scene in a wide angle provided the audience with orientation. Then, as tensions grew, camera angles came closer and closer until, at a scene's climax, the action played in closeups. The pattern remains valid today.

[5]Eliot Elisophon, *Color Photography* (New York: The Viking Press, 1961), p. 12.

- Camera usage and style vary from director to director. Some prefer a fluid, moving camera; others shoot a single "master angle" (usually a wide shot that covers action of the entire scene) and then break the scene into closer angles, to be assembled later by an editor. Each camera position is labeled a *set-up.* Since set-ups consume valuable time, they must be carefully evaluated for economical efficiency and for effectiveness.

- Playing a scene in a single wide angle is economical but has negative aspects. Usually such an angle is static, lacking in dynamics: actors frequently play key speeches in profile. Because of distance, audience involvement becomes difficult.

- To prevent the disorientation of two characters changing their relative positions in a frame, directors should avoid "crossing the line" by keeping the camera on one side of an imaginary axis bisecting the characters.

- Simple logic and consistency control the direction of character movement within a frame. When directors establish a right-to-left progression for, say, cavalry and Indians, any change of direction will confuse viewers unless they see the change actually occur on screen. When, for practical reasons, directors find they must change directions, a neutral, directionless shot often provides an effective transition.

- Camera coverage in drama usually is staged in complementary angles (for example, matching over-the-shoulder shots or closeups). Audiences have come to expect such professional coverage. More significantly, equal coverage usually matches the growing tension between characters.

- Since certain moments in drama are more significant than others, directors use their cameras to bring appropriate emphasis to those moments. They achieve such emphasis through closeness, separation, positioning, duration, variation, and visual composition.

- Close angles do not create significance; they increase or intensify whatever dramatic values already exist. They also clarify, allowing audiences to glimpse details and sense emotions they would be unaware of in wider angles. Finally, closeups create a feeling of intimacy, of emotional closeness, allowing empathy between the audience and a character.

- A character facing camera achieves greater impact than characters in profile. While over-the-shoulder shots do not have the impact of closeups, they create a strong feeling of *relationship* between characters.

- Emphasis may also be achieved by prolonging a moment. Slow motion is one method. It also creates a sense of grace, of poetic fluidity. Significant moments may also be prolonged through editing, expanding key actions or reactions by adding additional cuts. Similarly, dull moments may be shortened or eliminated through editing. One key device for reducing unnecessary or boring action is the timing cut: Directors or editors cut ahead of the boring moment to a character or action in another location after the boring moment has concluded.

- Emphasis changes many times in most dramatic scenes. Cutting between angles is the most common method for directing audience attention from character to character. Another method is changing (or racking) focus. Audiences give their attention to what is most easily viewed. When a foreground character appears sharp and the background character is out of focus, attention centers on the foreground character. When focus moves to the background character, audience attention follows.

- Camera may contribute to a drama's mood and atmosphere through position, movement, and lenses and filters.

- Camera placement causes spectator inferences. A high angle shot looks down on characters, figuratively as well as literally; it places them in a subordinate position, making them seem small or weak. A low angle shot, in contrast, looks up at characters, making them appear powerful and dominant. Because they create towering figures and dynamic diagonal lines, low angle shots provide a measure of theatricality.

- While the camera usually provides an objective view of action, occasionally it becomes subjective, providing the perspective of one of the characters. The most usual form of subjective photography is the POV (point of view) shot in which the camera literally assumes a character's angle of vision. A second form of subjective camera is demonstrated when the entire treatment of subject matter (lighting, sets, music, and so on) reflects a character's state of mind—the external mirroring the internal.

- Tilted or canted angles suggest disequilibrium, the world of a mad-man or a drunk—or perhaps someone wildly in love.

- Hand-held shots are associated in viewers' minds with news and special events coverage. Directors take advantage of this association, using hand-held shots to create a gritty, documentary look for appropriate dramatic sequences.

- Every camera move, like every actor move, should have a dramatic motivation. Forward and backward movements by a dolly, for example, usually echo the viewer's increasing or decreasing involvement with a dramatic situation. Trucking and tracking shots usually are impelled by the movements of characters. The majestic sweep of a crane shot brings an audience down from their overview and into the fictional world of the characters.

- Lenses and filters affect the quality of an image. Lenses control the optical qualities; filters modify the image either by making aesthetic corrections or refinements, by affecting the color balance, or by changing the exposure.

- Both wide angle and long lenses distort the image; the wider or longer the lens, the greater the degree of distortion. Wide angle lenses enlarge objects in the immediate foreground and diminish background objects, thereby creating the illusion of increased depth. Long lenses reduce depth, flattening the photographic field. Wide angle lenses are often used for orientation. Long lenses, because of their shallow depth of field, are used for selective focus.

- Star filters transform highlights into star-shaped flares, creating an effect that is bright, upbeat, glittery. Diffusion filters soften an image, concealing imperfections, idealizing its subject matter. Fog filters, originally used to create the illusion of fog, today have almost replaced diffusion filters. They create a soft, hazy, luminous image. Directors use fog filters in drama to separate flashback, fantasy, or dream sequences from reality. Color correction filters subtly alter the color values in a scene, thereby eliciting a desired emotional response.

C H A P T E R 8

Keeping them in suspense

The term *suspense* usually is applied to a genre of television shows or motion pictures designed to generate anxiety or apprehension. Such "thrillers" traditionally attempt to terrorize audiences by placing protagonists in sinister, frequently life-threatening situations. Exploitative feature films sometimes intensify shock values by adding scenes of gratuitous violence, bloodshed, and mutilation.

Since elements of the thriller occur so frequently in television and film, this chapter will examine them in considerable detail. But suspense has a far broader application than providing thrills. It is an essential part of all successful shows, the foundation of every dramatic scene, as necessary an ingredient as actors or dialog. Through an understanding of the nature of suspense, a director can deepen audience involvement and heighten a project's impact.

The four major parts of this chapter will examine:

- THE NATURE OF FEAR: studying its basis in the unknown and the unseen

- HITCHCOCK TECHNIQUES for generating suspense: delaying the revelation of what audiences want to see, scraping their nerves, and providing them with information that will provoke worry

- SCRIPT ASPECTS OF SUSPENSE: examining the victim, the antagonist, and the need for believability

- THE ESSENCE OF SUSPENSE: shattering many misconceptions

The art of creating suspense is also the art of involving the audience, so that the viewer is actually a participant in the film. In this area of the spectacle, film-making is not a dual interplay between the director and his picture, but a three-way game in which the audience, too, is required to play.   FRANÇOIS TRUFFAUT[1]

THE NATURE OF FEAR

All successful drama stirs us fundamentally. It touches basic hungers; it awakens our collective unconscious. When a particular show unaccountably makes us cry, often it is because we have been moved on a very primitive level, beneath all of the scaly, protective layers that make us "civilized."

When directors seek to create fear in an audience, they look for its primordial roots. What is the subject matter that makes all people afraid, no matter what their culture, no matter where they live? Many such deep-seated terrors go back to a time when we were all primitives: when we were children.

The Unknown

If you were like most youngsters, you were afraid of the dark. Why? Because you couldn't see what might be lurking there. Your imagination supplied terrifying possibilities. The Boogie Man. The ghost of Uncle Arthur. A grotesque monster. When, finally, you turned on a light, the room became reassuringly normal. Fright disappeared. Moments later, with the lights out, the Unknown again manifested itself and darkness conjured up the hobgoblins of imagination.

---

[1]François Truffaut, *Truffaut/Hitchcock* (New York: Simon & Schuster, 1966), p. 11.

What else were we afraid of as children? Graveyards. Coffins. Ghosts. Skeletons. All symbols of the dead. What is death? For many of us, it is (again) the Unknown.

When I was young I used to shiver at thunderstorms. The sudden, stroboscopic flashes of light were warnings of explosions to come, deep-throated rumblings and crashings that set the walls of our small home (and me) trembling. Some primitive cultures worshipped thunder as a god. The phenomenon is awesome and powerful. And it, too, represents the Unknown.

Fear of the unknown also confronts us on the most mundane levels. When we visit a dentist, most of us become tense, afraid of possible pain. The moment the dentist describes exactly what to expect—even when it's going to hurt—much of the fear vanishes.

For a director, fear of the unknown is a valuable tool when fashioning projects that seek to create terror. One of the earliest television series I produced was called "The Untouchables." Its violent, fear-oriented stories concerned activities of mobsters in the late 1920s and early 1930s. Significantly, five out of six scenes in every episode played at *night*. Had anyone applied simple logic, it would have been obvious that the lengths of those nights were absurd. The reason for so many night sequences, of course, had nothing to do with logic. Scenes of unexpected violence, where fear constitutes the essential subtext, play more excitingly in a darkened, shadowed world. In such a world, our childhood fears return to choke us. Have you ever watched a ghost story that played in the *daytime*? Has any hero in any story ever visited a haunted house at *noon*?

The Unseen

There's a special kind of dread of things unseen, unrecognizable, unassessable, whose grotesqueness can only be guessed at. In the motion picture *Jaws*, the sea monster swam concealed in the ocean depths. It is significant that in a story whose primary character was a great white shark, audiences never actually saw the shark until the film was almost two-thirds over. The opening sequence featured the shark's moving point of view under the water. Certain throbbing, Stravinski-like music became the shark's theme. Whenever we heard it, we trembled at the monster's presence. From time to time we saw results of the shark's depradations. But it wasn't until scene 178 (out of a total of 255) that we actually glimpsed the sea monster. The ocean, like the night, protectively concealed his presence, magnifying him, increasing our terror. Like the night, the ocean itself became frightening; the most innocent sea-scape might erupt into stomach-wrenching horror.

Using the Camera to Conceal.   Revealing only a shadow or a portion of someone's anatomy is the most obvious way by which a camera may conceal the

identity of a character. A *claustrophobic angle* is another. Ordinarily when a protagonist enters a new locale, the director provides a wide angle for orientation. Sometimes, however, directors deliberately prevent orientation. They fasten their camera angles close on a protagonist's face, placing blinders on the audience, not allowing them to see who or what may lurk in the vicinity. Such shots generate claustrophobia, an uneasy frustration at being confined. Sustained for a period of time, they build genuine apprehension.

Let's watch as Rachel approaches the decrepit old mansion and stares at it nervously. The angle changes. Now we're watching Rachel through a small upstairs window. As she glances up, camera moves back quickly, as if to avoid being seen. We suspect (and worry) that this angle may be someone's point of view. Our suspicion is confirmed a moment later when we see a gnarled hand pull a curtain across the window, blocking our view.

Now Rachel goes to the front door and opens it. The huge door squeaks, scraping our nerves in the tradition of such clichés. Once inside the mansion, Rachel walks slowly from room to room, *camera remaining close,* tracking her. Because the camera is restricted to a head-and-shoulders closeup, we wear blinders. Like a child in a darkened bedroom, we cannot see what is there. We grow apprehensive, anxious to survey the off-screen space, aware that Rachel may be in danger, eager to *see* that danger before it descends. The longer our view is restricted, the more disquieted we become. When, finally, Rachel turns a corner and screams, we're jolted by a shocking closeup of the maniac/monster/fiend.

Note that in this example, the director used both kinds of camera concealment. When someone watched from an upstairs window, the observer's *identity* was kept hidden, revealing only his gnarled hand. When the camera stayed claustrophobically close on poor Rachel, the villain's *whereabouts* remained a secret, denying the audience the chance to look around and assess the dangers.

The suspense values of a claustrophobic angle are twofold: (1) Things unseen are more frightening than things seen, and (2) delaying the moment of revelation also serves to build spectator anticipation. (More about delaying the revelation in a moment.)

The Viewer's Imagination.   When thrillers enter the realm of fantasy, directors confront a new set of problems. Recall the low-budget "shockers" you may have seen on late-night television in which special effects trickery or costume design appeared inept and amateurish and loathsome monsters emerged as nothing more frightening than a man in a green rubber suit. When a show becomes laughable, the director inevitably and rightfully inherits much of the blame.

Readers of best-sellers often complain that a motion picture or miniseries falls short of expectations. The reason, usually, is that a novel depends on the reader's *imagination* to supply its visuals: scenery, costumes, faces. So abundant is the reservoir of the human imagination that dramatic artists have difficulty competing. Most prefer not to try.

In so-called thrillers, the more familiar audiences become with antagonists, the less fear those villains engender. Imagine a diabolical fiend, a sadistic murderer-rapist who talks volubly with everyone, revealing in detail his innermost hopes and dreams. Compare him with an identical figure who never speaks a word. Now our imaginations go to work as we wonder what vile, unspeakable passions motivate his actions. While the first characterization might represent a more original approach, the second promises to generate far more terror.

When the director conceals or partially conceals a figure, the imagination adds dimension, transmuting the unseen into something far more terrifying than anything a special effects artist could devise.

HITCHCOCK TECHNIQUES

One of the acknowledged masters of screen suspense, director Alfred Hitchcock, used a variety of techniques to create apprehension and shock. Among these were: delaying showing the audience what they wanted to see, building a succession of incidents or creating elements whose only purpose was to scrape audience nerves raw, and providing spectators with more knowledge than a protagonist possessed, thus allowing them to worry.

Delaying the Revelation

In almost all of his films, Hitchcock capitalized on the fear of the unseen and the unknown, prolonging anxiety by putting off showing an audience what they wanted to see. Let's examine two examples from one of his less-celebrated films, *Under Capricorn,* the first utilizing camera and editing and the other simple staging in order to postpone a revelation.

The opening scenes created an aura of mystery concerning the character played by Ingrid Bergman, wife of the Australian businessman played by Joseph Cotton. The audience had never seen her and was anxious to discover the nature of her problem. At a dinner party, Cotton's business colleagues started to ask about her and then embarrassedly changed the subject. Moments later, we heard her footsteps on the staircase. Anticipation built as the footsteps came closer. All eyes fastened on the closed double doors leading to the hall. The footsteps stopped outside. The double doors started to slide open. But before we could glimpse Bergman, Hitchcock cut to a group shot of the dinner guests as they reacted. Now, certainly, we expected Hitchcock to cut to their point of view. But again the director denied showing us what we wanted to see. Instead, he slowly panned the faces of party guests as each reacted in dismay. When, finally, the director cut to Bergman, he again delayed the revelation, starting close on her feet and slowly tilting up. By the time he arrived at her closeup, it seemed anticlimactic. The revelation of Ingrid Bergman in a drunken stupor unfortunately did not justify all of Hitchcock's delaying tactics. The director had built our sense of anticipation to such a high point that what followed was a letdown.

Here's a more successful example from the same picture. Bergman, in bed, suddenly became aware of *something* beneath the covers. Instead of throwing back the bedclothes and immediately exposing it, she arose cautiously from the bed, staring in mute horror at a spot on the far side. She crossed slowly all the way around the bed, camera panning with her, delaying, delaying, delaying showing us the cause of her horror. When, after no less than twenty seconds, she reached the far side of the bed, she suddenly whipped back the covers, and Hitchcock cut to an extreme closeup of a hideous shrunken head there. The shock was extreme this time, justifying all of Hitchcock's delaying tactics.

In many suspense mysteries, directors conceal a killer's identity by showing only a shadow or a pair of legs. The plot purpose is to delay the revelation, but such concealment has a rich fringe benefit: It simultaneously creates an aura of fear because it stimulates the viewer's imagination to create a far more terrifying "heavy" than if he or she had been revealed.

A slow panning action is sometimes used by directors to build anticipation or apprehension. For example, a baby lies sleeping in a crib. Off screen, a window opens surreptitiously. When the camera pans slowly, slowly away from the child, we wait anxiously to see what the camera will reveal. As with other delaying tactics, the slow pan deliberately teases us, delaying the revelation.

Scraping Nerves

A jolting moment does not happen accidentally. Usually it is meticulously crafted by author and director. Shocking moments grow out of a succession of minor abrasions that make spectators nervous and uneasy. Notice that the element of *progression,* so intrinsically a part of drama, again manifests itself. When half a dozen minor irritations rub our nerves raw, we are off balance, edgy, apprehensive. Any major shock will now cause us to leap from our seats.

In a newspaper interview with Hitchcock concerning *Psycho,* the reporter asked why an abrasive motorcycle policeman wearing bizarre, mirrored sunglasses had appeared early in the film. Hitchcock's reply: for one reason only—to make people nervous.

Abrasions or irritations may arise from *characters, incidents,* or *atmospheric elements.* They may even arise from *editing techniques*. Verna Field, discussing her editing of *Jaws*, revealed that most editors develop a rhythm by which they cut film elements together. In *Jaws* she deliberately violated that rhythm, always cutting a moment before or after her normal instincts would dictate, thereby hoping to create uneasiness in spectators.

Because of its great capacity to evoke emotion, music heads the list of atmospheric elements capable of creating spectator disquiet. Audience shock during the stunning shower sequence in *Psycho* came primarily, of course, from the avalanche of brutal visual images, but the accompanying music contributed powerfully. High-pitched, almost discordant violins created in tone and quality the sound of a woman screaming, so nightmarish, so alarming in quality that it sandpapered nerve endings.

Probably the most familiar of atmospheric elements designed to make us nervous are thunder and lightning. Despite the fact that they have become stereotypical in ghost stories, so powerful is their ability to evoke primitive fears that they continue to disquiet us.

Wind is also effective in creating disquiet through a variety of disturbing noises: shutters or screendoors banging, creakings and groanings of wooden structures, tree limbs clattering against a window pane. Recall the effective use of wind in *Poltergeist* when it climaxed with the uprooting of a tree. Note that the wind cannot be seen and therefore the director must devise some visual manifestation of it—such as a lantern or a hinged sign that can blow back and forth, tree branches that can swing, or leaves or dust that can be blown about—in order to make the viewer visually conscious of the wind's presence. When an exterior light source (moonlight or a street lamp) throws shadows on an interior wall, supplementing the wind sound, uneasiness is transmitted from outdoors to indoors.

Suspense versus Surprise

One of the ways Hitchcock made audiences nervous was to tell them more than he told his characters. By knowing in advance that the villain was waiting to pounce, the audience could anticipate violence, agonizing for the unsuspecting heroine, unable to warn her of her impending doom, and stew in ever-increasing apprehension as she approached the fateful moment.

Like other directors of the genre, Hitchcock preferred suspense to surprise. He described the difference through the classic example of a bomb ticking beneath a desk as two executives talk. If the audience is unaware of the bomb, they will be stunned at the explosion. But how much more satisfying, claimed Hitchcock, to let the audience *in* on the secret. Aware of the bomb ticking beneath the desk, aware that it will explode fifteen minutes from now, the audience can participate in the scene, anxious to warn the victims-to-be of their danger. "In the first case we have given the public fifteen seconds of surprise at the moment of the explosion. In the second case we have provided them with fifteen minutes of suspense. The conclusion is that whenever possible the public must be informed."[2]

SCRIPT ASPECTS OF SUSPENSE

In drama as in any art form, no arbitrary principles may be applied to all stories all of the time. Certain characteristics have repeatedly manifested themselves in successful fear-inducing drama, however, and therefore are worthy of consideration. These characteristics concern the victim, the antagonist, and the believability of the production.

A theorem not found in any physics textbook: The degree of suspense generated in any story varies directly with the *vulnerability* of the victim and the *fearsomeness* of the pursuer.

The Victim

It is night. Frail, thirteen-year-old Beth, searching for her younger sister on an abandoned ocean pier, approaches an ancient building. Below, pilings creak loudly as if in warning. Beth shivers, swallows hard, and enters. Inside, a shadow moves wetly.

Beth, *stop!* Don't go in there! As audience, we sense danger. We're uneasy, nervous, apprehensive: prime components of suspense. Yet when I first wrote Beth's story as part of a magazine article, the opening paragraphs (considerably expanded from that above) created neither involvement nor worry. I rewrote them half a dozen times before realizing what the problem was. I had ignored one of the elementary principles of suspense.

Attempting to create teenage vernacular, I had given Beth the thought, "Why did the little creep keep coming here?" congratulating myself on having captured the typical sibling animus. Beth's character went downhill from there. Nowhere in that ill-fated scene did she do anything to make herself remotely sympathetic. When she reluctantly entered the old building, it appeared she was acting out of duty rather than concern.

Audiences have to *care* about the victim. If they don't care, they won't worry. The more they care, the more they will worry. It seems so obvious, doesn't it? (See Chapter 4 about "a person with a problem.")

With new words implying that Beth loved her sister, was actually afraid

---

[2]Truffaut, p. 52.

for her, was forcing down her fears in order to find her, the story vastly improved. For the first time, the reader became involved and started to worry.

Perhaps you have a picture in your mind of what Beth looks like: thirteen years old, skinny, wide frightened eyes, freckles. What if I changed her into a lady wrestler, a muscular, leathery woman of thirty-five or forty years? Think about it. Would you worry quite as much?

What if I performed transsexual surgery and changed her into a man? Would there be any difference in apprehension between a scared teenage girl and a seasoned, gun-carrying policeman?

The answer is obvious. We tend to worry more about vulnerable protagonists than those who can easily protect themselves. We worry more about the female of the species because of some distorted cultural notion that women are the weaker sex. Do you remember the classic suspense film, *Wait Until Dark*? Audience apprehension was excruciating because the frail heroine, Audrey Hepburn, was pitted against three cruel and sadistic killers. And she was blind.

In *Jaws*, Roy Scheider played the role of a police chief, theoretically a strong authority figure. But the director, Steven Spielberg, wisely built in a character weakness, a way to make him vulnerable. His enemy was a twenty-foot great white shark—and the police chief was acutely afraid of the water!

Jaws exploited vulnerability throughout. Do you recall the opening sequence? A beach party at night. A girl decided to go swimming. Alone. We became conscious of the unseen Menace swimming in ocean darkness. The girl shed her clothing, making her seem even more vulnerable. We held our breath, afraid to look.

Later the shark appeared in an ocean inlet where the police chief's own son swam. Our apprehension increased, for now the potential victim was someone we knew, someone we cared about. Someone extremely vulnerable: His hand was bleeding (blood attracts sharks), he was only a child, and because he was in the shark's milieu, he was not fully in control.

While vulnerability begins with the character defined by the script, it can be enhanced and exploited by the director—for example, in casting. The choice of Audrey Hepburn for the blind heroine in *Wait Until Dark* was brilliant. Would audiences have worried quite as much about an older, tougher, more authoritative woman? By selecting actors whose physical appearances suggest vulnerability, directors can ensure audience sympathy for their victims and vastly increase the suspense potential of their projects.

The Antagonist

Vulnerability is only half of the suspense equation. If the hero(ine) flees from a truly formidable antagonist, the director can build effective suspense. When the attackers/pursuers come from outer space, capable of concealing themselves in your best friend's viscera or masquerading as your fiancé (as in *Alien* and *The Body Snatchers*), paranoia is set aquiver. When they leave their graves (*Poltergeist*) to steal our children or terrorize our families, the viewer reaches for a tranquilizer (see Figure 8.1).

Remember *The Exorcist* and *The Omen* and *Rosemary's Baby*? There is no more fearsome adversary than the devil or his emissaries: dedicated to evil, powerful, crafty. Hitchcock used to say, "The better the villain, the better the picture!"[3]

Thus, to create fear-inducing suspense the director must involve the audience emotionally, make the protagonist vulnerable, and make the attacker or pursuer fearsome. An apparent contradiction to such requirements is presented on television each Saturday morning in the multiplicity of kids' cartoons. These hyperkinetic programs display the most fearsome antagonists imaginable—ghosts and living skeletons and green, scaly monsters—as well as heros and heroines who usually are young (and thus vulnerable). Yet these shows generate surprisingly little fear or suspense.

The contradiction is apparently reinforced by the many classic thrillers that featured antagonists who were normal human beings: neither demon nor sea monster nor alien from outer space.

To explain this contradiction, let's examine the third factor contributing to the suspense thriller—believability.

Believability

Believability cannot be computed mathematically; it depends largely on the abilities of the director and the writer to create the illusion of reality.

Jaws could have been ludicrous: a comic strip sea monster attacking swimmers. Yet the production team was so skillful that they made us believe it. I was fortunate enough to read five different drafts of the script as well as the novel from which the scripts were adapted—which perhaps explains my preoccupation with *Jaws*. The most significant development that occurred between the first script and the fifth is that the characters assumed dimension; they became more honest, less melodramatic. It is revealing that director Steven Spielberg remained a guiding, contributing force during the shaping of the *Jaws* screenplay. As a matter of fact, he wrote the third version himself.

The final script examined for the first time the minutiae of a police chief's daily routine: downing an Alka Seltzer for his queasy stomach, showing a secretary how to set up files, typing a drowning report, reporting a stolen bicycle—all unimportant to the plot but vital in converting spectators into

---

[3]Truffaut, p. 141.

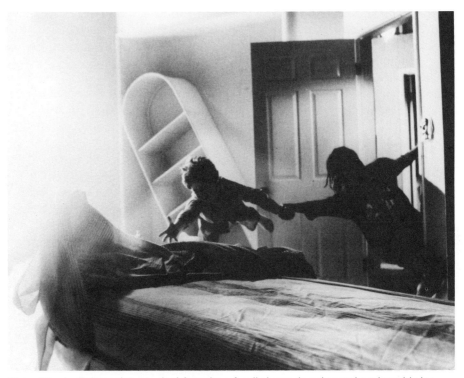

Figure 8.1   In *Poltergeist,* a typical American family is rendered acutely vulnerable by forces from beyond the grave. (An MGM release © 1982 Metro-Goldwyn-Mayer Film Co. and SLM Entertainment Ltd. Used with permission.)

believers. For the first time the audience explored the relationship between the chief and his wife and discovered that they loved each other: certainly not innovative material, yet essential in terms of making viewers care. Altogether, the director and the writers seduced the audience into believing a bizarre concept by surrounding it with believable people.

Saturday morning cartoons offer little suspense because we cannot accept them as reality. And since we cannot identify (other than superficially) with their one-dimensional characters, we remain spectators rather than participants.

In real life when your sister or your father loses a job, it's a serious matter. If someone should threaten to *kill* them, it would become mind-boggling. In a TV show or movie, if the hero becomes as real as a member of your family, you're going to worry when that person is threatened. When pressures build, your worry changes first to apprehension and then to terror.

THE ESSENCE OF SUSPENSE

Answer the following questions true or false:

1.   Suspense films necessarily deal with elements of fear and shock.
2.   A well-written, well-directed show does not need suspense.
3.   A show either has suspense or it doesn't. There's no in-between.

If you answered false to all of the questions, give yourself a perfect score. Let's clarify a few misconceptions about the nature of suspense. When asked by François Truffaut, "Is suspense necessarily related to fear?" Hitchcock replied, "Not at all."[4] Suspense does not deal solely in shock and terror. What we have discussed in this chapter concerns only a single genre in the dramatic universe, the thriller. In the minds of the general audience, the word *suspense* equates with *thriller.* "You're going to see a suspense film? Better take a tranquilizer to steady your nerves!"

Every well-designed dramatic program—whether on TV, the stage, or the movie screen—contains suspense. Will the lost child find her way home? Will the husband desert the wife who loves him? Will the executive sacrifice her moral values in order to gain promotion? Every story in which someone has a problem (and that's 98.8 percent of all stories ever written) engenders worry. And worry and suspense are virtually synonymous.

Every drama ever written evokes reactions that fall somewhere on the continuum in Figure 8.2. Between the beginning of a show and its final curtain, the action will move back and forth, generating mild interest at some moments and dark apprehension at others. Any show whose viewers remain for an extended period of time in the area of disinvolvement or casual observation is in serious trouble.

Most successful human interest drama generates concern and worry, and perhaps moments of apprehension and fear. In watching the award-winning movie, *Kramer versus Kramer,* for example, we worry first that Ted's need to care for his small son will destroy the career that means so much to him. After Ted changes his values, treasuring the newfound relationship with Billy, finding joy and fulfillment in his role as father, he loses his job—and our concern deepens. It turns to genuine apprehension when former wife, Joanna, appears and threatens to take Billy away from him. Our apprehension turns to anguish when the court rules in favor of Joanna. Is *Kramer versus Kramer* a suspense film? Unquestionably. Audience fears soar higher when

---

[4]Truffaut, p. 50.

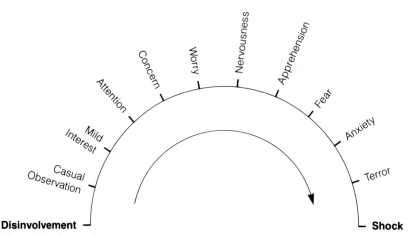

Figure 8.2   Every drama creates audience responses described somewhere on this continuum. Thrillers provoke those responses at the far right; human interest shows fall somewhere in the center; those at the far left usually fail.

that father-son relationship is threatened than during most blood-and-guts horror films. Ted Kramer becomes acutely vulnerable because what he loves most in this world may be taken from him. And Joanna becomes a "fearsome monster" by threatening to wrest Billy away.

Think of films you have seen recently. Did they make you worry? Then they were "suspense" films. Westerns, soap operas, science fiction, children's stories all make us care about a hero and fear an antagonist. When written, produced, and directed effectively, all are suspense films.

In addition to using the fundamental dramatic techniques discussed in earlier chapters, directors can heighten suspense by exploiting the specific elements that make an audience worry. The basis for that worry is contained in the threat posed by the antagonist. Any device, action, or visual image that reminds the audience of that threat will maintain or build dramatic tension.

In Hitchcock's *Strangers on a Train,* the character played by Farley Granger is tormented by guilt feelings concerning the death of his wife. In one scene where he sits in his den, we can read the titles of books on a shelf behind him. Hitchcock has placed prominently among them a book titled *Murderer,* commenting on the man's inner tension and reminding the audience. In another scene, Granger meets surreptitiously with Robert Walker, who plays the actual murderer. At the sound of police sirens, the two duck behind a gate. Hitchcock again reminds us of Granger's guilty fears by framing camera angles through the gate, now suggesting jail bars, and by casting on the wall behind them shadows that also resemble jail bars. In each instance, the director found ways to underscore Farley Granger's problem, to externalize his inner tensions, thus deepening audience concern.

CHAPTER HIGHLIGHTS

- The label *suspense* often is applied to shows that generate anxiety or fear. But the word has a far wider application. It is the foundation of all dramatic action.

- So-called thrillers achieve their success through exploitation of our most basic fears. Children (and many adults) are afraid of the dark because it conceals the *unknown*. The unknown lies at the heart of most fears. Graveyards, skeletons, ghosts, and coffins—frightening to many of us—are symbols of death, the greatest unknown of all. The unknown and the unseen are tools for directors. The mere use of night as a background for fear-oriented stories provides an atmosphere that enhances story values.

- Concealing antagonists usually make them more fearsome; the viewer's imagination magnifies them, increasing their power. Directors sometimes conceal the identities of villains by revealing only a portion of their bodies: legs, a hand, a shadow. Directors also sometimes conceal the antagonist by keeping the camera angle close on the protagonist (a claustrophobic angle). The viewer becomes frustrated at an inability to see where the villain might be lurking. When, finally, the villain is revealed, the moment frequently stuns.

- Director Alfred Hitchcock utilized these principles repeatedly in his films, delaying (through editing or staging) the revelation of what an audience wanted to see. He also devised scenes with the sole intent of making an audience nervous, building disquiet, thus making the moment of shock more traumatic. His suspense techniques included providing the audience with more information than he gave his protagonist, thus allowing the audience to worry.

- Many fear-inducing techniques begin at the script stage. The degree of suspense generated in a story varies directly with the vulnerability of the victim and the fearsomeness of the attacker. Vulnerability usually manifests itself through age, sex, or physical disability. Directors can add to a protagonist's vulnerability through casting or characterization.

- The fearsomeness of the pursuer or attacker is demonstrated in such films as *Jaws, Poltergeist, Alien,* and *The Exorcist,* featuring sea monsters, ghosts, aliens from deep space, and demons from hell.

- The final factor in the suspense equation is believability. The more audiences accept the drama as reality, the more terrified they will become.

- A major point: Every well-designed TV show, stage play, and feature film contain suspense; it is not limited to thrillers. Suspense is manifested whenever audiences worry about a protagonist. Every story in which a protagonist has a problem creates worry, provided the audience truly cares about the protagonist. Directors can exacerbate the worry by keeping audiences aware of factors that threaten the protagonist's goals.

P A R T 3 · *Directing Nonfiction*

NOTE: *Since most nonfictional television programs contain elements of drama, please read Part Two,* Directing Fiction, *before embarking on the following chapters. In particular, you should read Chapter 6,* Staging the Actor, *and Chapter 7,* Staging the Camera.

C H A P T E R 9

Questions and answers: The interview

*I*nterviews seldom stand alone; that is, they are usually part of a larger program.[1] For example, interviews sometimes appear as elements in news or sports programs, homemaker shows, documentaries, game shows . . . in short, as components of almost every television program type, with the exception of drama. They afford us the opportunity to meet a wide variety of people, to learn from their reservoir of knowledge, to be entertained by their stories, perhaps to become emotionally involved with them.

In preparing an interview, the director must begin with an understanding of the program's basic appeal. What aspects of the interview will attract viewers? Will they tune in to learn? For self-improvement? Or to be entertained? After pinpointing the interview's most appealing aspects, the director may then enhance or highlight those aspects through staging, set decor, camera and editorial treatment.

In this chapter we will discuss the three basic categories of interviewers. We will examine the various television programs that utilize interviews as well

---

[1]Exceptions include "Face the Nation" and Barbara Walters' specials, which are 100 percent interview.

This instrument can teach, it can illuminate; yes, it can even inspire. But it can do so only to the extent that humans are determined to use it to those ends. Otherwise, it is merely lights and wires in a box.   EDWARD R. MURROW[2]

as the appropriate directorial treatment for each. Finally, we will dissect a typical daytime interview show in order to examine the director's broad range of activities, in both preparation and on-the-air camera coverage.

THE INTERVIEWER

Many people believe that a director's function is solely to stage the action and call camera shots. To them, such concerns as the interviewer's style or personality or the guest's subject matter are inappropriate, outside the director's purview.

Such attitudes, of course, are totally incorrect. The director's goal is to build a program to its highest potential, seeking the greatest possible audience involvement. Accordingly, the director's province must be the entire show—all of its elements, including camera, music, lighting, scenery, editing, staging,

---

[2]Quoted by Fred W. Friendly in *Due to Circumstances Beyond Our Control* (New York: Random House, 1967).

performers, and performances. The interviewer's style of presentation is central to the success of an interview show and, therefore, a legitimate directorial concern.

Interviewers generally fall into one of three categories: the Sincere Inquirer, the Personality, and the Provocateur.

The Sincere Inquirer

Most interviewers take a secondary or background position, emphasizing their guest's unique knowledge or expertise. Such Sincere Inquirers allow their guests to star. They are creative listeners, attentive, encouraging, supportive, subtly leading their guests into conversational paths that have been prearranged. Dick Cavett typifies the Sincere Inquirer.

Usually, a production assistant has met with the guest prior to the telecast and conducted a preinterview. Preinterviews are designed to assess a body of information and to select specific facts, stories, and anecdotes as well as a theme for the broadcast. Such items may be chosen for their humor, human interest, or whatever characteristics make them unique or audience worthy. When the production assistant later relays this information to the host, the host prepares notes, perhaps on unobtrusive three-by-five-inch cards, for use during the broadcast. If the host meets a guest immediately before the broadcast, it is to extend a warm greeting rather than to labor through an exploration of possible discussion areas. In the televised interview, host and guest may now explore conversational areas with purpose and direction, yet spontaneously, with no sense of having travelled this road before.

Frequently, guests pinpoint certain taboo areas: topics they prefer not to discuss. This is often true of show business celebrities, many of whom rule out discussion of controversial aspects of their private lives. If the host expects to conduct a pleasant, upbeat interview, or wants ever to interview this celebrity again, he or she must respect the guest's wishes and avoid discussion of taboo subjects. Frequently showbiz celebrities exact a "price" for their appearances: a plug for their latest film or television series. Sometimes such appearances include film clips, which the director must view prior to broadcast. If language or actions in the film clip seem questionable, the director must have the material approved by station management.

With the multitude of details and time strictures in preproduction, a director is often tempted to take the guest's word that material is inoffensive. A word of advice: Don't take anyone's word! When directing a live show for NBC, I once accepted the star's solemn assurance that film she had brought back from Europe ("home movies") would pose no problems. Innocently I bypassed my directorial responsibilities and instructed our film department to run the material on cue. When aired, the film seemed harmless enough—

until a Folies Bergere sequence appeared, featuring a number of bare-breasted showgirls! Of course we quickly cut away from the film—and the hostess giggled in some embarrassment. The station management didn't giggle at all.

If you believe that in a two-shot the camera-right figure receives primary audience attention (as many directors do), then you should place the guest at camera right.[3] Since the Sincere Inquirer defers to the guest, realizing that the interview will succeed or fail based upon the guest's effectiveness, the director should favor the guest in camera treatment. The host's introduction may occur at some distance from the guest, in another portion of the set. Following the introduction, the director may cut to the guest (assuming a two-camera operation), allowing the host/interviewer to enter this new shot and sit down beside the guest. Or the director may simply pan the host to the guest and hold this two-shot for the start of the interview. It is important to provide the audience with a closeup of the guest early in the interview, perhaps at the moment of introduction. Beyond the obvious function of showing the audience what the guest looks like, a closeup allows the audience to feel "close," establishing a sense of personal involvement.

In basic interview coverage, camera angles always will cross, so as to achieve the impact of full face rather than profile. The camera on the left photographs the performer on the right; the camera on the right photographs the performer on the left. Note cameras 1 and 3 in Figure 9.1. If the camera on the left photographed the performer on the left, it would provide unsatisfying profile shots.

Notice that when interviewer and guest are seated two or three feet apart on a couch or in chairs, a medium two-shot fits the three-by-four screen proportion almost exactly. When they sit farther apart, the camera must widen to accommodate both figures. This wider angle is inferior from two aspects. First, since the performers are farther away, the picture loses detail and facial expressions. Viewers lose emotional closeness, becoming spectators rather than participants. Second, the center of the frame in the wider angle is empty; the most valuable part of the camera frame features an expanse of blank wall or empty couch. In staging action, experienced directors always try to place their performers within the aspect ratio of a camera frame.

Since most interviews are conducted from seated positions, it is imperative that cameras photograph the performers *at their level*. Either cameras must pedestal down so that the lens looks performers in the eye, or the couch or

---

[3]In theory, the spectator's eye moves across the frame from left to right.

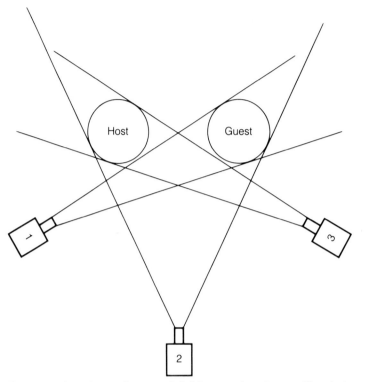

Figure 9.1   In order to photograph full faces rather than profiles during an interview, the righthand camera (3) photographs the host, the lefthand camera (1) photographs the guest, and the center camera (2) maintains a two-shot.

chairs must be placed on a small raised platform (a *riser*), bringing guests up to camera level. Risers have a secondary benefit: Because couches or chairs are higher, they make the acts of rising and sitting much easier for host and guest.

The Personality

Unlike the Sincere Inquirer, the Personality seldom if ever assumes a secondary role. Instead, he or she *shares* audience attention. In many cases, because of humor, flamboyance, or personal magnetism, the Personality attracts more interest than the guest. Johnny Carson and Joan Rivers are examples of such personalities. Note that they sit at camera right, rather than their guests.

The director's use of cameras for the Personality differs from coverage of the Sincere Inquirer. Instead of favoring the guest, cameras divide attention, attempting to highlight first the guest and then the host as each sparks audience interest. Ideally, such an interview should be covered with three cameras: cameras 1 and 3 on individual shots, the middle camera holding a two-shot (see Figure 9.1).

If the director is limited to two cameras, one should favor the guest and one should favor the host. Repeated cuts from a two-shot to a single and back to a two-shot can become tedious. More importantly, such a pattern minimizes the host's impact by playing him or her constantly in a two-shot. When the host is a celebrity, such treatment will weaken the show and will probably motivate the host to seek a new director. In a two-camera situation, then, the director should live dangerously. After orienting the audience with a two-shot, the director should instruct the wide-angle camera to provide closeups of the host. The director then must juggle closeups. Such a situation can cause adrenalin to flow when the dialog quickens, when speeches overlap, when one (or both!) performers decide to stand or move about the set. With competent camera operators, such a situation can be gracefully handled by zooming out to an angle that is wide enough to accommodate the action. Playing a two-camera interview in closeups isn't always "safe." It requires intense concentration from the director. It can make the director appear inept or incompetent when action unexpectedly boils out of the close angles. But those angles provide energy and impact, creating excitement, bringing the interview to life. Such a result is worth some risk.

One of the advantages of working with the same personality over an extended period of time is that director and star each come to understand the other's needs. The star realizes, for example, that standing suddenly will cause camera problems. Accordingly, the star will "telegraph" his or her movement by first leaning forward and then rising slowly so that the camera operator can follow the movement. When displaying a small object for closeups, the star knows where the director will want it placed. Since most stars are eager for their shows to become successful, they cooperate with their directors to make interview segments visually effective.

Realistically, the needs of director and star are not always the same. Friction sometimes occurs. It is important for aspiring directors to realize that the qualities that make a star effective as a performer are closely related to personal ego. The more successful the star, the more inflated the ego can become (although this is not always the case). I emphasize again: A skilled director is more than a mere stager of action and manipulator of cameras. A skilled director also displays talent in the often sensitive area of human relationships. Such a director is able to get along with people, even stubborn or unreasonable or childish people. Skilled directors understand how to persuade others to do their bidding, sometimes through humor, sometimes through flattery, sometimes through patient explanation. There are times, too, when directors must be firm. Controlled, polite—but firm.

The Provocateur

Some interviewers use the key entertainment element of conflict to arouse audience interest and elicit information from a guest. Mike Wallace in his early network interviews was a prime example of the Provocateur in that he goaded guests into making statements they might not otherwise have made. By stating blunt truths, by refusing to accept cop-outs, by provoking anger and emotionality, Wallace was able to knock aside a guest's defenses and stimulate honest, incensed, sometimes fiery reactions. Barbara Walters also sometimes acts the role of Provocateur.

Provocateurs do not always respect guests' wishes regarding taboo subject matter—although many do. Many state candidly that they will pry into sensitive areas, that, since these are areas of intense audience interest, they intend to explore just as exhaustively as the guest will allow. Thus, the guest knows what is coming and that he or she is expected to draw the line when the host goes too far.

With the Provocateur, the director must be alert, instantly ready to catch unexpected reactions. Most of us are trained from childhood to conceal emotions; we build protective walls around ourselves to shield us from remarks or actions that might shatter our equanimity. The Provocateur's goal is to shatter the protective wall, to cut through defensive devices, and to elicit honesty. With a camera trained on the guest's face, the director must try to anticipate reactions that betray true feelings, the twitch of a facial muscle, eyes suddenly watering, lips clenching to prevent speech. The director must try to *be* there when a guest suddenly comes apart, erupting emotionally, spilling feelings and honesty all over the studio floor.

Countless books have been written about cameras, lenses, switchers, and a director's commands to the crew. It is easy for directors to become so caught up in the mechanics of directing that they lose sight of the single most important broadcast element: the people in front of the cameras. Directing a live or videotaped program can be hectic, frenetic, busy. Under such circumstances, directors sometimes cut back and forth willy nilly, maintaining visual variety but overlooking what the program is all about. Good directors listen. *Really* listen. They concentrate on the interaction between performers so that their cameras will be on the right face at the right time. Such concentration is doubly essential in interviews conducted by a Provocateur.

THE INTERVIEW SPECTRUM

Watch a day of television and you will see interviews in almost every program category. In sports broadcasts they are a favorite halftime activity: questioning coaches about first-half glitches, their estimates of opposing team strengths and weaknesses, and their predictions on the contest's final outcome. Game shows inevitably interview guests before the competition begins, searching for quick audience identification—a "handle" for each contestant. In panel shows, interviews generally consist of probing for information gained by experts in the pursuit of their professions as well as for their personal opinions on newsworthy issues. Newscasts often include interviews with disaster victims, witnesses to catastrophes, or perhaps local celebrities. Sports commentators frequently question local coaches or ballplayers. On talk shows, the interview comprises the major part of the program, often slanted toward humor, seeking entertainment rather than information. The interview manifests itself briefly in comedy or musical variety programs as a way of allowing audiences to become acquainted with guests. In daytime programming, interviews comprise one of the major elements of the homemaker show.

Sports

While audience interest usually derives from the spoken words of the person interviewed, a director often may heighten interest by introducing the element of spectacle (see Chapter 2). Sports figures discussing game strategy in front of a neutral background may be fascinating or incredibly dull depending entirely on the personality of the interviewee and the content of the discussion. The wise director provides a measure of "insurance" by contriving a more colorful backdrop, thereby adding visual appeal to prevent the interview from degenerating into "talking heads." In the 1984 Olympic Games, directors used *chroma key* to place scenic or graphic backgrounds behind their program hosts.

Conducting interviews on the playing field provides color. During halftime (in basketball or football), with teams off the field, there is usually little competition from distracting background action. However, care must be taken that other halftime activities do not compete for spectator attention. A marching band, for example, generates sound, motion, and color, the primary ingredients of spectacle. Briefly clad cheerleaders constitute another element of compelling visual appeal. Appearing in the background of an interview, such diversions can cause restlessness and dissatisfaction. Audiences either lose interest in the interview, irresistibly drawn to the colorful background action, or uneasily divide their attention.

In television newscasts, sports commentators often interview coaches or ball players. When such interviews originate on a playing field rather than in the studio, visual interest is vastly enhanced. Such question-and-answer sessions are frequently staged with the commentator in the studio and the interviewee at the ballpark, responding on camera to the commentator's questions, which he or she hears through an earpiece.

Even when both commentator and guest are at the playing field, spectator interest is weighted heavily in favor of the guest. Usually such interviews are conducted with a single camera. The director frequently begins such an interview with a single shot of the commentator as he or she begins an introduction, widening to a two-shot at the appropriate moment. Beginning close prevents the awkward situation of a guest standing with nothing to do or say, "with egg on his face," while waiting for the commentator to conclude introductory remarks. Once the camera has zoomed out to a two-shot, interest usually fastens on the guest.

After a brief exchange between commentator and guest (played in the two-shot), the camera's movement should follow the pattern of viewer attention. As interest in the guest increases, the camera should zoom slowly in to a close shot and should hold there. By placing the commentator slightly downstage (closer to camera), the director clearly favors the guest, with the camera providing a three-quarter view of the guest's face rather than an ineffectual profile. Occasionally, the camera may pan to the commentator, paralleling viewers' interest in his or her questions and observations. If the discussion is an extended one, the director may want to zoom back to a two-shot from time to time, for purposes of orientation and visual relief.

In my television classes in directing drama, there is an almost compulsive tendency among students to fasten their cameras on the face of the character who is speaking. About halfway through the semester they come to understand that dramatic significance often lies on the face of the person *reacting*, who may not speak more than a word or two in the entire scene. In drama, the camera angle ideally reflects audience interest. In other forms of television and film, instructional or entertainment, the same rule applies. Audience interest dictates what appears on the screen—not the source of the words. In a sports interview, some beginning students might pan the camera to the host/commentator every time he or she phrased a question. Such literal camera movement is unnecessary, awkward, and probably dizzying. As in drama, there is no supreme law requiring the audience to see the person speaking. They can hear the question; they know perfectly well what the person looks like. So the camera can remain on the guest's face because that's where viewers' primary interest lies. Yes, occasionally it is visually refreshing to pan to the host as he or she adds commentary or phrases a new question. But such camera moves should be the exception, not the rule.

If it is practical, the sports interview can be further enhanced through the addition of videotape or film. Visuals relating to the guest's message, depicting specific team actions on the playing field, add impact to the interview and increase audience appeal. When videotape or film is not available, still photographs of sports action also can underscore spoken comments and provide effective visual variety.

In sports as in any interview, the choice of guest remains supremely important. A ball player with a sense of humor, vitality, and an infectious grin that compels us to like him is certainly preferable to Barnaby Bland, who speaks in a monosyllabic monotone. As discussed in Chapter 2, audiences are attracted to life. Performers with *aliveness* compel us to watch. In an interview, dynamic personalities command our attention; those who radiate energy create vibrations that do not allow boredom.

Panel Shows

Panel shows satisfy viewer curiosity, emotional or intellectual. They provide information that may help us achieve goals, impress friends, or simply enlarge our knowledge of the world. At times, when conflict divides panelists into armed camps, such shows also provide an element of drama.

The purpose of the panel show directly parallels that of an interview: to extract information from guests or to provoke discussion. Although panel formats vary, the content usually consists of variations of a question-and-answer pattern, which of course defines the interview. Thus, a panel show *is* an interview show, with a greater number of guests.

Positioning.   Panel shows generally feature a host who coordinates the flow of information plus expert panelists. The placement of panelists within a set depends upon how many there are and what their relationship is, either to the host or to one another. For example, when a panel of investigative reporters questions a political celebrity, the director places the cerebrity in a position where he or she may confront the team of interrogators, as for example, on "Face the Nation." The reporters, allied in purpose, are seated together. (See Figure 9.2.) The celebrity, target of the questions, perhaps assuming a defensive stance, sits opposite, either alone or beside a program host. Such positioning of panelists seems almost too obvious for comment, yet the staging principle should be understood since it applies to the composition of any panel show, no matter what the chemistry of its experts or how diverse its elements.

In a situation where a host questions experts, where there is no clear division into separate, allied groups, the director may place the team of experts either facing the host or to either side of him or her. Where experts are allied by profession or a commonality of interest, they should be grouped together for easy audience identification. Thus, a host interrogating union members and management about a current work stoppage would place union members on one side of a table facing management personnel on the other.

Identification for the audience may be further facilitated either by placing small identification cards in front of the panelists or by superimposing name and title when each is introduced. When superimposing name and title, the director should occasionally repeat such identification, reminding the audience of panelists' identities, especially when there are more than two guests or when guests are so prominent that their names will attract additional viewers.

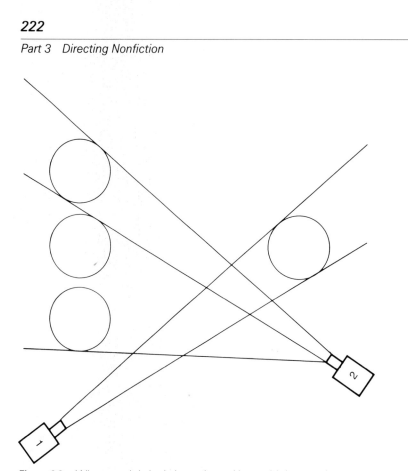

Figure 9.2   When a celebrity is interviewed by multiple questioners, one camera covers the celebrity, the other provides either a group shot or single shots of the questioners. A third camera would allow both a group shot of questioners as well as individual closeups.

Setting.   The setting for a panel show generally should be simple and utilitarian, reflecting the character of the program and its host and focusing attention on the table and chairs in which panelists sit. The table facilitates the panelists' use of notes, conceals unsightly laps and legs, and provides a base for identification cards.

Sometimes, directors (or producers) create a warmer, more relaxed atmosphere with a den or living room setting, guests seated in sofas and easy chairs. "Wall Street Week" on PBS combines both patterns, with a host querying "regular" experts seated at a table and then moving into a living room setting to meet a special guest expert, seated on a couch. In this new setting, host and regulars also occupy couches and easy chairs. Easy chairs and couches sometimes present staging problems. They are often difficult to get into and out of. Placing boards beneath the seats is of some help. Also, as discussed previously, placing the couch or chairs on risers facilitates rising and sitting.

In some cases the setting must also provide for the concealment of cameras. Where panelists sit at a table conversing with a host or with one another, cameras must be able to move deep into the set in order to photograph the action (see Figure 9.3). Since there will be some risk of cameras photographing each other, the setting (together with lighting) must provide concealment. In instances where it appears that the opposing cameras must certainly photograph each other (see Figure 9.4), long lenses that allow cameras to shoot from a distance can prevent such an accident. Finally, the director should make certain that each camera's tally light has been covered or extinguished. When cameras are hidden in shadow or behind a lattice, a bright red tally light appears as the devil's eye, gleaming in darkness.

Some network shows place their cameras on platforms or ramps some distance behind and *above* the level of seated panelists. When they photograph panelists with long lenses, at an imperceptible down angle, there is no longer danger of cameras photographing each other. Instead they shoot below the opposite cameras. (See Figure 9.5.)

Camera Coverage.   In the basic situation of a celebrity being questioned by the press, camera treatment is fairly simple (see Figure 9.2). Basic two-camera coverage would direct one camera toward the guest with the second recording both three-shots and singles of the press panel. Addition of a third camera would allow the director greater flexibility, permitting tie-in shots past the celebrity to the questioners and the freedom to cut between three-shots of the press panel and individual shots of its members.

Camera treatment of the six-member panel (and host) seated around a table is somewhat more complicated. As indicated in Figure 9.3, camera 2 shoots a master establishing angle as well as a single shot of the host seated at the head of the table. By moving slightly to the left or right, camera 2 can also pick up two-shots, three shots, and four-shots of the host and panel members. (Figure 9.6). Camera 1 shoots the complementary angles, past the host to panel members (Figure 9.7). Guests seated on the camera-left side of the table would be covered by cameras 2 and 3, paralleling the patterns indicated in Figures 9.6 and 9.7.

In photographing the six-member panel, complications quickly arise when panel members turn away from the host to address one another. Cameras 1 and 3 must move downstage—that is, toward camera 2—in order to shoot complementary angles on the panel members addressing one another (see

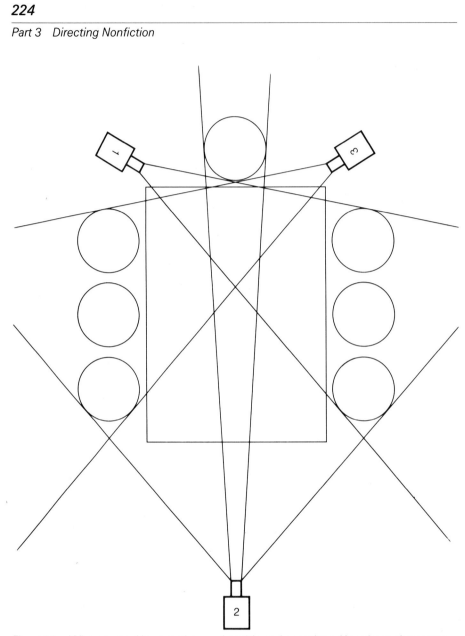

Figure 9.3   When a panel is seated around a table and questioned by a host, the center camera (2) provides orientation shots as well as closeups of the host. Cameras 1 and 3 provide angles on panelists.

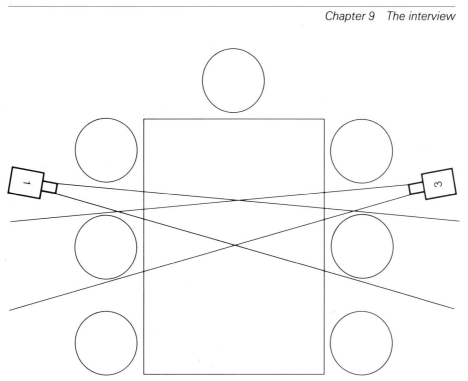

Figure 9.4   When panelists discuss issues with one another, cameras 1 and 3 must truck to complementary positions, shooting across the table. Long lenses prevent the cameras from photographing each other. Maintaining appropriate, corresponding looks becomes a formidable problem, so that panelists will appear to be speaking to (looking at) one another.

Figure 9.4). If the angles are not complementary, one of two possible mishaps may occur: The panelists may not appear to be addressing one another, that is, the direction of their looks will seem incorrect. Or the cameras will *cross the line*. Remember that in complementary angles each figure must occupy the same frame position in each angle. Imagine a line that bisects both figures. So

Figure 9.5   Cameras mounted on raised platforms avoid the problem of photographing each other. When cameras are placed some distance behind panelists, utilizing long lenses, their down angle is minimized.

long as both cameras remain on the same side of that imaginary line, the figures will remain in their same relative positions (see Figure 9.8). When one of the cameras inadvertently crosses the line, a jump occurs—that is, the figures appear to jump from one side of the frame to the other (see Figure 9.9). As discussed in Chapter 7, such a cut is usually awkward and disorienting, the mark of an amateur director.

Finding complementary angles quickly, in the midst of sometimes heated discussions among panelists, requires careful coordination between camera operators, director, and technical director. Such coordination is facilitated by experience. Keeping the same key personnel on a program from week to week assures optimum production values and minimizes the number and severity of director ulcers.

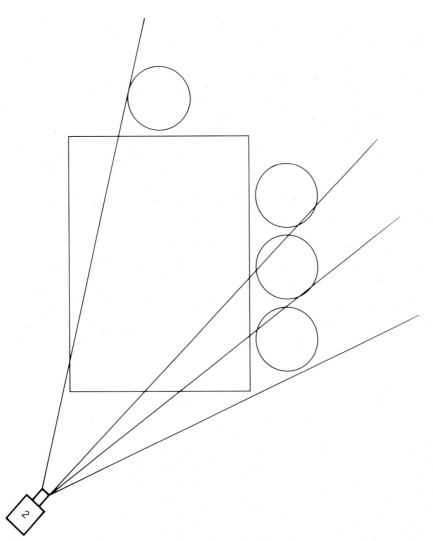

Figure 9.6   On a taped show, camera 2 may move laterally so as to provide two-shots, three-shots, or four-shots of the host and panelists—on either the right or the left.

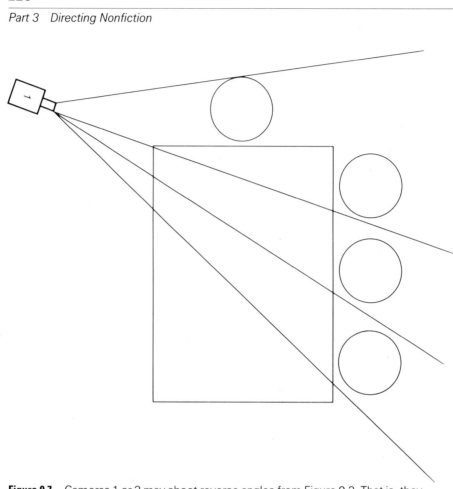

Figure 9.7   Cameras 1 or 3 may shoot reverse angles from Figure 9.3. That is, they provide angles past the host toward the panelist(s). From almost identical positions, they may provide closeups of panelists when they direct their attention to the host.

Newscasts

Interviews in newscasts, like those in magazine format shows (such as "60 Minutes" and "20/20") or documentaries, rely for their effectiveness upon immediacy, veracity, and authority. We will discuss news interviews in some depth in Chapter 11.

Game Shows

While the interview is but a minor part of game shows, its purpose is an important one: to make the viewer root for contestants. In discussing drama

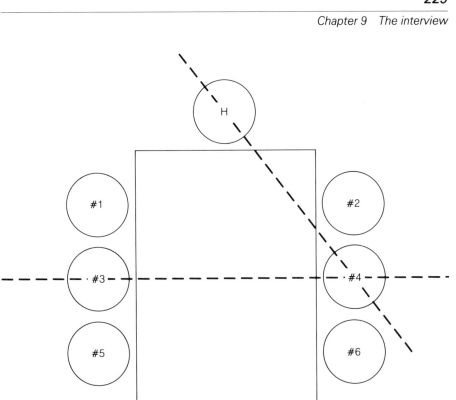

Figure 9.8   Performers will change positions in the frame when a camera crosses the imaginary line that bisects them. So long as both cameras remain on the same side of line, both performers will retain their original two-shot positions. When Host addresses Guest 4, for example, the imaginary line bisects them. When Guest 4 questions Guest 3, the line bisects them.

earlier, I indicated that in order for a play to be successful, spectators must identify with a protagonist. The stronger the audience's emotional involvement with a character, the more powerful will be their rooting interest, their need to see that character win his or her battles.

The game show uses many elements of drama; it provides an arena of conflict and a number of sympathetic protagonists. Awareness that a contestant is a newlywed or a working mother or a newly recruited marine transforms that contestant from a total stranger to an empathetic figure. The director can intensify emotional involvement by providing viewers with close shots of the contestant. Creating physical closeness helps to intensify emotional closeness. By identifying with contestants, the viewer can participate in the game more wholeheartedly.

Figure 9.9 When Host addresses Guest 4 and a camera crosses the imaginary line that bisects them, the Host will appear on camera left in one shot (a) and camera right in another (b).

Realistically, game show viewers divide their attention; part of their consciousness identifies with contestants, the other remains in den or living room, competing with them. Such a splitting of consciousness is characteristic of most audiences; a portion of their minds always remains aware that they are spectators.

Interviews in musical variety or comedy shows occur essentially for the same purpose as the game show interview: to win audience empathy, to promote a feeling of closeness between audience and guest performer. As with the Personality interviewer, close shots of both interviewer and guest allow a sharing of emphasis.

THE MARTHA McCULLER SHOW

You have been assigned to direct "The Martha McCuller Show." A staff director at a local television station, you're aware that Martha McCuller has hosted homemaker shows at other stations in your city. She's an articulate and attractive woman in her middle thirties and comes to your station with a sponsor (a local bank) for two of her thrice-weekly afternoon programs. Your program director advises you that she has a reputation for being "difficult," but he's sure you will have no problems. (You resolve to talk to the director of her latest show.)

You meet Martha McCuller; you're charmed by her. She's gracious, cordial, and apparently delighted at the prospect of working with you. (Certainly your program director was wrong!) You also meet her production assistant, Terry, a bright, no-nonsense woman in her early twenties. Terry worked with Martha (you're on a first-name basis by now) on her earlier shows. At this first meeting you discuss the program format. Most shows will divide into two major segments that will deal with fashion, makeup, exercise, gardening, interior decoration, cooking, or marital counseling—subject matter of interest primarily to homemakers. While some of the segments will feature demonstrations (such as fashion modelling, gift wrapping, pruning roses), most will consist of guest interviews. Terry will give you a detailed outline (names of guests, commercial information, and so on) on the morning of each show day.

After Martha leaves, Terry discusses a confidential matter: We must make certain that Martha looks as attractive as possible on each show. Will you please talk to your lighting crew? You assure Terry that your lighting director is a genius in such matters.

Your assurance is more than a "pat on the head" designed to keep a star happy. You know that a major part of any show's success depends upon its star. If audiences relate strongly to a personality, they will watch that personality's show, even if the show itself is less than extraordinary. Wise directors provide tender loving care, trying to make a star feel secure so that he or she will function effectively. They do everything possible to maximize their star's personal appeal. Understanding these facts of life, you discuss Martha's appearance with your lighting director immediately, perhaps ordering video-tapes of Martha's earlier shows in order to study the lighting.

The setting for "The Martha McCuller Show" will appear to be her home. In the comfortable living room will be two primary staging arenas: a conversa-tional group (couch, chairs, coffee table) and a desk where Martha will deliver commercials. Adjoining the living room will be a small, latticed patio with wrought iron chairs and a glass table, either for interviews or demonstrations. (See Figure 9.10.)

Later, Terry delivers to you a cartridge containing the program theme, a bright, lively melody that effectively sets the mood. You send the name and the publisher of the melody to your station's Music Clearance Department. They will handle legalities, determining whether song is ASCAP or BMI, whether the station will have to pay fees, and so on.

Your program director advises you that you will have one hour for lighting and camera rehearsal. You're delighted; it's more time than you expected. You check with your station's art director. He has already drawn plans for the "Martha McCuller" set. He gives you a copy. Construction begins immediately. The first show will air next Monday.

Early Monday morning you receive a telephone call at home. It's Martha. Will you be a darling and try to help her? She's deeply concerned. There is simply no way she can rehearse the program and talk to her guests while the lighting director and crew are lighting the set. It will be pandemonium, utter chaos.

You swallow hard and try to reassure her. You and the lighting director have already prelighted the set but, realistically, he will have to see each program's specific action before he can fine-tune the lighting. He's eager to make the show look just as rich as possible and he wants to do justice to the show's star, to make her look as beautiful as possible. Well, Martha under-stands and appreciates that, but . . . . You ask if it would be possible for her to talk with her guests in the dressing room, away from the lighting activity. You suggest meeting Martha an hour prior to rehearsal so that together you can discuss and plan the physical action of the show. Then she will be free for makeup and to meet her guests. When she's done, she should come to the set and walk through the action, allowing the lighting crew to make final adjust-ments. You hope this will be comfortable for her.

She's not sure it will be. In your heart you suspect that part of the reason for this early-morning call is apprehension. First-show jitters. You also under-stand that this is a test of your future working relationship. You try to mix kindness with authority. You assure her there's simply no other solution. Most

Figure 9.10   The setting for "The Martha McCuller Show."

of the station's shows aren't allotted as much rehearsal time as she's getting. You don't know how she did it; she really must have clout. But the studio is in use immediately prior to her rehearsal/lighting time, so you and she will just have to make the schedule work. Ultimately she accepts your suggestions. You're a darling and she appreciates your help. She'll meet you an hour before rehearsal time.

You sit down, push aside your cold scrambled eggs and pour yourself another cup of coffee. First crisis averted.

Prior to rehearsal and lighting time, you preview the one-minute film commercial that Martha will use in the show. She will do two commercials, the first live, the second on tape. You note that the taped commercial contains two seconds of so-called *freeze frame* after the announcer's final words, a continuation of picture after the sound portion has concluded. Thus, the commercial has fifty-eight seconds of audio and sixty seconds of picture, allowing you two seconds in which to cut or dissolve to Martha before the tape runs out. You write down the announcer's final words since they will be your cutaway cue.

Since the booth announcer (the staff announcer on duty) will have a few words at both the opening and the closing of the show, you make certain that he has his copy and has familiarized himself with it. (He hasn't but he will claim that he has.) Since his announcement is divided into two parts ("KBEX welcomes a new personality to its family of stars, Martha McCuller . . ." and ". . . brought to you by the City-State Bank, with a branch in your neighborhood"), you advise him to wait until he sees the City-State Bank logo (identification) on his booth monitor before reading the second half of his opening.

Prior to rehearsal time, you meet with Martha and Terry and discuss the content of the first show. Martha would like to interview her first guest, a famous author, in the living room and her second guest, an aging movie star, in the patio section. She suggests beginning at the couch with her guest. You suggest that since this is her first show it might be gracious to spend a quiet moment welcoming the audience to her new home, perhaps beginning in the patio and then walking into the living room to greet her guest. Martha applauds the idea.

Martha's notes (based on a preinterview conducted by Terry) will be placed on the coffee table in front of couch. No preinterview was held with the second guest. Her appearance was arranged by a press agent who sent along a mimeographed list of credits plus suggested discussion topics. Ordinarily, such limited (and predigested) preparation would worry Martha. This star, however, has worked with Martha before. They are old friends and Martha knows exactly what she wants to discuss. Terry suggests that you ask the prop department to place a pitcher of iced tea and glasses in the living room for Martha to share with her guest. You will be happy to make such arrangements, but in the future would Terry advise you of such needs ahead of time, to prevent possible disappointment?

The first (live) commercial will use another prop, a steel safety deposit box. The property person will place it on Martha's desk after she has begun her first interview. You have read the commercial and blocked the camera shots on paper. You will stage it with Martha and cameras when rehearsal time begins.

When Martha goes to makeup, you walk to the stage where the show will be televised. You spend a few quiet minutes by yourself, before the crew arrives, visualizing the action as you and Martha have discussed it. You make a few tentative markings on the floor and a few notes on the program outline that Terry personally delivered to you this morning.

Later, after you and Martha have walked through the essential moves of the show and indicated where she and her guests will work, the lighting director and crew finish lighting. You take a few minutes to examine Martha's makeup and lighting on camera. You have invited the makeup artist to come to the control booth to study Martha's makeup on camera. You both agree she looks magnificent. Her lighting will come almost entirely from the front, filling in facial imperfections. There will be some modelling, some shadow area, but it will be softened with fill light.

The show's opening titles have been videotaped. You have put the program theme on the tape. Titles will be keyed over live shots of Martha moving busily within her living room. At the conclusion of titles, Martha will acknowledge the audience and begin the program. Under titles for this first show, Martha will pour tea for her guest (seated on living room couch) and then will cross to the patio area to greet viewers. Along the way she will pass her desk with its bank logo and camera will zoom in to a full screen closeup of the logo. You decide to open on camera 2 with a medium full shot of Martha and guest. But you work backwards. That is, you carefully position camera 2 for its zoom to the bank logo and then ask the camera operator to swing around—*without moving the base*—to a shot of Martha and her guest. After the zoom to the bank logo, you will cut to camera 1 framing the patio area as Martha enters.

Once Martha has welcomed her viewers, camera 1 will pan or truck with her as she moves into the living room, crosses to the couch, and introduces her guest. You will then cut to a two-shot at the couch (on camera 2), followed quickly by a closeup of the guest. Two-shots at the couch (on 2) will favor Martha, seated at camera left. Closeups of the guest will be taken by camera 1. Since the opening pattern will probably be the busiest of the program, you rehearse it several times, making sure that the camera operators and others are secure.

You have arranged for the couch to be placed upon an unobtrusive six-inch riser so that Martha and guests may sit or stand more easily, so that there will be less separation between a standing Martha and a seated guest, and so that cameras will not produce severe down angles when photographing interviews.

On future shows when Martha interviews two or more guests at once, you will be careful to place them on the same side of her, perhaps with guests on couch and Martha seated in the upstage chair. Were guests to be seated on both sides of Martha, you would have a difficult time covering the interview effectively with only two cameras.

At the conclusion of the first interview, camera 1 (wide) will carry Martha to her desk. She will then sit, address the audience directly, camera moving in slowly to a closeup. At one point she will unlock and lock a safety deposit box. In rehearsal you position the box at Martha's right (camera left) so that it will face camera 2, which will provide tight shots. Following the live commercial, camera 1 will pan or truck with Martha as she crosses into the patio.

Now it is eight minutes before air time. You know from experience that performers need a moment or two to catch their breath between rehearsal and performance. Even if you desperately need another three minutes to rehearse a move, you wisely call a break so that the lighting crew can make final adjustments and the cast can straighten seams, brush hair, and powder noses. You carefully set eight minutes on your stopwatch before you leave the control room and go to the stage. Now you reassure the cast, making performers feel comfortable and relaxed, giving them any final directorial points. With stopwatch in hand you know exactly how much time is left. A cast left too long alone on the stage begins to get nervous.

At a minute or so before air time (yes, you're cutting it awfully close), you wish them well and hurry to the control booth. As you enter, you remind your audio person that the program theme will be on tape. You check to make sure that camera 1 is in the patio and that camera 2 is positioned for the zoom. You take a deep breath and grin at the technical director (TD) seated beside you.

At two seconds before program time you roll your titles. A moment later, a red light blinks on, indicating that your studio has "channels." Simultaneously the program titles appear on a preview monitor. You have previously instructed your TD to matte the opening titles over camera 2—on the *effects bus*. Now you command quietly: "Cue Martha. Up on effects. Fade music under, cue announce!"

"The Martha McCuller Show" is on the air.

CHAPTER HIGHLIGHTS

- Interviews seldom stand alone; they are usually part of a larger program unit (news, sports, homemaker programs). Interviews provide information or entertainment from the guests' reservoir of knowledge.

- Hosts of interview programs fall into three basic categories: the Sincere Inquirer, the Personality, and the Provocateur. Sincere Inquirers take a background, supportive position, allowing the guest to star. Most allow a production assistant to conduct a preinterview, selecting facts and anecdotes as well as a theme for discussion. Thus, in the broadcast, the interview will be structured rather than floundering aimlessly.

- With Sincere Inquirers, directors should favor the guest in camera treatment. In order to present full-face pictures, directors cross their cameras: the left camera photographing the performer on the right and vice versa. Placing couch or chairs on a riser assures that cameras will look performers in the eye. Directors search for stagings that will fit (approximately) the screen's aspect ratio of three units by four units. Two-person interview patterns fit this proportion nicely.

- Because of their humor, personal magnetism, or celebrity status, the Personality interviewers attract as much (or more) attention than their guests. Directors acknowledge their status by giving them equal or preferred camera treatment. With three cameras, the center holds a two-shot; cameras 1 and 3 favor host and guest in single or over-the-shoulder shots. With two cameras, coverage becomes more difficult. To avoid the painful repetition of a two-shot followed by a single, the director must "live dangerously," occasionally placing both cameras in close angles.

- The Provocateur takes off the kid gloves, probing into sensitive areas, provoking guests into statements they might not otherwise make. Directors must be sensitive to guest reactions so as not to miss key moments, a catching of breath or a tear quickly brushed away. All good directors concentrate deeply on the action before the cameras, listening intently, taking their cues from the performers rather than from their own whims.

- Each program type (news, sports, panel show, and so forth) presents different visual opportunities for directors. Sports programs provide a colorful backdrop for interviews. The playing field, marching band, cheerleaders, players themselves, all add richness.

- In one-camera interviews, the camera should follow the focus of spectator interest. Generally, it is the guest who attracts more interest so that is where the camera should be aimed most of the time. If the host takes a slightly downstage position, the guest will then favor (partially face) camera rather than present a profile.

- Panel shows are a variation on the interview pattern, guests exchanging views or providing information. In staging panel shows, directors place together panelists with a similar attitude and in opposing positions (across a table from one another) those having conflicting points of view. To prevent audience confusion, placards or superimposed titles should identify panelists from time to time.

- Concealment of cameras presents a major problem since they frequently must photograph panelists sealed directly across from one another. Lighting and the set may provide concealment.

- Directors of homemaker shows—as with most other program forms—perform a wide variety of functions. Their sphere of action is not limited to a control room.

C H A P T E R 10

Show and tell: Demonstration

Demonstration programs inform, but you should recognize that almost all programs inform, even those whose only avowed purpose is entertainment. We learn about foreign lifestyles from motion pictures filmed abroad. We gain insights into sociological or psychological problems in our culture from certain television shows or feature films. We even educate ourselves in new vocabulary, new styles of dress, new modes in home decoration, new hairstyles, and new emotional experiences from these same "noneducational" entertainment forms.

A primary difference between demonstration and entertainment programs lies in the program goal. Demonstration programs—instructional, educational, or industrial—aim to teach rather than entertain, to provide information that may add to their viewers' reservoir of knowledge or instruction that may add to their skills. The spectrum of demonstration programs is wide, primarily because demonstration (like interviews) often appears as an element within other program types (such as homemaker shows).

As entertainment programs also educate, so do educational programs also (in varying degrees) entertain. As successful teachers understand, the informational pill often requires sugarcoating in order to stimulate or maintain student interest. In directorial terms, sugarcoating simply means the application of principles described in Chapter 2: utilizing such classic elements of audience appeal as spectacle, humor, surprise, conflict, curiosity, sex appeal, or personal involvement through dramatization.

When you are in a good working mood, images swarm through your busy imagination. Keeping up with them and catching them is very much like grappling with a run of herring.   SERGEI EISENSTEIN[1]

In this chapter we will examine the nature of the demonstration program, dividing our examination into three primary discussions:

- CREATING SPECTATOR INTEREST: a brief glimpse at the roles of audience and director

- ELEMENTS OF DEMONSTRATION: the director's techniques for creating vivid and understandable instructional shows

- TWO DEMONSTRATION PROGRAMS: a structural analysis of the cooking show and the fashion show.

CREATING SPECTATOR INTEREST

The basic goal of television or film programs is communication—the director transmitting to an audience a message that is entertaining or instructive, or both. The success of the communication process depends on many factors. Two of the most significant are the skill of the Sender and the interest of the Receiver.

---

[1]*Film Form—Essays in Film Theory* (New York: Meridian Books, 1957), p. 261.

The Sender

Viewers will watch demonstration programs that deal with their favorite subject matter. If fine art intrigues them, they will watch a television program about art appreciation. If art lies outside their sphere of interests, they will avoid it—unless the director or the producer has managed to incorporate elements of such extraordinary appeal that they compel audience attention. If, for example, the art show is hosted by an internationally famous movie star, disinterested viewers might tune in. While such an example is extreme—and outside the province of most directors—it demonstrates the importance of the mode of presentation.

If a program consists of a single lecturer in a monotone exhibiting little-known paintings and demonstrating their compositions on a blackboard, casually interested viewers will certainly yawn and tune out. At the other extreme, if that program consists of "living paintings" from the famous Laguna Art Festival, enhanced by music and lively commentary from an engaging host, those same viewers will probably watch in fascination.

The point is obvious. Viewer interest varies in proportion to the Sender's showmanship and creativity. When talented directors use the classic entertainment elements effectively, minimally interesting subject matter is often warmly received. Warning: While the director has the responsibility to shape and interpret the message, he or she is frequently tempted to highlight only the color, to allow significant content to become minimized or lost. Elements of entertainment provide more fun; they are titillating. But, like frosting without the cake, such programs are unsubstantial and ultimately unsatisfying.

The Receiver

Of the elements of audience appeal discussed in Chapter 2, the one most applicable to demonstration programs is *curiosity*. Most of us lead hectic lives. Our days bulge with the pressures of professional, educational, or personal activities. We watch entertainment programs for an escape valve. When we taken the time to watch educational or instructional programs, our purpose is more specific, more goal oriented. We label it "curiosity" but in truth our curiosity is frequently mixed with self-interest.

Most of us seek to improve our knowledge of quasars or Jungian psychology or classical music in order to gain respect from peers, to be accepted into the world of sophisticated, well-educated people, or to win admiration from members of the opposite sex. We seek new or improved skills in order to gratify personal or avocational interests or else to improve our professional statuses, to help us make more money. If a television program helps us to achieve those goals, we watch with a sense of inner pride.

Understandably, we tend to select programs that require less effort and that provide more entertainment. However, when the reward is high and the motivation sufficiently strong, we will dig in, despite a lack of sugarcoating; the accomplishment outweighs the effort.

ELEMENTS OF DEMONSTRATION

Most of us learn best by doing. When programs can stimulate viewer participation—creating projects that require a hands-on experience for spectators—they will usually succeed in achieving their broadcast goals. Shows aimed at young children often use this principle beautifully, presenting projects that require paper and scissors or crayons, to be used by viewers in "games" that teach skills or inform. Since the art of instruction—especially as it relates to student participation—belongs more appropriately in a teaching text than in one devoted to directing, I will not pursue it further.

A recurring motif in this volume is the director's need to present program material in the most visual manner possible. The principle applies more to demonstration programs than to almost any other directorial category. Other than viewer participation, visualization creates the greatest audience impact and provides the most effective instructional tool. Creating appropriate visuals becomes the motivating factor for directors in programs that demonstrate objects or a skill or concept.

Demonstrating an Object

When audiences can see an object for themselves—a gyroscope, for example—together with a demonstration of ways in which the object can be used, they gain an understanding that would be impossible from mere "talking heads." Seeing the gyroscope spin at an impossible angle or on the point of a needle, virtually defying gravity, creates a vivid mental picture. Enlarging that understanding with film depicting how gyroscopes are used in the navigation of ships or airplanes, holding the vessel to course despite ocean currents and wind, demonstrates effectively because it demonstrates visually.

Closeness.   As discussed in Chapters 6 and 7, close angles intensify dramatic values. They create emotional closeness or familiarity and they provide impact. When introducing an audience to an unfamiliar object, all of these values are helpful.

When placing the object before your closeup camera, look at it as if you had never seen it before. When an object is presented at a flat angle, its shape

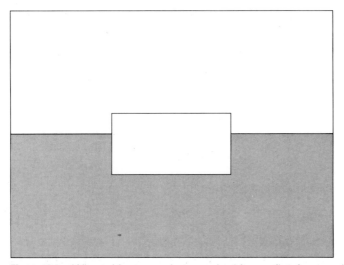

Figure 10.1   When objects are photographed from a flat, front angle, they become difficult to recognize.

and dimensions are difficult to ascertain (see Figure 10.1). When the object is turned slightly or if the camera is raised so that the viewer can recognize three dimensions, the image will be more clearly delineated (see Figure 10.2).

Lighting, too, can provide dimension and recognizability. If an object is a significant part of your demonstration, ask your lighting director to key it from a 45-degree angle and then to check it on a monitor (or from the control room) to make certain that the object is crisply defined.

Separation.   Sometimes an object in a close angle tends to become involved or lost in its background. Separation may be achieved through color, lighting, or texture.

When the color of an object is too close to the color of its background, separation becomes difficult. Changing the color or tone of one or the other is an obvious answer. Also, by taking some (or all) light off the background, it will appear darker, providing better separation.

Backlighting the object separates it from its background, providing a rim of highlight and creating a three dimensional image. Backlighting also throws a shadow pattern on the floor (in foreground) that may help to define the object's shape.

When the background is "busy"—that is, if its pattern is small, convoluted, or intricate and its colors varied—the object is easily lost in the com-

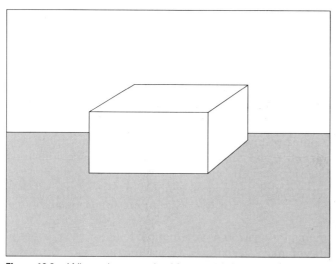

Figure 10.2   When photographed from a 45-degree angle and lighted so as to provide dimension, an object's shape and character may be easily discerned.

plexity of the background (see Figure 10.3). Generally, the key for easy recognition is simplicity.

Motion.   The simple act of picking up an object and putting it to use automatically solves many recognition factors. The object then changes position, lighting, and background. The audience also may determine its size in relation to a performer; in limbo, it could be any size.

Motion also demonstrates the object's practical aspects. The gyroscope, for example, reveals more about itself when spinning on a suspended thread than through a hundred beautifully composed camera angles on the still object. A stationary automobile is little better on television than a magazine advertisement. When that same car races up a scenic mountain road, it creates more than static beauty; it suggests speed, control, power. Viewers understand the object as much by what it *does* as by how it *appears*.

TV commercials utilize the demonstration process as a major sales tool. By seeing a product in use, and the happy reactions of users, spectators learn (are sold on) the remarkable effectiveness of the product. Interestingly, the reactions of others are usually what sell the product, not the specific qualities of the product itself. When a homemaker is thrilled at the effectiveness of a detergent or the rich taste of a new coffee, viewers tend to identify with her, sometimes in spite of themselves.

Figure 10.3   Intricate backgrounds create problems in recognition.

Demonstrating a Skill or Concept

Nowhere is the need for visuals more apparent than in demonstrating something that is itself nonvisual—an idea, a method, a concept, or a skill. If a program deals with the art of interior decoration, for example, words alone are virtually worthless. The director of such a program must insist on videotape, film, or photographs—or televise the program directly from the site to be refurbished—so that viewers can study the decoration problems firsthand. Creative planning could add greatly to such a program. With a photograph of the bare room, for example, the director could matte possible groupings of furniture into the room so that spectators could actually see what worked and what didn't. The decorator might then explain the specific reasons why one furniture grouping was effective and the other was not. But explanation without visual demonstration would fail to make its point, no matter how skilled the explainer.

Demonstrating ideas often calls for some degree of dramatization. Many industrial films teach employees such concepts as merchandising, salesmanship, how to resolve office conflicts, and stress management. Rather than put together films that simply lecture employees, producers sometimes build story situations in which new principles are dramatized, creating characters with whom an audience of employees can identify. I once directed an industrial film in which a girl accepted a job as a magician's assistant. When the magician trained her, she made every mistake in the book. As she learned how to learn, so did the audience.

Classroom methods of demonstrating a concept often work well on television. Experienced teachers use visual aids such as videotape, film, or still photographs in educating their students. Still photographs, when used with imagination, provide unusual opportunities for visual demonstration.

When using photographs, many directors try to keep their cameras moving so as to help create an illusion of reality. They either start wide and dolly in slowly, or start close on some feature of the photograph and dolly out. Sometimes, if the photograph is large enough, cameras can pan slowly from one feature of the photograph to another, the movement bringing life to the inanimate. Such treatment works far better, of course, when there are no human figures in the photograph frozen in position. On some occasions, music or sound effects can help create the illusion of three-dimensional reality in a still photograph. Bringing in music as a director dissolves to a photograph creates dramatic impact. Since the camera is focusing on a flat plane rather than dimensional subject matter, dollies in or out become somewhat difficult; be sure that your camera operator can handle the chore.

Other classroom devices also work on television. A blackboard, easel, or any surface on which pictures may be sketched help to turn a verbal description into a visual one. Audiences, like students, need help in reinforcing ideas. A picture adds another dimension; it redefines an intangible concept, even if it is nothing more sophisticated than chalk on a blackboard.

Whenever possible, a skill should be performed *from the viewer's point of view.* Students of instructional programming have labelled such a shot a "zero-degree camera angle." The shot creates far greater learning impact than an objective angle since it seems to make the viewer a participant. Realistically, angles photographed from the learner's point of view are sometimes difficult to accomplish.

For demonstrating a skill, all of the described principles for demonstrating an object hold true. When an expert demonstrates how to prune roses, for example, viewers must see each of the cuts made by the pruning shears. When the expert explains that each cut should be diagonal, slightly above the bud that will later become a branch, it is critically important for the audience to *see* the bud and to *see* the diagonal cut. It is essential that the branches stand out clearly from the background. Backlighting, a contrast between foreground and background, and simplicity of background will all help to make the expert's demonstration visually effective.

The Director as Audience

In addition to staging action and calling camera shots, the director of a demonstration program plays another essential role, that of audience. In preparation and rehearsal, the director watches the demonstration with a critical eye. If the expert does not present material clearly and understandably, the director must ask for changes.

Since the director is a relatively disinterested observer, he or she can be objective in assessing the manner of presentation, asking such questions as: Does the expert go too fast, not giving viewers time to assimilate the material? Does the expert lead the audience carefully from the known to the unknown, from the simple to the complex? Are his or her explanations confusing? Do they involve too many esoteric words or phrases? Are the explanations visual? What can the expert do to make the demonstration *more* visible? By asking the questions an audience would ask, the director prevents a breakdown in communication.

The Expert

When demonstrating where and how to prune a rosebush, the gardening expert must be as aware of your problems as you are of his or hers. The expert must know, for example, which camera will take close shots so that action can be angled to that camera. You can help the expert (and yourself) by placing a monitor near the work area. Now your expert can see when a hand or shadow covers the significant action or when it is angled incorrectly to the camera. During rehearsal, allow your expert to experiment in showing action to the camera, becoming comfortable with the physical set-up, even a little proud of his or her ability to accommodate your needs.

While experts are highly skilled in their own fields, they are often unskilled (and uneasy) when appearing before television cameras. Nervousness can mar the effectiveness of their contributions. Remember, directors are responsible for the overall impact of a program. They do not simply "direct traffic" on stage. Their function is not limited to calling camera shots. Therefore, as director, you must make the expert feel welcome and secure. A cup of coffee helps. So does a smile.

TWO DEMONSTRATION PROGRAMS

The element of demonstration appears in programs covering a wide spectrum: from cooking shows to documentaries, from homemaker shows to industrial films. We will examine in some detail a typical demonstration show and an atypical one. Whether you have any interest in these two specific program types or not, they will nevertheless provide insights to a broad range of other demonstration programs.

A Typical Demonstration Program: The Cooking Show

Literally and figuratively, the cooking show has become the meat and potatoes of many local television stations. It has also appeared on daytime commercial networks ("The Galloping Gourmet") and repeatedly on PBS ("The Julia Child Show"). TV stations may produce such a show inexpensively on a daily basis, featuring local epicurean personalities.

The director may bring visual appeal to cooking shows in three areas, all of which may be described by the word *appetizing:* the food, the host(ess), and the setting.

The Food.   A key concern in the preparation of food is that the audience be able to see it clearly, vividly, and up close. The obvious answer is to zoom the camera in to an extremely close shot. Unfortunately, the solution isn't that simple. Since most normal work areas are at waist height, a camera, even at the top of its pedestal, cannot gain a steep enough down angle to provide an effective view of the food. The angle does get steeper as the camera moves closer, and it is possible for work/display areas to be lower than normal (although low counters cause problems for a performer's back). These, however, are generally unsatisfactory, second-best solutions.

Many cooking shows utilize a large, double-mirror "periscope" for one of their cameras (see Figure 10.4). Through such a device, the camera is able to shoot from an acute high angle, providing viewers with an excellent perspective on the food. Such a large piece of equipment somewhat limits camera movement, although the camera may pedestal up to shoot between the two mirrors or may move to either side.

Most cooking shows use two cameras. One generally stays wide, covering the host and providing orientation; the other provides close shots of the food in preparation. Thus, it is seldom necessary for the closeup camera to move from its mirror position except when shooting live commercials or titles. Such an arrangement is comfortable for the host in that he or she only has to play to one camera that represents the viewer.

Most professional cooks and chefs are aware that an attractive appearance is as necessary to a dish as its taste. As a director, you should be equally aware. In all steps of preparation, stove, sink, and counters should be immaculate. When fat has been trimmed from meat, for example, or vegetables peeled, debris should be immediately cleared so that work areas remain spotless.

Of course, food should be arranged on plates or platters as artistically as possible. Garnish often adds eye appeal. Parsley, carrot curls, or fruit baskets may not be utilitarian but they effectively dress up the completed dish. Even the choice of china is important in creating eye appeal. If the host needs prompting in this area, don't be shy.

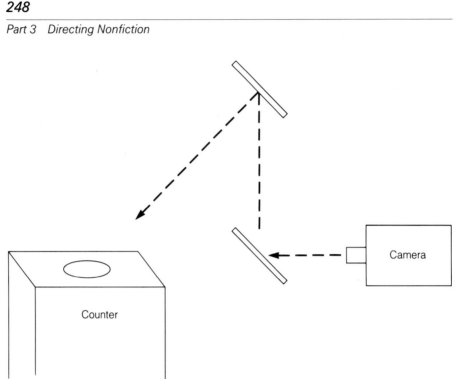

Figure 10.4   In order to provide effective down angles on food preparation, many cooking shows utilize a system of double mirrors.

Commercial photographers learned many years ago that one of the secrets of making food appear appealing was to use plenty of light. Backlight, in particular, creates the glisten and sparkle that most of us associate with taste appeal. Glance through any magazine that features food advertisements and note the glisten that "sells" the food. If your lighting director isn't aware of such fine points, pass along the word. Most cooking shows feature a special downstage area where the completed dish is proudly displayed. More than any other, this is an area for special care and attention by your lighting director.

Since many recipes require considerable preparation time, it is often advisable to "cheat" in a live telecast by having on-hand examples in various stages of progress. Thus, the host can prepare cake batter on camera and then avoid an hour's baking time by producing a second cake which he or she has prepared prior to airtime. No need to apologize for taking shortcuts. Audiences understand the exigencies of a half-hour live telecast. Now, the host can decorate the cake, concluding the recipe with a grande finale of fancy frills and trimmings instead of a deadly wait or the promise to finish tomorrow.

The Host.   In my years in live television I directed three different cooking shows. Two of the three had hosts who were truly marvelous cooks. The third was a mediocre cook but a delightful personality. Which of the three shows had the highest audience ratings? Beyond any question, it was the third.

People relate to people. True, we watch a cooking show primarily to learn. But learning need not be tedious. As Julie Andrews sang in *Mary Poppins,* "A spoonful of sugar makes the medicine go down!" When the learning process includes elements of entertainment, the medicine goes down easily. When a host brings humor, a personal zest, or style to a show, it lifts the show beyond the ordinary. Caution: A sense of humor cannot replace cooking ability. Audiences still tune in primarily to learn kitchen skills. But if five cooks have approximately equal talents, the one with a twinkle will steal the Nielsen points.

One of the delights of "The Julia Child Show" was her ability to laugh at herself when she misread a recipe or dropped a soufflé. The error made her human; her self-deprecating remarks endeared her to us. But those qualities would not have been so meaningful had she not been recognized initially as a superb cook.

The kitchen's immaculate appearance should, of course, be reflected in the appearance of your host. In dress, hairstyle, and work habits, he or she should create an appetizing image. Studio lights tend to work against that image; they are hot and cause perspiration. If your show occasionally breaks for filmed or taped commercials, those breaks are ideal opportunities for your host to blot that perspiration.

Since you're aware that a star's popularity and a show's success often go hand in hand, you should try hard to make your host look good. Make certain that the lighting is flattering. Try to create an ambience on the set that is warm and supportive. If the star is nervous or insecure, ask your crew for help in making him or her comfortable. Build confidence through sincere compliments; create humor to reduce tension; generate a feeling of competency. Your host will come to understand that the crew are professionals who know exactly what they're doing; they're not going to let anything go wrong.

The Setting.   For a cooking show the setting should be cheerful and utilitarian. Whether modern or period, most designer kitchens use plenty of brick and wood with bright colors (paint or paper) for accent. As in all well-designed sets, your kitchen should not be too "busy"; avoid too many small, fussy details that obstruct easy readability. Thus, ceramic tiles are seldom a good choice. Most kitchen sets place oven and refrigerator to the side or in the background so that the primary work area can be in the foreground, usually a countertop and adjoining gas stove top.

One of the financial fringe benefits of cooking shows is the opportunity they present for merchandising tie-ins with local grocery markets. Since major food distributors always are seeking display space in markets, the cooking show is often able to attract national advertisers through the promise of such space. Local grocers usually are happy to provide displays in return for being mentioned in the advertiser's cooking show commercials. Thus all parties benefit. Merchandising sometimes includes appearances by the host at the market and on-the-air contests involving market and product.

While the director must respect the host's involvement with advertisers and merchandising (stars frequently receive a percentage of advertising dollars), commercial efforts should not impinge upon the content of the show. When this happens, audiences begin to feel that the program has become one long advertising message. To prevent such a reaction, directors should separate the work area from the commercial area so that the host must physically leave the work area in order to begin a commercial pitch. Such an area usually adjoins the downstage countertop and is of the same decor as the kitchen.

An Atypical Demonstration Program: The Fashion Show

Fashion shows, like other demonstration elements, usually are presented as part of a larger program format. They appear occasionally in newscasts in coverage of couturier showings. Since their appeal is primarily to women, they appear frequently in homemaker shows, sometimes as a part and sometimes as the entire program.

Fashion shows are unlike other demonstration programs in that the ambience becomes almost as significant as the product demonstrated. In this respect they are much like magazine advertisements and TV commercials. In truth, their goal is often as much to sell as to educate. The drama surrounding the presentation, the character of the models, the setting, the music, and the commentator create an atmosphere that shapes the spectator's receptivity.

The Models.   A popular fallacy: Successful models are always beautiful. Not so. They are *sometimes* beautiful. More importantly, they wear clothes with style. By their demeanor, they make fashions appear attractive, important, necessary. Part of a model's effectiveness relates to her figure, usually lean and strikingly tall. The most sought-after fashion models are five feet, nine inches or taller. Part of their effectiveness relates to facial expressions.

When directing a fashion show, notice that the finest models create ambience as much from their expressions as from their physical demeanor. They wear clothes proudly; their faces proclaim, "I feel marvelous wearing this gown; I feel rich and sensuous; I love myself." Models also express these thoughts in their movements, in the way they walk, in their gestures such as pulling a collar about the throat or pointing out specific apparel features as they are described by a commentator. By their movements, facial expressions, and attitude, they create an unmistakable sense of beauty.

Directors sometimes are presented with an inexperienced or lackluster model. While most TV directors don't have the time to give lessons, they can suggest what a model should be feeling in the hope that the model will have the dramatic capabilities to bring it off. Inexperienced models often are so concerned with the physical movements necessary to the staging of a fashion show that they cannot give thought to much else. Wise directors therefore keep their staging simple. When possible, they voice their opinions in the selection of models.

The Staging and Setting.   Logically, decor should complement the fashions. Thus, if the gowns are formal, the setting should echo that formality, perhaps with "marble" columns, arches, or a circular staircase. The elaborateness of the setting, of course, depends on budget, the resourcefulness of the art director, and the set pieces available in the storage barn. Less formal attire might utilize a garden setting with lattice or a gazebo and greenery as space (or money) will allow.

Male models seem to function more effectively when using props. Tennis rackets or golf clubs, for example, give them something to do with their hands while modeling sports attire. When modeling suits or formal attire, they appear more natural carrying a briefcase, overcoat, or a corsage box. When the budget allows, such handsome props as a Rolls Royce or classic old car will not only add elegance to the setting but will also give the models something to relate to.

Imagination sometimes provides answers to budget problems. I once directed a fashion show featuring bathing suits. We tried to put together a beach setting. Because of time and budget limitations, it was impossible. Instead, we directed a spotlight into a pan of water, throwing shimmering reflections on a bare cyclorama. We introduced each model in a master angle, shooting through a small fish tank (borrowed from a neighborhood pet store), with multicolored fish and seaweed in sharp focus in the foreground, the model blurred and indistinct in the background. The camera then racked focus to the model. After a moment, we cut to the second camera, which provided a closer angle, eliminating the fish tank. But the underwater illusion was maintained with the ripple effect on the cyclorama and a few rock cutouts in the foreground.

Traditionally, the staging of fashion shows divides into two parts: (1) the revelation of a new model in a new gown and (2) a closer inspection of the gown and its features. The revelation can be as simple or as elegant as the setting allows. For example, if the fashions are formal, the model might appear at the top of a staircase. Camera 1 would follow her in a full shot as she descends the staircase and moves downstage (toward camera) to a spot that you have carefully marked on the studio floor. In this second, foreground position, you cut to a closer angle, perhaps a waist shot. As the model turns, revealing features of the gown, camera 2 follows her movement. Camera 2 may tilt down to the model's feet, revealing features at the hem, and tilt back up to her head and shoulders.

While camera 2 photographs this closer angle, your floor manager cues the next model to take her place at the top of the staircase where she waits, unseen by camera 2. Camera 1 meanwhile is lining up on the waiting model. When the first model has completed her stint, you cut to camera 1 as the floor manager cues the second model to descend. The first model now exits, unseen by camera 1. And the pattern is repeated. (See Figure 10.5.) A principle that serves directors well, in fashion shows as in other forms of staging: Entrances are interesting; they create anticipation. Exits are boring. The conspicuous exception is the final shot in many dramatic films in which an exit has traditionally marked the bittersweet fadeout. (Recall the final shots in many Charlie Chaplin comedies and in most Westerns.)

In maintaining the mood generated by the gowns, the formal setting, and the music, it is often effective in a fashion show to dissolve rather than cut between camera angles. A dissolve seems less abrupt, more fluid.

The Commentator.   The commentator in a fashion show does far more than provide descriptions of various garments; he or she sets the pace for the program, tying together all of the elements. Commentators work far more effectively off camera than on because they must refer to notes and their presence often interferes with the mood generated by setting and models.

Careful coordination between commentator and director is essential. The director usually has no idea how much time the commentator will take in describing each gown. Therefore the commentator must provide a cue when to cut or dissolve to the next model. Usually a polite "thank you" to the on-camera model signals completion. Generally, the fashion show coordinator or commentator provides the director with a list of gowns to be exhibited and specific features of each so that the director may anticipate the commentator's words. Thus, when the commentator describes lace at the neckline, the direc-

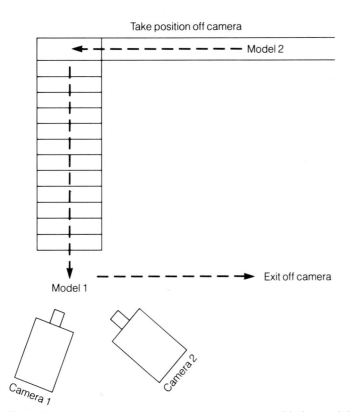

Take position off camera

Model 2

Exit off camera

Model 1

Camera 1

Camera 2

Figure 10.5   In this staircase pattern, camera 1 pans with the model down the stairs in a full shot. Camera 2 provides closer coverage.

tor will be waiting and ready to cut to a closeup. Providing the commentator with a monitor also helps ensure effective coordination. By watching the screen, the commentator knows exactly what is being photographed at each moment, enabling him or her to adjust commentary to match.

The Music.   Like the setting, music must complement the mood generated by the fashions. Easy rock and roll or muted jazz might be appropriate for sports attire. Formal fashions might require something more stately: violins or harps or popular classics. Remember, the music must fit comfortably behind the commentator's voice; it cannot be strident. It is a background to the show, not the show itself.

CHAPTER HIGHLIGHTS

- Entertainment programs educate; educational films entertain. The latter create interest through such classic elements of audience appeal as humor, spectacle, conflict, curiosity, sex appeal, or personal involvement through dramatization.

- Viewers normally watch subject matter in which they are interested. Subject matter of minimal interest requires greater creative effort by director and producer in order to entice viewers.

- When demonstrating objects, directors must photograph them for maximum recognition, utilizing such factors as closeness, appropriate angle, separation from background, and movement. Separation may be achieved through a differentiation in color and by backlighting. Movement that indicates how an object is used most clearly reveals its nature.

- In demonstrating a skill or concept, the director must create a presentation that is essentially visual. Visuals include videotape or film, still photographs, physical demonstration of a procedure (such as pruning roses), dramatization through actors, and even a chalk board.

- Experts bring knowledge and skill to a program but often lack familiarity with television procedures. Sensitive directors try to make them feel secure. Directors also try to react as a typical audience would, making certain that the expert's presentation is not too fast, too esoteric, or too complex for easy assimilation.

- A cooking show is a typical demonstration program. Directors sometimes use mirrors for down angle shots of food. They ensure that food presentations appear attractive and appealing, in both preparation and lighting. The host's personality is a major factor in the success of a cooking show; humor may be as important in attracting audiences as culinary ability.

- A fashion show represents an atypical demonstration program—atypical in that ambience becomes almost as important as the fashions themselves. The setting should reflect the character of the clothing being modelled. Thus, formal gowns require a formal setting. Models "sell" their apparel as much through facial expressions as through physical movement.

■ Camera coverage of fashions divides into two parts: a wide shot for entrances and to establish an overall impression and closer shots to accentuate specific apparel details. Generally, in fashion shows as in other program forms, entrances are interesting; exits are not.

■ A fashion commentator usually works off camera, timing commentary to the director's coverage (or vice versa). A studio monitor helps the commentator synchronize words with picture.

C   H   A   P   T   E   R   11

The news program

News has come into its own. A decade ago many TV stations aired two daily quarter-hour newscasts, one at the dinner hour and another in late evening. Now those same stations broadcast two or three hours of news each day. To be sure, much of it fails to qualify as "hard" news. Many stations boast feature reporters, restaurant authorities, consumer advocates, medical or health advisers, entertainment reporters, and political commentators. The newscasts also include sports and weather experts, chosen as much for audience appeal as for their expertise. When you add to this potpourri the personal magnetism of anchorpersons and the colorful computer graphics that enhance these "news" programs, you must conclude that, in most cases, they have become a new form of variety hour—news-oriented entertainment specials.

Because of the multiplicity of elements and the complexity of their visual structure, these programs have become tests of concentration for their directors. While concentration is an essential characteristic of all directors, the term seems particularly appropriate for news directors since they must coordinate script, local cameras, remote cameras, videotape, timing of sound elements, computer graphics, personalities, and more.

A second characteristic marks successful news directors: *awareness*. Once a newscast begins, a dozen disparate elements hang in the air. A weather reporter on remote at the county fair is having trouble with crowd control. A newsroom executive hurries in with revised script pages. The producer is on the phone to a remote, advising a performer to stand by. The technical

News, or orientation to reality, is essential to the happiness and emotional balance of democratic man. Disorientation is one of the things we have most to fear.

HARRY SKORNIA[1]

director has punched up the incorrect graphic. The aware director has a dozen eyes, tracking on-the-air elements as well as those in the control room. The latter are significant because they will affect or become on-the-air elements in minutes or seconds.

Aware directors are conscious of the problems of other members of the production team. If the audio engineer has difficulty with a microphone, that difficulty automatically becomes the director's problem. If the producer has miscalculated, cramming too many elements into a script, that timing miscalculation also becomes the director's problem.

A key part of awareness is knowledge. Successful directors work to build a knowledge of the functions, goals, and problems of other members of their news teams. Such knowledge provides security. If something goes wrong, they are better able to adjust or to compensate. Knowledge transforms technicians into directors.

This chapter includes two primary discussions. The first, addressing itself to knowledge, will deal with the individual elements of a newscast. The second will concern specific directorial and editorial functions in the field and in the studio, in preparation and on the air.

---

[1]*Television and the News* (Palo Alto, Calif.: Pacific Books, 1974), p. 2.

THE ELEMENTS

While the material in this chapter is based largely on personal observation of the news operation at KHJ-TV, a Los Angeles independent station, it directly parallels news procedures at other, larger stations, both independent and network. The difference lies primarily in scope and size. Where KHJ-TV has four field units, KNBC has over a dozen. Where KHJ-TV has a news staff of 40, KNBC has a staff of approximately 240. Scope and size, however, are not necessarily determinants of an effective operation. The KHJ-TV nine o'clock newscast, for example, has won dozens of Golden Mike awards for excellence in a variety of categories. (Golden Mike awards are presented annually by the Radio Television News Association.)

Most viewers would be surprised at the depth and complexity of the typical television news-gathering operation. The discussion here divides into three parts: visual content, preparation, and paperwork.

Visual Content

Television stations recognize the acute need for visuals as a way of dramatizing news stories. Showing an anchorperson simply telling (reading) a story fails to realize the promise of a visual medium. Watching such "talking heads" is little better than hearing the same story on the radio. Therefore TV stations search for ways to add a visual dimension. When such visualization is not available, stories frequently are dropped from the lineup.

The ideal way to dramatize a story is through videotape or film, creating impact because it places viewers at the scene of an event. In the news operation, videotape has almost completely replaced film; it is cheaper, faster, more flexible.

Videotape.   How can a local TV station offer its viewers videotape of major news events happening thousands of miles away? If the station is affiliated with a network, it receives each day an "affiliate news feed from a network satellite: usually sports, some hard news and many softer news items. The affiliate feed will sometimes include a promo for the local station to air, promoting that evening's network news."[2]

In addition to receiving visual material, affiliates may also contribute. If a newsworthy event happens locally, the local station covers the event with its field units, recording the material on videotape. The station then ships the

---

[2]Director Jay Roper with NBC News.

videotaped news material to its New York headquarters for possible distribution (via affiliate news feed) to other stations. Satellite use is expensive; if an event is not sufficiently newsworthy, networks use other means of distribution. If the event has major national significance, however, the network usually sends its own director and crew to handle coverage. In the latter case, the material would be transmitted to New York via a satellite *uplink,* for later airing on network news programs and satellite distribution to affiliates.

Independent stations also exchange video material via satellite. They form a network of their own called *INDX* (pronounced "index"), an acronym for Independent Exchange. Member stations both receive and contribute material. WPIX in New York functions as the origination point for daily INDX transmissions.

About the middle of the afternoon, independent stations receive (via telex) a list of stories that will be transmitted by INDX that day. Such advance notice helps stations plan the pattern of their newscasts. An hour or two later (usually about five o'clock), the satellite material begins coming in. The station records the material on two separate videotape machines, for protection in case one breaks down and to expedite editing. Each item carries a slate describing the story and its exact length. On the average, approximately forty minutes of material is transmitted each day. According to KHJ-TV executive producer, Bill Northrup, only about 10 percent of that material is actually used by the station.

A local TV station tries to serve the interests of its community; it therefore places a mix of local and regional news in the foreground, allowing world and national news to take a background position. To provide visuals for such stories, the station must rely on live or videotape coverage from field units, material borrowed from other local or regional stations, still photographs, or artwork and computer-generated titles.

Still Photographs.   Still photographs generally are used to provide visual inserts, appearing in a corner of the frame with an anchorperson. They usually come from the wire services.

Wire service photographs, while fulfilling a distinct need, also create problems. In most cases they are the wrong aspect ratio; vertically oriented eight-by-ten-inch photos do not comfortably fit TV screen proportions. Also, because they are black and white, they seem out of place in a color telecast.

Many stations employ graphics artists to work magic on these unsatisfactory still photos. With sophisticated computers, these artists first rephotograph the still, placing it into computer memory. Second, using an incredible electronic wand, they extend the black and white background imagery so that the photo fills a horizontal aspect ratio. Third, they add color to the background—whatever color they feel appropriate to the subject matter. Fourth, sometimes they print a title (such as the subject's name) at the bottom of the frame. Of course they have considerable freedom in terms of lettering: a choice of size, form, color, and style. Sometimes the graphics artists place a solid band of color behind the lettering. When finished, they have accomplished a casual miracle, in minutes transforming a drab black-and-white vertical still into an attractive, horizontal, color-oriented graphic. Later, on the news program, the technical director will insert the picture into the anchor person's frame using *DVE (Digital Video Effects).*

Most TV stations have voluminous files of such inserts—photographs or generic graphics (for example, a drawing of the sun radiating heat waves)—which are numbered, placed in an electronic "frame storer," and which can be called forth at a later date to add visual information to an appropriate story.

Still photographs in full color sometimes are extracted from videotaped stories for which there is insufficient broadcast time—or whose content doesn't warrant more than minimal coverage. The single frame insert replaces videotape; the newscaster succinctly describes the story in ten or fifteen seconds instead of a more time-consuming videotape version.

Printed Material.   Often news figures must be identified for an audience, by either name or title. Computers such as the Chyron generate such printed material, usually in color. The director indicates when titles are to be matted into a picture (usually across the bottom of frame) and when they are to be removed. Other computer-generated printed material is used in sportscasts, listing scores of completed (or ongoing) ball games. As the sportscaster ticks off the scores, the director cues changes from one graphic to the next. When used in ball games, character generators have their own operators, constantly providing the director with a flow of statistical information.

Opening and closing title patterns on news programs also draw from computer memory, combining dynamic still photographs of the station's news team with imaginative graphics.

Local TV Cameras.   Newsworthy local events usually are covered by three-person ENG crews: camera operator, sound technician, and reporter. On a day-to-day basis, independent stations do not employ the services of directors to stage such coverage; the reporter in consultation with the camera operator generally handles such chores.

One of the advantages of the single-camera, three-person unit is that it is compact, lightweight, self-contained (usually in a van), able to move quickly from one locale to another. Such units maintain constant radio contact with the newsroom so that they can keep the producer informed of their progress and any unexpected problems. Also, after completing an assignment, the field unit may be dispatched by radio to cover a story breaking suddenly in another location. Most such units are constantly on the move, videotaping interviews, fires, award ceremonies, accidents, political speeches, and arrivals and departures of celebrities. Usually they leave the TV station in the morning and do not return until night.

Field units dispatch their stories to the newsroom in two ways: by microwave link, transmitting picture and sound as an event is actually occurring, and by recording the event on videotape. In the second circumstance, the tape is subsequently microwaved to the station, "bulk feeding" it, along with other material recorded that day, or is picked up by a courier who will deliver it to the TV station. When the signal is transmitted by microwave, it is recorded at the newsroom. In both cases, the coverage is evaluated by the news producer and edited per his or her instructions.

Sometimes, when an event occurs at the time of the news program, it is transmitted live (via microwave link) to the TV station where it is incorporated into the newscast. Such a practice is common during local elections, with sports or weather personnel on location, with reporters providing updates on major catastrophes and other events.

The balance of the news program is supplied by studio cameras covering live performers in the news set. One practice currently in vogue ties together studio anchor personnel with reporters on location. The reporter's picture is fed into a monitor within the news set. (These monitors usually are on hydraulic lifts so they may be raised into view or lowered out of sight during a program.) With the monitor raised, anchorpersons may address or question the distant reporter directly. Sometimes no monitor is used; the reporter on location is chroma keyed onto a wall behind the anchorperson or wiped in using digital video effects (DVE). Once the questioning is finished, the director usually cuts directly to the reporter so that he or she becomes the sole focus of attention.

Weather Reports

Just as the location reporter was chroma keyed onto the wall behind the anchorperson (or inserted via DVE), so are maps and graphics frequently displayed directly behind weather reporters. When a weather map is keyed behind a reporter, he or she must glance occasionally at an off-camera monitor in order to know where to point—to orient himself or herself in relation to the map. Some weather reporters hold a concealed switch in one hand in order to cue changes in the graphics. Others use word cues to signal the director when to make changes.

When backgrounds contain movement—as is sometimes the case with satellite weather tapes—the director rolls the videotape full screen with the weather reporter keyed over it.

Preparation

The various elements within a news program come together slowly. Some major events such as political conventions are planned weeks before the date of broadcast.

Feature stories and local news events for Tuesday usually are discussed on Monday afternoon. The stories to be covered by field camera units are also determined at this meeting. The news director, the executive producer, the producer, and others discuss and evaluate ideas for future feature stories. Sometimes the concepts for these features originate with the personalities who will be reporting them.

Let's examine in depth a news program that is one hour in length, airing at 9:00 P.M. Beginning early in the day, its structure slowly takes shape. By late morning, the producer and the staff have read copy from a number of Associated Press (AP) or United Press International (UPI) news wires and identified those three or four national or international stories that will probably be included in the broadcast. A telex will later confirm that INDX will provide video material for these stories. Aware of local events being covered by field units, the producer is able now to assemble a list of known "availables" for the night's broadcast: stories covered by each of the field units plus features in work. (See Figure 11.1.) To this list will be added INDX material for national or international items, once they have been specified (mid-afternoon). The pattern will change a dozen times between now and nine o'clock as some stories fall by the wayside and others suddenly break, sometimes only minutes before the broadcast.

By late morning, material from the field units begins to filter in. The producer screens each piece of incoming material, evaluating its impact and probable running time. Writers are assigned to provide copy; editors are assigned to cut the videotape footage down to size, eliminating dull material, heightening drama. The length of the videotape will be tailored to fit the news copy rather than the other way around.

The newsroom atmosphere early in the day is relaxed and casual; writers joke with one another about events in the news. As the day progresses, the relaxed atmosphere gradually changes. By late afternoon, it has become quiet, businesslike. By early evening, as the staff makes final changes in the rundown and hurries to assemble a final script, the casual atmosphere has been replaced by mild tension. No panic, no loud voices, simply a sense of urgency, a need to get a lot of work completed in a limited time.

At 3:30 the executives assemble for a production meeting. At some stations the director attends this meeting, a first glimpse at the news pattern with which he or she will deal. At other stations, the director will not arrive for another hour or two.

At this production meeting (and there may be others, depending on

AVAILS FOR THURSDAY JULY 12, 1984

PAGE 1

R   BRADLEY REACT   CALLS A NEWS CONFERENCE TO SAY MONDALE'S
    U-1   CHOICE OF FERRARO IS A BOLD AND COURAGEOUS
    CHUCK   STROKE....
    WRAP   LOS ANGELES
                      OTHER FERRARO REACT.....INDEX IS TRYING TO
                      GET MAUREEN REAGAN, INDEX WRAP ON MONDALE/
                      FERRARO NEWS CONFERENCE, KIVU WILL SEND
                      FEINSTEIN, SCHLAFLY, AND FEINSTEIN...T.
                      SAN FRANCISCO
                      WE ALSO DO AN MOS ON WHAT PEOPLE THINK OF
                      THE CHOICE AND WHETHER THEY WILL OR WILL
                      NOT VOTE FOR THE TICKET BECAUSE OF FERRARO...

                      LOS ANGELES

P   OLYMPIC COMPUTER   STORY ABOUT THE NEWEST DIOMECHANICAL RESEARCH
    U-1   AND TRAINING TECHNOLOGIES NOW AVAILABLE AT
    CHUCK   THE U.S. SPORTS OLYMPIC MEDICINE LABS.....

                      EXPOSITION PARK

P   OLYMPIC BRIEFING   FINAL MEDIA BRIEFING BEFORE THE SUMMER GAMES..
    U-2   BOTH UEBERROTH AND USHER ATTEND...UEBERROTH
    JIM   TALKS ABOUT THREATENING LETTERS THAT HAVE
    WRAP   BEEN RECEIVED BY THIRD WORLD COUNTRIES.....
                      WE ALSO PREVIEW THE OLYMPIC ARRIVAL CENTER
                      AT LAX...

                      BEVERLY HILLS, LAX

R   DELOREAN   JUDGE THROWS OUT ONE COUNT OF THE COCAINE
    U-1   CONSPIRACY INDICTMENT AGAINST THE AUTOMAKER
    CHUCK   BUT ALSO RULED THE JURY WILL BE ALLOWED TO
    WRAP   DECIDE HIS GUILT OR INNOCENCE ON EIGHT
                      OTHER CHARGES...WE HAVE ARTIST IN THE
                      COURTROOM...TALK WITH WEISSMAN AND RE AS
                      THEY LEAVE THE COURTROOM FOR THE DAY.

                      LOS ANGELES

J   OLYMPIC VACATION   A STORY ON HOW MUCH IT IS GOING TO COST
    U-4   A FAMILY OF FOUR TO ATTEND THE OLYMPICS
    NANCY   IN S. CALIFORNIA...AND HAVE A GOOD TIME.
    WRAP

                      BEVERLY HILLS

J   ICE CREAM   TODAY IS NATIONAL ICE CREAM DAY..WE GO OUT
    U-3   TO AN OLD FASHIONED ICE CREAM PARLOR IN
    KAREN   BEVERLY HILLS AND TALK WITH KIDS ABOUT ICE
                      CREAM AND HOW THEY FEEL ABOUT IT....
                      DOES IT DO THE TRICK ON A HOT DAY...

                      BEVERLY HILLS

Figure 11.1   A list of available stories is distributed to the news staff early in the day. "Availables" note the ENG camera unit responsible for each story as well as the assigned writer. (Courtesy KHJ-TV.)

late-breaking stories), the "final" assemblage of stories is discussed, evaluated, and arranged into a broadcast sequence. The newscast is divided arbitrarily into seven or eight sections, depending on the number of commercial breaks. Certain fixed, continuing patterns (which vary from station to station, depending on the programming philosophy of each) determine how elements are structured. For example, at KHJ-TV sports generally concludes the third section and is updated at the end of the newscast. The weather forecast begins the next-to-last section. As with all news programs, the headline story, the news item of greatest significance to viewers, begins the lineup.

Paperwork

After a sequence is determined at the production meeting, the producer distributes a rundown sheet listing each story and its position in the sequence, plus the writer, talent, and certain necessary technical information. (For a portion of a rundown sheet, see Figure 11.2.) When late-breaking stories create ruptures in the pattern, revised rundown sheets are distributed.

To some, the newsroom would appear to be a paper factory. Paper spews forth from a dozen sources. Six or eight wire service teletypes provide coverage of sports, hard news, soft news, feature stories, weather, and human interest items. A dozen typewriters and word processors grind out script material, contributing to the avalanche of paper. In addition, papers lie inches deep in baskets and bins, on desks and on the floor, pinned to bulletin boards and taped to the walls above desks. Without paper, a news program could not happen.

An hour or two after the rundown sheet first appears, script pages begin circulating—about seven or eight o'clock. While the majority of the stories were written earlier in the day, many were later revised or polished due to time limitations, an updating of news facts, or a change in the talent who would read the material. When the producer adds late-breaking stories to the lineup, others are necessarily deleted.

Script pages are printed in large type and numbered according to the section in which they appear (see Figure 11.3). Copies go to director, technical director, audio engineer, talent, producer, executive producer, TelePrompter department, and others. The *TelePrompter* people will later feed the script through a motor-driven device containing a small television camera. This camera relays the image of the news copy to TelePrompter screens mounted on each camera. A sheet of glass in front of the lens, angled at 45 degrees, enables performers to read the reflected news copy but still direct their vision to the lens, apparently speaking directly to the home viewer.

When script pages are first distributed, many are incomplete. These mostly blank pages, called *shooters* (by some stations), indicate what material will later appear there. As the copy for each story is completed, pages are

Figure 11.2   A rundown sheet describes the sequence of stories to appear in each section of a newscast, the talent, the writer, and the type of video coverage anticipated. (Courtesy KHJ-TV.)

distributed to replace the shooters. By air time, most (but seldom all) of the script pages have been completed.

In some newsrooms, journalists write stories on a computer (word processor) where they are stored. The computer later generates TelePrompter copy for use during the broadcast. The director works from a hard-copy printout. Typing stories directly into a computer represents "state of the art" in terms of TV news operations.

THE DIRECTOR AT WORK

In directing on-the-air news programs, the role of directors is more integrative than creative. They must combine a dozen disparate elements into a crisply cohesive whole. Because these visual and aural elements appear so quickly, offering little opportunity for leisurely examination, and because

```
ANDREWS OLYMPICS    3 00

CK ADDA OLYMPICS            THE SUMMER OLYMPIC
                           GAMES OFFICIALLY BEGIN 2D
                           IN JUST FIVE DAYS...
                           AND, TODAY ANDREW █
                           AMADOR BEGINS A SPECIAL
                           FOUR-PART SERIES,
                           'HOW TO COPE WITH THE
                           OLYMPICS, AND STILL
                           HAVE A GOOD TIME.'

                              IN PART ONE, ANDREW
                           LOOKS AT THE █HASSELS
                           OF OLYMPIC TRAFFIC---
                           AND HOW WE CAN GET
                           AROUND IT.

VTR--SOT FULL                   --SOT--

AT TOP SUPER BEACH
AT 1:26 SUPER ANDREW
AT 2:13 SUPER MALONEY --QUICK--

ANDREWS OLYMPICS 2-2-2

 OUTQ: NO █ONE WILL SUCCEED
 TRT: 2:28                           2U
                                     A
 LIVE TAG              IF, DURING THE GAMES
                      YOU WANT TO GET
                      AROUND THE L-A BASIN
                      WITH THE LEAST AMOUNT
                      OF DIFFICULTY---CALL
                      ONE OF ███ THESE NUMBERS.

TAKE FULL CG          THEY ARE CAL-TRANS
                      HOTLINE NUMBERS FOR
                      OLYMPIC TRAVELERS...
                      IN THE 2-1-3 AREA CODE,
                      CALL 6-2-0-5-6-5-7...
                      IN ORANGE COUNTY, 7-7-
                      3-9-5-2-6...AND█, IN
                      THE 8-0-5 AREA, CALL
DROP FULL C█          6-5-3-1-7-9-5.
```

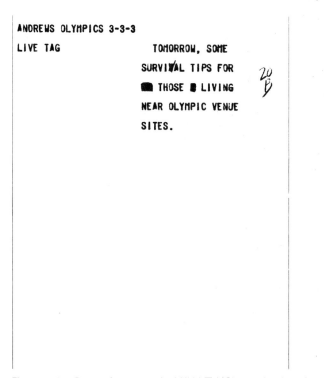

```
ANDREWS OLYMPICS 3-3-3
LIVE TAG              TOMORROW, SOME
                     SURVIVAL TIPS FOR
                     THOSE  LIVING
                     NEAR OLYMPIC VENUE
                     SITES.
```

Figure 11.3   Pages from a typical KHJ-TV (Channel 9, Los Angeles) newscast. (Courtesy KHJ-TV.)

each element directly affects others, news directors' concentration must be intense and coordination keen. Directors' prebroadcast preparation must be so meticulous that most of the possibilities for error will be eliminated.

News directors also work in the field, covering special events.

In the Field

A psychotic robber has slain half a dozen customers and holds others as hostages in a neighborhood market. A local television station has sent a director, camera crew, and reporter to cover the grisly event. Police have surrounded the market. From time to time, a police lieutenant calls through a bullhorn. The fear-crazed robber does not answer.

Upon arriving at the scene with a remote crew, the director's first function is to assess: Where is the drama? How can that drama best be transmitted to an audience? What subject matter will best convey the sense of fear that has descended on the scene?

A second responsibility falls on the director's shoulders: staying out of the way of police so that they can do their job. After a quick appraisal, the director places one camera on top of the remote truck, the high angle providing excellent orientation. From this vantage point, viewers will be able to see the market, police cars, and police personnel, plus curious and frightened by-standers. Cameras at ground level can focus on the reporter and provide close angles on the market, police lieutenant, and bystanders. If in an exchange of gunfire police officers are killed or wounded, the director has another respon-sibility: treating the mayhem with taste, avoiding gruesome shots of blood and dead bodies that would offend home viewers.

After the director and the reporter have created a visual and word picture of what transpired earlier, a long wait begins. The director suggests interviews with witnesses. Such interviews personalize an event; they reduce major catastrophes such as fires and floods to the level of people with whom specta-tors can identify.

The reporter talks to an elderly woman who was actually in the market at the time of the robbery. She's extremely nervous and upset, almost inarticu-late, trying to describe events but breaking down and running off in the middle of the interview. Next the reporter interviews a teenage boy who arrived on the scene minutes after the carnage took place. He saw little or nothing but he's bright, full of words, eager to expand his moment of impor-tance. Finally, the reporter grabs a brief moment with the police lieutenant who is reluctant to talk; he merely states his concern for the hostages and that he has radioed headquarters to send a SWAT team.

All three of the interviews proclaim immediacy. While the teenage boy had little factual information to contribute, his words still provided viewers with a sense of being there. Weak as his interview was, it still proved superior to no interview at all.

The interview with the elderly woman was most effective of the three. It contained immediacy and veracity of such crushing emotional force that viewers would be shaken, would feel the terror and panic that such an event could evoke. Her words communicated far more than facts; they created emotional involvement, transforming viewers into participants.

The interview with the police lieutenant provided a note of authority. It gave viewers a sense of being on the inside, of having special knowledge which even on-scene spectators did not have.

Experienced directors try to stage on-site interviews with as much location atmosphere in the background as possible, thus visually enriching the inter-view. On occasion, overly zealous directors manufacture background color, trying to add richness when the interview or location seems lacking. Most responsible executives prohibit such practices.

Most field interviews are staged or recorded under circumstances less calamitous than the market massacre. These day-to-day interviews usually have no director assigned; the cost factor would become prohibitive. Since single-camera interviews are a necessary part of today's news spectrum, we will discuss them briefly here, despite the fact that they touch only rarely on a director's world. You may find yourself working as a camera operator, as talent, or as a field producer—and such essentially directorial knowledge may prove helpful.

When videotaping interviews with a single camera, it is essential to provide some degree of editorial flexibility. In any interview, certain words, phrases, or speeches are unimportant or confusing; they get in the way of more important thoughts. It's necessary to be able to delete such clutter, but this is possible only if someone has anticipated the editor's needs.

The primary angle, of course, favors the person being interviewed. A second camera angle, usually favoring the interviewer, provides the editor with something to cut to, thereby eliminating unwanted material. Accordingly, after an interview has concluded, camera operators usually shoot a reverse angle: an over-the-shoulder shot favoring the interviewer. If the person interviewed cannot (or will not) remain for the reverse angle shot, the camera operator generally shoots a closeup of the interviewer alone, faking it, reacting appropriately to the thoughts expressed earlier. This gives the editor something to cut to in order to clean up or sharpen the interview. There is nothing unethical about manufacturing such a shot since it does not change either the message or its implications.

When covering speeches by newsworthy figures, the need for editorial flexibility remains; newscasts usually have time only for a few sentences. Therefore, experienced camera crews shoot some relevant cutaway material, frequently shots of the audience listening or applauding or of the press photographing the speaker. Sometimes an extremely wide shot serves the purpose; from such a distance we cannot distinguish lip movements so the editor may cheat and place any necessary words into the speaker's mouth.

In the Studio

The following specific directorial pattern approximates the patterns used by many news directors at many local TV stations. However, practices vary from station to station and from director to director, so the following procedure will not be 100 percent accurate for every news operation.

At KHJ-TV, director Chris Stegner arrives approximately four hours before the newscast. He times his arrival to the issuance of the rundown sheet, which is where his preparation begins.

Stegner is thirty-four years old. He studied television and film at the University of Wisconsin and began his career at a UHF station in the Chicago area. Directing sports took him to Los Angeles where he entered the news field.

The rundown sheet is a blueprint for Stegner's treatment of the newscast. He plans his camera positions, section by section, based on knowledge of the news set and where each newscaster will function. He marks this information on the rundown. Later he will transfer these markings to his script. Stories in the first section carry the page prefix *A*, in the second section *B*, and so on.

Stegner's camera pattern follows the pattern for interviews as shown in Figure 9.1. Camera 1 generally photographs the anchorperson on the right. Camera 3 generally photographs the anchorperson on the left. Camera 2 generally holds a two-shot. (See Figure 11.4.)

Notice that the rundown sheet specifies by initial the name of the performer reporting each story. The initials *W* and *P* stand for KHJ-TV newscasters, Wendy Gordon and Paul Bloom. Thus, generally, all talent indications for *W/P* (both Wendy and Paul) will use camera 2; *W* (seated on the left) will call for camera 3 and *P* (seated on the right) for camera 1.

The *A* below the camera marking denotes that there will be a visual insert. Visuals from the Adda computer (used at KHJ-TV) will be shown in the control room on two monitors: *A* indicating the channel in use or on the air, and *B* which previews the upcoming visual. Thus the marking *1/A* indicates camera 1 with a visual matted over it from the Adda computer (screen *A*). Note that the Adda visuals are indicated by subject matter at the extreme right side of the rundown sheet.

In checking the rundown sheet, the director notes that most stories have the VTR column checked, indicating that videotape will provide visual material, but he doesn't concern himself with the VTR material now. He will mark his roll cues and note specific timings later, after he receives his script.

Planning camera coverage for a news program coincides exactly with the principles used for other live programming. Specifically, the director starts with the last item in each section and works his way forward. Such a procedure becomes critical only when a camera must move to a new position to accommodate a sports or feature reporter.

Notice that the last item in each section of the rundown (Figure 11.2) is a "tease" for upcoming material. A tease is exactly what the word suggests: words or pictures designed to intrigue, to keep viewers watching despite an upcoming commercial or station break. On this news program, the tease for the third section of news (section C) occurs in the sports area. Since the sports area is located at the camera-right side of the set (Figure 11.4), it should logically be covered by camera 3, which is closest. The item immediately before the sports tease is introduced by Wendy. Ordinarily, she would be photographed by camera 3. But if 3 will be needed seconds later for the sports tease, it would make better sense to photograph Wendy on camera 2. In that case, 2 would have to move right to take 3's position. (Are you still with me?)

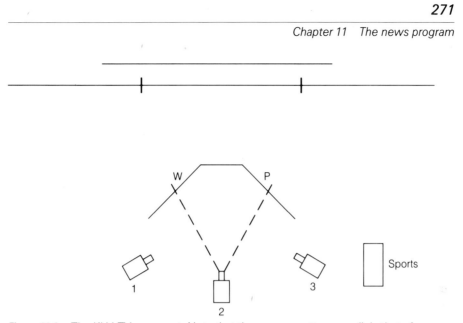

Figure 11.4   The KHJ-TV news set. Note that the camera pattern parallels that of an interview show. Cameras 1 and 3 cross to provide individual shots of Paul Bloom (*P*) and Wendy Gordon (*W*) while camera 2 provides a two-shot.

Camera 3 will be needed for the first item in *C* section. After that, the director will release it to move to the sports area. After determining his camera pattern in the rundown, the director makes a script note after C-1: *Send 3 to sports area.* Once camera 3 has moved out of the main news set, camera 2 may take its position. Thus, item C-3, a shot of Wendy, will be taken by camera 2.

When script pages begin to arrive, the director transfers markings from the rundown sheet to the script. As indicated earlier, some of the pages are shooters, to be replaced later when the copy has been written. Shooters merely contain the page number, the name of the story, and its running time. While the director seldom sees a completed script before airtime, he is not concerned; most of the necessary information has already been provided in the rundown—and all camera moves have been plotted.

In addition to camera shots and camera instructions, the director also marks *roll cues* in his script. Years ago, when most stories were recorded on film, directors needed five seconds for their roll cues. That is, they had to roll the film five seconds before a commentator finished speaking so that the film would be up to speed by then—and the director could cut to it. Directors used to rehearse all news copy with commentators, timing their speech with a stop watch in order to find the appropriate word on which to roll film. Today, with videotape players capable of attaining the necessary speed almost instantly, no such rehearsal is necessary.

Editors routinely place what is known as *digital leader* at the head of each videotape story. Digital leader displays a succession of numbers indicating how many seconds remain before the picture appears. We have all seen digital leaders on television when the director mistakenly cut to a videotape too early.

For news programs, videotape usually is rolled down to number 1 or 2. When the technical director previews the videotape channel on a control room monitor, the number 2 or 1 can be clearly read. Some digital leaders deliberately omit 1, replacing it with black so that if a director (or technical director) inadvertently cuts to the tape early, no numbers will be seen by viewers. Some directors omit the digital leader altogether, preferring to roll the videotape down to its first frame. Since the tape gains speed so quickly, only a second or two of video material will be lost.

During the newscast, the director follows the talent's commentary on his script. A couple of words before the videotape picture is scheduled to appear, the director calls, "Roll!" The TD rolls the tape. A second or two later the picture appears—and the director cuts to it.

Sometimes videotape material is silent with the talent providing commentary. Sometimes the videotape contains sound: music, effects, or speech. Sound on tape is abbreviated *SOT* (see Figure 11.3). Sometimes a videotaped story contains sound from beginning to end. Sometimes the sound appears at a point within the story and continues to its conclusion. Sometimes sound appears, sustains for a brief period and then cuts out, the videotape continuing silently as the studio talent resumes commentary.

For the director, such intermittent sound elements demand the utmost in concentration and coordination. If, for example, sound appears at eighteen seconds into a story, the director must start a timer when the picture first appears and must alert the sound engineer to be ready for the SOT eighteen seconds later. A sharp audio engineer won't need such warning; the script states exactly when the SOT appears. But meticulous directors leave nothing to chance. In addition, the director (or an associate director) must recite a countdown to the floor manager so that the latter can signal the talent, so that the talent can finish speaking before the SOT occurs. When the director (or associate) recites the countdown for the floor manager, the recitation also prepares the audio engineer to open his or her pot (sound channel). When such sound elements appear many times in a single program (which is usually the pattern), they can tax the crew's coordination.

Experienced directors always punch a timer (or stopwatch) when tape appears, whether the tape contains sound or not, whether they have an associate sitting beside them or not. The script always indicates *TRT*, total running time, so the director is forewarned. He or she must cut away from videotape before it runs out—or look like an amateur. The only way directors can *know* when the tape will run out is if they have started a stopwatch.

The script (Figure 11.3) provides SOT "out cues," sometimes called "end cues." They state the ending phrase in an SOT segment, usually two or three words, so that the director will know exactly when either to cut away or to cue another sound source (such as an anchorperson).

While the timing of many live programs often rests on the director's shoulders, such is not the case with news. Either the associate director or (in some cases) the producer must get the show off the air on time. He or she has "back timed" the script as carefully as possible, considering the late arrival of some pages. The term *back timing* is inherited from radio. When associate directors (ADs) back time a script, they work with both known and unknown factors. They know the running time of each videotape segment, of opening and closing titles, of commercials, and (when scheduled) the time needed for a station break. But the time for commentary by performers must be estimated.

Starting at the end and working forward, ADs calculate exactly when the director must hit closing credits. Prior to that, and still working forward, they estimate as closely as possible the time at which each segment of the newscast must finish. They mark these approximate timings in their scripts. Knowing that every show contains some elasticity, they cue performers (through a floor manager) to stretch or tighten their commentary, so that show timings will correspond to the timings in their scripts. Usually the last element in a news program contains some flexibility, expanding or contracting to accommodate the clock. At KHJ-TV, a sports update usually provides such a buffer. When content must be stretched, the anchorpersons ask questions of the sports authority.

CHAPTER HIGHLIGHTS

- The most effective news programs utilize as many visual elements as possible. For national or international stories, network affiliates receive videotape coverage from a network satellite. When major events occur in their territory, stations also contribute stories via the satellite.

- Independent stations rely on INDX (Independent Exchange) for videotape coverage of distant news events. Like network affiliates, they also contribute material. Stations receive approximately forty minutes of material each day but use only about 10 percent.

- The bulk of local stations' news coverage is local or regional, using videotape borrowed from nearby stations or from their own three-member ENG units. These field units either transmit stories directly to the TV station or record material for later use. If no videotape is available, stations use still photographs as inserts, sharing the frame with talent.

- In late morning, the producer prepares a list of available stories based on assignments given to ENG units, features already in work, and material to be provided by INDX. As stories come in from field units, they are evaluated by the producer and assigned to writers and editors.

- In mid-afternoon, a production meeting determines a final news sequence, subject to change by late-breaking stories. This sequence is distributed in the form of a rundown sheet describing each story and noting the talent and visual elements involved. Stories are grouped into sections, divided by commercial or station breaks.

- The director's work divides into two spheres: the field and the studio.

- When a news break occurs, the field director assesses the nature of the event and how best to transmit its drama to an audience. Interviews often personalize an event. Since most interviews are staged with a single camera, directors usually photograph a second angle featuring the reporter. The second angle gives the editor something to cut to in order to eliminate unnecessary verbiage.

- News directors usually begin their preparation with the rundown sheet. From the information contained therein, they are able to mark most camera angles.

- The traditional pattern: Camera 1 (on the left) photographs the talent on the right. The reverse is true for camera 3. Camera 2 generally holds a two-shot. The director blocks cameras section by section, usually beginning with the *last* angle and working forward.

- When the director indicates cameras on the rundown sheet, he or she also usually indicates a visual insert. For example, 3/A indicates that camera 3 will be used and that a visual insert from the Adda computer will be matted over it.

- When script pages arrive, the director transfers camera markings to the script and adds *roll cues*. When videotape is called for, it must be "rolled" by the director a second or two before the picture appears. Digital leader at the head of each story displays a succession of numbers indicating how many seconds remain before the picture appears. Most directors set the leader at one or two seconds, which allows the tape to attain speed before the picture appears.

- Some videotapes contain sound elements. Sound on tape (or SOT) sometimes begins a story and sometimes occurs in the middle of a story. Astute directors always start a timer (or stopwatch) when videotape appears. Since scripts always state the exact number of seconds before SOT occurs, the timer enables the director to cue the audio engineer as well as performers on the set. Scripts also contain "end cues" or "out cues" stating the last two or three words in an SOT element. When directors hear these words, they automatically cue the upcoming sound source.

C   H   A   P   T   E   R   *12*

"And now a word from our sponsor": Commercials

*T*elevision commercials reach out and touch almost everyone. Their slogans and jingles have become part of the American vernacular. They are repeated by youngsters barely able to walk, who become aware of such social calamities as ring around the collar well before kindergarten.

So stunning are the production values in some commercials, so meticulous is their preparation, so powerful is their motivating force, that they have become "an American art form . . . ahead of most TV programs in being in tune with the United States."[1] As shaped by some of the country's most creative directors, they provide viewers with such diverse entertainment elements as humor, music, spectacle, drama, famous celebrities, and extraordinary visual style. A case in point: the Pepsi-Cola musical commercial with Grammy winner Michael Jackson, which cost approximately $2 million, a sum once considered high even for a feature motion picture.

Presented with script and storyboard, directors must express their message creatively, with optimum impact and sales effectiveness, pleasing themselves, advertising agency, and client. The director's challenge is compounded by the need to cram a message into thirty or sixty impossibly short seconds. Of necessity, they must be high-density seconds; directors must distill the actions

---

[1]Albert Book and Norman Carey, *The Television Commercial: Creativity and Craftsmanship.*

I don't mind the commercials. It's just the programs I can't stand.

TV CRITIC JOHN CROSBY[2]

and emotions of performers. Each gesture must count. Each word must contribute. Each facial expression must advance the premise.

Because many commercials demonstrate the newest styles, technologies, and cinema techniques, they often become a stimulus for directors in other entertainment arenas. On occasion, they propel their own directors into more prestigious projects such as feature films. (I do not mean to denigrate the status of commercials; successful commercial directors receive respect from their industry peers as well as substantial financial rewards.)

The world of TV commercials offers its directors both opportunity and frustration: the opportunity to achieve near perfection in terms of realizing a script's promise and frustration in terms of limited creative control. A storyboard, client, or agency executive, for the most part, will hold directors to preconceived patterns and parameters.

This chapter will discuss what commercials sell, what they *really* sell. We will examine national and local production structures including such practical aspects of the director's world as the sample reel, backgrounds for commercial directors, the storyboard, casting, set design, an analysis of the preproduction

---

[2]Quoted by Robert Hilliard, *Writing for Television and Radio* (Belmont, Calif.: Wadsworth, 1984), p. 41.

meeting, and the problems encountered by directors in production and post-production. We will also examine special requirements in photographing the product and directorial techniques that set commercials apart from other directorial fields.

WHAT DO COMMERCIALS SELL?

To the casual viewer there is a single, obvious answer to the above question. Commercials sell a product. A narrator describes its advantages; we see it displayed handsomely; a playlet dramatizes how it can simplify our chores or enrich our lives.

Directors of commercials quickly discover that selling a product usually is secondary to selling a lifestyle, showing viewers how to make themselves enviable. John Berger, in his delightful *Ways of Seeing,* calls the state of being envied "glamour."[3] According to Berger, advertising provides viewers with an image of themselves as they might be, transformed by the product, thereby becoming enviable. Thus, commercials sell but one thing: the happiness that derives from being envied.

At first glance, Berger's assertion seems simplistic. Yes, it is certainly true for blue jeans that make us appear sexier. It is true for hair shampoos that make our hair lustrous and manageable. And perhaps for detergents that will give us whiter, brighter sheets, thus making us the envy of neighbors. But what about such products as underarm deodorants or headache remedies or medications for hemorrhoidal relief?

If we are to believe commercials (and most of us do!), such remedies will make us feel like our old selves again, jovial, good-natured, ready to tackle the world. If the commercials don't make those statements in so many words, the attitudes of their participants do—suddenly released from the depression of congested sinuses, smiling, inhaling deeply, able now to win the love of beautiful men or women or to battle the dragons of Wall Street. In short: enviable.

In view of this attitude, directors in preparing TV commercials must give as much thought to the ambience of the world they are creating as to the specific needs described in script or storyboard. The ambience—created by camera, wardrobe, lighting, photography, music, choice of performer, acting, set, and set dressing—provides an upbeat dream world filled with delightful, fantasy characters who have a single purpose: to be envied. By buying the

---

[3]John Berger, *Ways of Seeing* (New York: Penguin Books, 1977), p. 132.

product, the TV viewer can enter their luminous world and win the envy of friends and neighbors.

Soft drink commercials frequently depict a joyous, fun-filled never-land in which attractive teenagers rollick and flirt, kiss, play ball, dance, wash cars, splash one another in the surf, or picnic on sundrenched beaches—creating a lifestyle that viewers can achieve for fifty cents. Coffee commercials sometimes sell taste, sometimes price, sometimes quality. More often they sell ambience: a man and woman alone in a mountain cabin, snowed in, savoring the pleasure of coffee shared in love.

Despite the fact that they play in a few seconds rather than in minutes or hours, playlets such as the mountain cabin coffee commercial are literally drama and utilize principles discussed in earlier chapters on staging the actor and staging the camera. One of the three basic functions of camera is to create mood or atmosphere, achieved through lighting, filters, choice of angle, and camera movement. A low angle will make a truck appear strong and powerful in the same way it brings those dominant characteristics to an actor. A wide angle lens will make a new model car appear longer and sleeker in the same way it makes a modest soap opera corridor appear endless. Fog filters have become almost a cliché in commercials, creating a luminous, dreamlike quality that in the audience's minds ultimately becomes associated with the product itself.

For the director, achieving any kind of ambience, positive or negative, requires creative as well as technological know-how. Skilled cinematographers create daily miracles in adding sparkle to foods, beauty to fashion models, and glamor to kitchens. Use of gels in lights or fog filters on cameras can transform the mundane into the mythic. But directors cannot always rely on the expertise of others. From analysis of the script and discussions with agency personnel, together with their own personal "vision" of what the commercial must be, the director coordinates all of the production elements so as to create a specific mood or atmosphere. Sometimes such an atmosphere is defined in the script. Sometimes not. But a director's ability to find the specific ambience that will make characters glamorous (enviable) and their lifestyle desirable lies at the heart of his or her commercial success.

THE PRODUCTION PATTERN

Television commercials are produced and directed on two levels: national and local. National commercials are usually first aired on network television. The most lavish cost hundreds of thousands of dollars and include colorful locations, extravagant visual or graphic effects, accomplished actors, dancers, and original music or jingles. They are capsulized versions of a Broadway musical or Hollywood melodrama with a single major difference: Their goal is to sell a product. If it delights audiences but fails in motivating them to buy, the commercial is a flop.

On the local level, commercials usually are filmed or taped by local advertising agencies or by TV station staff directors. Typically, such commercials advertise new- or used-car dealers, local markets, tire dealers, department stores, loan companies, and so on. Since audiences are necessarily smaller on a local level, dollars expended by advertisers are considerably fewer. The production scope of local commercials is thus considerably more modest than for national ones. Directors must work with relatively simple scripts and within relatively tight production schedules.

The National Commercial

Major commercial campaigns are prepared by advertising agencies with the consent and approval of their clients. Before a script or storyboard reaches a director's hands, its concepts have been pondered by agency and advertiser, evaluated and reevaluated, written and rewritten, tested and retested for style (do they properly reflect the advertiser's image?), for sales impact, and for their ability to capture and hold a viewer.

Most directors of national commercials either work for a production house or for themselves; sometimes a director *is* the production house. Usually when agencies solicit bids from production houses, it is because those houses provide the services of directors in whom they are interested.

The Sample Reel.   When advertising agencies consider which director to hire for a specific campaign, they frequently study sample reels submitted by various directors, assessing their past work, searching for directorial styles and backgrounds that seem appropriate for the upcoming campaign. As in other fields, directors tend to be typecast. Those who are experienced in food commercials tend to be hired for other food commercials. Those experienced in high fashion will inevitably be offered other high fashion commercials. Specialization is so taken for granted by agencies that they often joke about it. Typical is the story in which a director is called in for an interview and the producer asks, "Have you ever worked on breakfast cereals?" When the director answers, "Yes," the producer asks, "Hot or cold?"

Since hundreds of thousands of dollars frequently hang in the balance—as well as the security of a valuable advertising account—agencies often use directors who have worked for them before, whose style, creativity, and dependability are known quantities.

Aspiring commercial directors inevitably ask how it is possible to assemble a sample reel without having directed commercials. This, of course, represents the classic chicken-and-egg paradox. You cannot get a job until you have experience. You cannot gain experience without getting a job. Catch 22.

Getting Started.   Seldom if ever do commercial directors begin their professional careers as directors. Usually they gain some measure of success in a related field and then move into directing. According to Tony Asher who has functioned as a producer for both advertising agencies and production companies, directors of national commercials usually have backgrounds in art direction, cinematography (or still photography), and editing.[4] Because word-oriented people such as writers tend to rise in an advertising agency and dominate its hierarchy, the visually oriented art directors often veer into other realms, specifically directing. Broadcast art directors (as opposed to print art directors) are basically "picture people," and therefore able to translate a commercial message into effective visual language.

Many directors are actually director-cinematographers. Many began as cinematographers and then, because of their unique abilities, expanded their craft to include directing. Actually, says Asher:

> A sizable number of commercials don't require the direction of any talent [actors]. They're made up of animated stills—close shots of food, or cars driving along a road while the voice-over describes the product. These directors don't have to say to actors: emote. Most of them are essentially skilled still photographers. They don't direct talent. They're storytellers in the visual language. They're painters.

Like cinematographers, film or videotape editors develop a keen visual sense. They come to understand the theory and practical application of fitting angles together so as to build effective dramatic sequences. As Asher says,

> Editors get such a good sense of how and why a film is working. Over and over again they find themselves in that situation where they simply can't make a sequence work and they complain: 'if only the director had shot seven more frames of this or a reverse angle of that.' They really understand why something works or what it would take to make it better.

Many, perhaps most, editors aspire to become directors. So do many, many members of the production world: writers, actors, producers, cinema-

---

[4]Tony Asher has worked on the Mattel Toys account for Ogilvy & Mather and for Paisley Productions.

tographers. Asher recalls a T-shirt he saw at a guild screening. It depicted Jojo the talking dog in conference with his agent. The dog was explaining: "But what I really want to do is direct!"

Hiring a Director.   Just as most people get several estimates before hiring someone to paint their homes, so do advertising agencies secure estimates or bids on what a contemplated set of commercials will cost. (Usually several commercials are filmed at one time; such a procedure is more cost effective.) Before agencies make any decision concerning which director to use, they assess the budgets submitted by producers at the various production companies.

Let's assume that you are a director associated with a major production house. Before your producer submits a bid, she automatically checks directly with you, asking that you read the script and study the storyboard. She asks for your estimate of how many hours you feel you would need to shoot the material, if you foresee any unusual production problems, and so forth. Based on your answer and the production elements called for in the script, the producer then submits an estimate to the advertising agency.

If the submitted budget figure is within the ball park, the agency then obtains the client's approval. Traditionally, the client first screams that the budget is far too high but after some haggling eventually approves it. Once the client has approved both budget and director, the agency invites you to its offices for a first meeting with the agency producer. From this moment forth, you and the agency producer become a team, working closely through preparation and production. It is imperative that you both see eye to eye on the look, feel, and style of the commercial.

During the weeks that follow, you find it impossible to get the commercial out of your mind. You examine its content in the light of your own professional experience. You study the implications of the storyboard.

The Storyboard.   A storyboard is simply a series of drawings (frames) prepared by the agency's art department, illustrating various key moments in the commercial: camera angles, actions by performers, how the product itself should be displayed. Many believe that storyboards came into being because clients lacked imagination, unable to visualize how a commercial would look merely from reading a script.

> A storyboard has more value than making the commercial clear to the client. It is a blueprint for all the pertinent artists, artisans and mechanics to see, if not follow. This is the most articulate manner in which the advertising agency can present its thoughts to all

concerned, both in the agency and outside. The board is a guide, a direction.[5]

During preparation you probably discover more effective ways of shooting certain elements than have been presented in the storyboard. When you have ideas for changes—no matter how slight—you must discuss them with the agency producer. Chances are, he will initially resist them. After all, the client has approved the storyboard as is. Changes can be disruptive. And yet you have been hired because of your creativity and expertise. Your reaction is a fresh one, providing agency executives with a valuable new perspective. If you are persuasive, the producer will take your suggested changes back to his own creative staff—and to the client—for approval. Once (and if) they are approved, you should try to get such changes incorporated into the storyboard, so that everyone will clearly understand your intent and there will be no recriminations later.

Sometimes the producer will suggest that you shoot the questioned element (an action, line of dialog, piece of business) two ways: as presented originally in the storyboard and as you would like to change it. Such duplication is costly in terms of time, patience, and money. Yet it happens again and again. Since commercials must please executives with a variety of needs and pressures, it is not always possible to satisfy everyone with a single stroke. That is why directors sometimes print multiple takes—in order to keep everyone happy, accommodating different opinions regarding line readings or specific actions.

While many directors rail against storyboards, claiming that they limit creativity, that they reduce the directorial function to little more than "painting by the numbers," storyboards do provide subtle insights that might be difficult to obtain otherwise. Agency creators usually are bright. When you study their concepts as defined in storyboard drawings, you must try to recognize their goals as well as the reasons for stagings or camera angles that appear less than optimum.

If the lawnmower is drawn way back in the frame with lots of green grass in the foreground, you might say that there is insufficient identification of the product and you would be right. However, in

---

[5]Ben Gradus, *Directing: The Television Commercial* (New York: Hastings House, 1981), p. 55. All quotations appearing in this chapter from *Directing,* copyright 1981 by Ben Gradus, are used with permission of Hastings House, Publishers, Inc.

this case, the agency/client wants to emphasize the successful lawn, and this is a compromise.

The storyboard is quite useful in creating a communication with the agency to determine what the sketches mean. Understand each frame with all its nuances—our business is nuances. The nuance is the director's stock in trade; that's what he's hired for, since the storyboard has the facts.[6]

Producer Tony Asher describes two primary criteria that determine a director's latitude in relation to a storyboard: the director's reputation and the nature of the product. Directors who have won Clio awards (awarded yearly for excellence in TV commercials), whose services are in constant demand and whose talents are universally recognized, are allowed considerably more creative freedom than are relative newcomers. In some cases, they are allowed almost total freedom in shaping a commercial. Says Asher:

> If you're dealing with certain kinds of products, almost every word of copy is scrutinized by lawyers and network continuity departments and government agencies. Anyone can complain, "That's an odd way of saying those words." The agency's answer is, "That's the only way they'll approve those words. They have to be in *exactly* that sequence and we have to say them *exactly* that way! This shot can't be any higher than that because it has to include the full table so the kids will know how big the toy is and we have to have a wide angle shot to show how many people are in the room." Almost every shot is required. So the freedom you have to be creative is limited.

Casting.   While casting patterns differ depending on the agency and the amount of preparation time, a tentative selection of performers is often made before the director is hired. An agency may have its own casting director or it may have hired an independent. In either case, the casting director will have called in performers to read for the commercial's key roles. Such early sessions usually are supervised by the agency producer.

Some agencies videotape performers who seem physically right for a part and whose abilities make them likely candidates. (The largest agencies build libraries of such videotapes, constantly updating them, weeding out ineffective or undependable actors.) Often the director is asked to look at these preselected videotapes and render an opinion. For creative, conscientious directors, such a procedure can be frustrating. Since as director you must

---

[6]Gradus, p. 56.

work closely with actors, under conditions of extreme pressure, and since you are responsible for obtaining the best possible performances, you will usually want as much voice as possible in selecting the performers. Often directors suggest performers with whom they have worked, whom they believe superior to those previously selected. The agency must respect the director's experience and usually will call in such performers for a reading.

You are always consulted for the final decision. So is the client. Such decisions usually are made at a major preproduction meeting that takes place a week or two prior to shooting.

Set Design.   Final approval of set design also is given at the preproduction meeting. Like casting, set design sometimes begins before a director enters the picture. When you have the opportunity of conferring early with the set designer (or art director), you and the agency producer examine and approve preliminary sketches based on script or storyboard, discussing such important aspects as color, dressing, camera needs, and the staging of actors. Because time is critical, long crosses (say, from a kitchen cupboard to stove) must be shortened; each fractional second must be evaluated. Highly significant is the social level of the family inhabiting the set. Whether it is wealthy, middle class, or just beginning its climb up the economic ladder is of tremendous importance to client and agency. Usually the economic status is spelled out either in the script or in a preproduction agency booklet that defines the characters, their lifestyles, attitudes, economic status, and so forth.

Many directors prefer to shoot on location, in actual buildings rather than in manufactured sets, feeling that the ambience will contribute significantly, especially to a slice-of-life commercial. Locations usually are more difficult to work in than a soundstage setting, requiring more production time and affording less flexibility, but many directors feel that the values gained more than outweigh the difficulty and expense. When locations are used, Polaroid pictures are taken for approval by agency executives and the client.

When a location is contemplated, you visit the locale in order to determine its appropriateness to the script/storyboard as well as any potential production problems. Is there space to park trucks? Where will the sun be morning and afternoon? Will billboards or advertisements need to be covered? On interiors, will there be room for camera and lights? Will the windows need gels (gelatin sheets placed over windows to reduce the brilliance of incoming light)? Will acoustics create sound problems? Will dialog have to be looped (recorded again, synchronized with lip movements)? Will the art director have to make structural changes? Will the location have to be dressed up or down in accordance with the economic status of its supposed occupants?

The Preproduction Meeting.   After all of the *pre*preproduction meetings comes the preproduction meeting itself at which most key decisions are made. The meeting usually is attended by representatives of the client and the agency as well as some production team members such as director, cinematographer, hairdresser, home economist, casting director, wardrobe person: production by committee.

> Usually, it's the agency producer who conducts the meeting. He has an agenda, and nowadays those production meetings are sometimes very elaborate. You're given a book—you think it's a meeting of the U.N.—and the book has everything written out in it and people turn solemnly from page to page like they're in a religious ceremony. The simplest things are stated over and over again. But, there is an agenda and (the producer) usually makes that agenda and conducts the meeting.[7]

The meeting addresses itself to each detail and aspect of the commercial, from the color of a kitchen to the upholstery in a car. Should earrings be diamond or should they be gold? Should fingernails have polish or should they be natural? Should a blouse have long sleeves or short? It is at this meeting that you lay out your staging plans, frame by frame, set-up by set-up. If there are deviations from the storyboard, they will be discussed at great length. You try to sell your ideas for possible improvements. Final casting decisions are often made at this meeting as well as approval for locations and set plans.

At preproduction meetings some directors dominate; others sit quietly, absorbing viewpoints of agency and client, synthesizing ideas, clarifying items of confusion or disagreement. From this point on, you become captain of the ship, pulling all of the production elements together for the "shoot."

Production.   Good directors who prepare meticulously visit their sets or locations a day or two before production begins to make certain that all details are as they have planned. (Some visit their sets or locations many times, soaking in atmosphere, visualizing the action, making preparatory sketches.) No director likes surprises. Discovering a mistake two days before the shoot is okay; there is time for the mistake to be rectified. Discovering that same mistake on the morning production begins can be disaster. No matter that it's not your mistake. It's going to cost precious time to fix it.

Directing commercials differs in one significant aspect from directing other fictional or nonfictional forms: the number of "bosses" on the set. At

---

[7]A director quoted by Gradus, p. 113.

one point or another, the following keenly interested individuals may visit your set, studying, evaluating, and perhaps trying to correct or modify your procedures. From the advertising agency: creative director, senior copywriter and copywriter, art director, producer, account supervisor, and account executive. From the client: the advertising manager, the brand manager, and others.

All of these so-called bosses are nervous. Nervousness seems to be endemic to the advertising industry. Many fear for their jobs. Many fear that you will go over budget. Many fear that their promises to the client will not be realized. Many worry that you will change the character or style of their commercial. Many worry that the commercial itself is unsound. All look to you as either culprit or savior.

This apprehensive audience presents two problems for the director. The first constitutes an invasion of your territory. Client or agency visitors sometimes register disapproval of a line reading or piece of action, voicing their disapproval either to you or to a member of cast or crew. Voicing comments directly to you would not be a problem except that opinions sometimes differ; an agency exec may suggest one thing, the client another. Moreover, it is disconcerting and time consuming to receive suggestions from half a dozen sources. Wise directors generally insist that all comments or suggestions be funneled through one person, usually the agency producer.

When client or agency visitors speak directly to cast or crew, it is a far more serious matter. As indicated earlier, everyone wants to be a director. When commercials are being filmed or taped, everyone wants to comment. Sometimes the comments are spurred by boredom, sometimes ego, sometimes the need to correct what appears to be a mistake.

Directors cannot allow guests to speak directly to cast or crew. All such comments must be funneled through them (the directors), quietly, away from the set. The cliché that "a ship can have only one captain" applies forcibly to any company filming commercials. Comments from offstage undermine the director's authority; actors begin to seek approval from multiple sources. Although directors are hired and paid by an agency, they must insist on autonomy on the set. In his excellent book, *Directing: The Television Commercial,* Ben Gradus recalls a speech he often recites to the agency/client group.

> I'm here to make the best possible commercial and to please all of you in the process. I trust you will all have helpful suggestions and I promise to listen seriously and respond. However, there can be only one director on the set if the actors and crew are to perform their best. All ideas and objections should be channeled through one representative, in this case preferably the agency producer. Then the cast and crew will not become confused and neither will I. Hence-

forth, no one but I will address the cast and crew directly and, please, all suggestions should be presented to the agency producer, who will relay them to me. I will listen.[8]

The second problem presented by the apprehensive agency/client audience is shock or consternation at how you are staging a scene or your choice of lighting or camera angle or whatever. Such a reaction should never happen.

More than anything else, a director is a communicator. Earlier I mentioned that directors don't like surprises on the set. Neither do agencies or clients. If directors expect to work again, they must spell out their intentions in great detail to the agency producer. If the storyboard indicates a closeup that the director doesn't feel is necessary, the director must communicate that feeling to the producer rather than have someone realize the omission the following day in the projection room. Perhaps the director can convince the producer of the validity of the change. Perhaps. If the client has already approved the storyboard, chances are that the producer will insist on shooting the sequence as indicated. If the director feels strongly about such a departure, then he or she may elect to shoot the sequence two ways: as defined in the storyboard and as the director prefers. The ultimate decision, then, will be made later in the editing room.

Postproduction.   More and more often, TV commercials are being edited in videotape. Even those photographed on 35-millimeter film are now transferred to tape, since computerized editing is both effective and incredibly fast. In addition, optical effects may be tried, changed, and incorporated in the commercial without the wait (or expense) of sending film to an optical house.

Directors theoretically are allowed to work with the editor and put together a "first cut." After the first cut, the film is then turned over to agency personnel and the director will move on to other projects. While most directors shoot a commercial with a clear idea of how they would like the film (or tape) to be assembled, the wise ones also respect the input of the editors. Editors bring to a project an objectivity that is impossible for a director who has spent weeks thinking of little else. The best editors have a sense of showmanship, an instinct for what plays and what doesn't, as well as a sense of dramatic rhythm in building sequences. While directors don't always accept editors' suggestions, they would be foolish not to consider constructive ideas.

---

[8]Gradus, p. 100.

They therefore listen respectfully and incorporate those suggestions which they feel will improve the spot.

> Neither the director nor producer nor any agency person can bring to the editing the unique perspective that the editor can. He alone has not been encumbered with the past, with the meetings and the dicta and the nonsenses and the difficulties of shooting and the preconceived ideas. He alone can truly measure good from bad in terms of audience acceptability and effectiveness with total disregard for politics and personalities and problems. His should be a strong voice and vote.[9]

The Local Commercial

Because commercials produced for a local or regional market reach a far smaller audience than those aired nationally, budgets are smaller and production schedules tighter. Only one element increases: pressure on the director.

The nature and scope of such a commercial depend, logically, on the size of the market. A town of 50,000 will see far more modest local commercials than will, say, New York or Denver. In the larger markets, directors may work with major advertising agencies, local agencies (large or small), or, on occasion, directly with the client. Sometimes these directors are employees of the agency or the client. More often, they work for the local television station or cable outlet.

While most local advertising agencies are enterprising, responsible, and often extremely sophisticated, a few are "schlock artists," intent on squeezing three commercials into the time normally required to produce two, on badgering directors into taking shortcuts or giving more of their time than should be legitimately expected. Directors with self-respect either walk away from such exploitation or refuse to go beyond the expected norms.

The simplest local commercials consist of nothing more elaborate than a series of slides with a staff announcer reading the copy. Others may use film or videotape of used car lots, restaurants, or markets with local personalities making the pitch. On occasion, the local director gets the opportunity to be genuinely creative.

Let's imagine that you are a staff director for a TV station and an advertising agency approaches you either directly or through your station's

---

[9]Gradus, pp. 187–88.

management. Perhaps you have worked with members of the ad agency on certain local shows. They liked your work. When they decided to create a series of local commercials, the agency's creative director thought of you.

While the agency will be using some station facilities, you will be employed as an independent contractor. In other words, the commercials will not be done as a part of your normal staff work. You will be paid extra for them and will probably direct them on your own time. The amount of money you receive will not purchase a Mercedes 350 SL.

Your station is delighted to see you direct the commercials. Such cooperation with a local advertiser tends to strengthen relationships and encourage future purchases of airtime on your station. The program director will try to arrange your work schedule so as to accommodate agency needs.

The account executive hands you mimeographed scripts for three one-minute commercials. (Storyboards are rare on a local level.) A prominent mortgage loan company will be advertising on TV for the first time. The exec grins guiltily: The company's president will work on camera in all three spots. Two of the three commercials depict young couples anxious (but financially unable) to buy their first home; the president closes these commercials with a personal sales message. The third consists in its entirety of a heart-to-heart pitch from the president.

You realize that the effectiveness of these commercials will depend in large part on the effectiveness of the company president. You ask the essential question: Can he act?

The account executive shrugs. He *says* he can. It turns out, of course, that the loan company's decision to advertise on television was prompted by the assurance that the president himself would create the company image. Now it will be up to you to "get a performance."

The president's office will be built at the station. Some wood-paneled flats, greenery, a bookcase, and a handsome desk. When you talk to the station's art director you specify that the desk must be large and expensive. (Big executives have big desks—and you know that the man has an ego.) The office must also seem comfortable, not intimidating. Maybe pictures of the wife and kids.

The young couples are selected from the local university's drama department. They will receive small change for their efforts, but it's worthwhile for them. The commercial provides professional experience that will look good on their resumés. You and the agency exec select two couples (and a standby in case of illness), both wholesome and engaging.

The following week, using a minimal VTR crew from the station, you tape the young couples looking wistfully at small but attractive new homes. (Local commercials usually are shot with videotape; it's cheaper than film, flexible, and can be edited quickly with a full range of optical effects.) To tape this location material the agency has purchased two hours of crew time. You asked for more. The agency couldn't afford it. It's a tight schedule, a fraction of the time you would have for a national commercial.

Aware of the pressure, you brought your actors here yesterday and meticulously rehearsed the sequences. (With professional actors you would have to pay for that privilege.) The taping goes well; viewers' hearts will go out to these attractive young kids aching for a home of their own. You cover the action in as many angles as time will allow, making certain the audience sees how much in love the couples are.

You have had two meetings with the president of the loan company, a white-haired gentleman with a warm, ingratiating manner. You discussed the commercial copy with him; he seemed comfortable with it. You explained that the material would be placed on a telePrompter so that he could look directly into the camera lens but still have the security of reading his material. (Tele-Prompter material is reflected onto a glass surface fixed at a 45-degree angle directly in front of the camera lens.)

At these earlier meetings you were impressed with the president. He had authority. He spoke well. Most of your doubts disappeared.

They return in full force the minute rehearsals begin. The president seems nervous, apprehensive. You try to kid with him, to build his confidence, to put him at ease. But his mind is elsewhere. The scripted action is simple. He will begin his pitch seated at the desk. At one point he will rise, move around the desk and downstage where he will pick up the company logo.

He seems to improve during rehearsal, becoming comfortable with the action. But the minute you attempt a take, he tightens up. The material suddenly sounds memorized and phoney.

You change a few words, making them more colloquial, clearing the changes with the agency exec who tries to conceal his own apprehension. Again, when you try for a take, the president tightens up. The words sound hollow. You know you're facing disaster so you decide on a little ruse. You change the action slightly and announce that you want to rehearse the new pattern. You privately instruct your technical director to roll the videotape on a secret word cue from you. No, you won't be in the booth. You'll be out on the stage, watching the apparent rehearsal.

Without the pressure of a take, the president is relaxed and comfortable. Unaware that videotape is rolling, he speaks the words warmly and with assurance. He's marvelous. Later, when the agency people see the tape, they congratulate you on your ingenuity.

While directors of national commercials most frequently begin as cinematographers, art directors, or editors, directing for a local TV station or cable outlet provides superb training. Also, superior local commercials may provide the beginning point for a sample reel. This is not to imply that directing on a local level is easily achieved. Most jobs in the highly competitive entertainment industry are difficult to obtain. Yet talented new people find their way into television every day of the week, every week of the year, so it can be done.

PRODUCTION TECHNIQUES

While production techniques for commercials do not differ substantially from techniques for other dramatic or nondramatic forms, one area of special directorial concern is the product itself.

Displaying the Product

For most advertisers, understandably, every element in a commercial takes second position to the product. No matter how lavish the production values, how catchy the jingle, how famous the guest star, if the product is not displayed handsomely, in a manner that creates a positive audience reaction, the advertiser will be unhappy. Often the product or its logo is the last shot in a commercial, the image that will remain longest in an audience's mind. You can understand the advertiser's need for perfection.

Directors often display small products "in limbo," that is, on a stand with a curved backing so that no floor line or horizon line is visible. At the station where I directed, such stands were called "gizmos." Sometimes the product is displayed in the same manner as many high fashion models—upon a sheet of seamless paper that curves back behind the product and up out of frame, again creating a bland, neutral background, generally of a pleasant pastel color, never taking attention away from the product.

Occasionally, other objects may be placed within the frame to enhance the product, to lend their own emotional colorations. An orchid, for example, beside a perfume bottle, might suggest exquisite beauty or delicacy. Bright red, polished apples with leaves and stems beside a can of applesauce might make the product seem more appealing. While such trimmings can add color and appeal to a product, be sure always to clear your concept first with the agency executive. What seems to be a first-rate idea to you may be counter-productive, for legitimate merchandising reasons.

Backgrounds also add their own colorations to a product. I was once assigned to direct a car commercial in which the script called for a "Beauty Shot." I asked the agency representative exactly what the term meant. Apparently inexperienced, he hemmed and hawed, telling me just to make the car look great. Since the car had a sleek, classic look, I asked our art director to bring in Greek columns (cutouts) which we arranged to form a colonnade. With the car brilliantly lighted in front of a cyclorama, the colonnade created a simple, yet classically rich setting, thereby lending richness to the product itself. The agency rep nodded when he saw it. Yes, that was what he had in mind all along.

As you watch TV commercials, be aware of how much backgrounds contribute to the ambience. Note how often car commercials are photographed in front of expensive mansions or elegant clubs or restaurants. Even in relatively confined studio commercials, an inventive background can enrich a product. A tweed or leather background, for example, might enhance an aftershave lotion. An artificial grass mat creates an outdoorsy background for a package of golf balls. Since the product shot is of such concern to advertisers, most directors and agency producers give it extraordinary attention. I recall a beer commercial in which the agency producer spent fully half an hour patiently coaching the gentleman who was going to pour the beer. The beer glass was illuminated from beneath—through a hole in the base of the gizmo—so as to highlight the bubbles. All that would be seen of the gentleman was his hand. But because the head on the beer had to be perfect, the manner of pouring became critical.

When the commercial features food, a home economist usually is hired (or on the company payroll) to make certain that its presentation is appetizing. The economist usually supervises the entire food background: tablecloth, place settings, silver, candles, flowers, and so on. When the food is to be served hot, multiple items usually are kept in ovens just off camera so that a dish may be whisked from oven to camera, in time to capture on film the heat radiating from it. Directors who specialize in food commercials understand the importance of highlights. Sometimes they spend literally hours lighting a closeup. One director I know used to brush certain food products with oil, causing them to glisten attractively.

Packaging of the product often demands special attention. Standard cartons as they are displayed in stores frequently contain so much copy that they appear "busy" when photographed in their usual state, so crowded with visual material that the impact is diminished. Most advertising agencies provide special packaging for commercials, closely resembling the product as routinely packaged and sold in stores and yet simplified for greater readability and impact. When photographing them, directors make certain the packages are perfect: clean, dust free, without flaws in design or lettering, no matter how minute.

Foil packaging or products that contain metallic or mirrored surfaces pose special photographic problems. Since their surfaces may reflect lights, the camera, or even the director himself, they must be surrounded by "tenting," a light cloth that will be invisible when reflected and will eliminate distracting reflections. The cloth must contain, of course, a small opening through which the camera can poke its nose in order to photograph the product. When photographing metallic surfaces such as watches, jewelry, or silverware, the glisten and sparkle become part of the sales appeal, so plenty of high intensity lighting is essential.

> There are times when the package has to be placed in closeup into an exact spot during a scene. Often a good way to do this is to have the fingers *remove* the package from its correct final placement, running the camera in reverse. . . . However, keep one piece of rhythm in mind. If you study the movement carefully, you will note that the hand will slow up toward the end of placing it down. Therefore, when playing the action in reverse and picking it up instead of placing it down, start the pickup slowly and then, after it is off the table a couple of inches, move it out faster. If you don't do it this way, there will be an unnatural jump of the product into place in the final straight-on version.[10]

Reversing camera action is a useful technique for commercial directors since it assures that action will conclude exactly where needed and lighted to perfection. When the storyboard calls for an automobile to drive toward camera, for example, stopping with the radiator grill in a tight closeup, such a shot can best be achieved by reversing action. Thus, the car would start in camera closeup, tight on the gleaming grill, and would back away.

Directorial Techniques

Tony Asher has produced literally hundreds of commercials and worked with dozens of directors. Here are his words concerning common directorial problems in commercial production:

> **Q.** Is there any special talent that directors need in order to tell a whole story in thirty seconds?

> **A.** A sense of proportion, obviously. A sense of *reduced* proportion. More specifically, they must know how much material they can get into a commercial. Very often agencies try to include too much.

> **Q.** But agencies have stopwatches. Don't they time their material?

> **A.** What happens is, you write yourself a nice commercial. And it runs thirty-four seconds and you say, "Hey, that's no problem. We

---

[10]Gradus, p. 47.

can certainly cut that down." And then somebody puts in four lines of mandatory copy. And "Member F.D.I.C." And somebody suggests a short musical intro. Now, people do put stopwatches on these things but they read the copy in their heads, silently—and not leaving the right pauses for this and that.

By the time it gets to the director, it's been sold to the client that way and the client's satisfied that he's included his nine essential points. If the director can't get all of those points in, he's going to be the one who has failed. Well, the director puts his own stop watch on the material—visualizing the way it will probably play—and he always comes out with something like forty-four seconds.

Q. And that's when the agency trims the material?

A. Well, the director says, "What's going to go?" And the producer says, "Nothing can go. It's been sold to the client. It's got to be delivered just that way." And the director will sometimes say: "Hey, guys, it's not going to work. We're not going to take the job on that basis. We can't deliver what's on this storyboard in thirty seconds." What happens, of course, is that eventually a whole scene is taken out—or if four points are supposed to be made, one of them gets lost and only three are made. So, for a director, having the ability to know in advance how material will play—that's crucial.

Examine the best commercials on TV. You'll find that usually they make a single point. By taking the full thirty seconds to make it, advertisers are able to dramatize their message with impact. Trying to cover too much territory in a limited time creates only confusion.

Telling a story in a minute or thirty seconds creates other directorial problems. Every moment has to count. Returning to the Tony Asher interview:

Q. How do you cram it all in?

A. You have to work with shorthand. You have to understand how to get from a raised eyebrow or a gesture, what might take 30 seconds or a minute in a feature film. Certain things happen simultaneously that might not happen simultaneously in real life. Or you're able to use a tiny gesture to communicate something that you didn't see nine-tenths of—but you understand what happened earlier because you saw the final moment. The really good directors understand how little you can get away with and still successfully communicate an idea.

Q. How do you learn that?

A. By doing it—or by studying others who know how to do it. You ask yourself, "Why do I know he just got through washing a car?" Well, because his pants are wet and he's got a sponge in his hand. To find ways to make those things clear in nonverbal, non-time-consuming ways is really tricky. Sharp directors do that. They create impressions without actually showing a piece of action. It's *economy*, really. Economy of words, economy of motion, economy of visual image.

Q. Does a director plan all of those economies before walking on the stage?

A. Absolutely. Frame by frame. Line by line. Action by action.

CHAPTER HIGHLIGHTS

- Commercials sell more than a product; they sell a lifestyle. They demonstrate how viewers can achieve glamor, the state of being envied. In order to sell such an elusive quality, directors often must create a glamorous ambience through use of camera, performer, music, setting, plus any other elements capable of affecting audience response.

- Directors of national commercials frequently come from three related fields: art direction, cinematography, and editing. Local TV stations or advertising agencies often provide invaluable training.

- Advertising agencies usually present directors of national commercials with storyboards, graphic depictions of the essential commercial action. While many directors feel that storyboards limit creativity, they also recognize that storyboards provide subtle insights and clearcut avenues of communication. Creative directors often suggest improvements, but because the storyboard has previously been approved by the client, directors are only occasionally successful in selling their concepts.

- In preproduction, directors often discover that preliminary casting has been done before they enter the scene. Many large agencies maintain videotape libraries of actors from which selections sometimes are made. Agencies consult both directors and their clients in determining final casting. During preproduction, directors select locations, work with art directors on set design, and plan their staging.

- Final approval of casting, set design, storyboard changes, wardrobe, and other details are made at a preproduction meeting attended by advertiser, agency, and director, plus key members of the production team. The director communicates his or her vision of the commercial, move by move, detail by detail, so that there will be no last-minute surprises during production.

- Since the shoot is usually attended by both agency and advertiser, the director must maintain control of cast and crew, preventing interference from visitors. Suggestions regarding staging or line readings should be funneled through the agency producer who will present them to the director in private.

- In postproduction, directors work closely with editors, preparing a director's cut. Since seasoned editors bring both skill and objectivity to a project, wise directors welcome their input.

- In the pressurized field of local commercials, directors face the dual problem of limited time and limited money. Scope depends upon the size of the market. Many local directors work for television stations or local agencies.

- In facing the differences between commercials and other entertainment forms, directors must give primary importance to the product. Enhancement can be achieved through appropriate backgrounds, accompanying props, effective lighting, and use of simplified-for-camera packaging.

- Experienced directors understand the inflexibility of time and refuse to shoot commercials containing excessive material. In order to cram a story into limited time, directors use a kind of visual shorthand, condensing actions that cannot be dramatized in full.

C H A P T E R   13

The musical program

Music evokes emotion; it is probably more evocative than any other art form. Rock concerts make our pulses pound. Movie love themes sometimes make us cry. Beethoven symphonies exalt us. In any program in which music is a major component, the director faces the obligation of communicating not just the music itself but something of the emotion generated by it. As we shall see, it is usually unsatisfactory merely to photograph the instrument that produces the music. A notable exception is when that instrument is the human voice and the performer is exquisitely talented. Emotion may be expressed through technical means (camera, lighting, lenses, editing); through scenery, props, and wardrobe; through imaginative use of related imagery; and through the skill and sensitivity of the artists.

Musical programs present an additional challenge. Since music is written primarily to be heard, its target is the ear. This book has stressed (and will continue to stress) that one of a director's continuing goals is to express concepts in visual terms, to pictorialize. Thus, when directing programs in which the primary element is music, directors face a paradox. How can they effectively pictorialize the instrument, whether it be an electric guitar or a human voice? Do they wander far afield, creating visual imagery evoked by the mood of the music? Or do they simply photograph the sound-producing apparatus? Do they cut to videotaped silhouettes of lovers walking on a fog-shrouded beach or lightning splitting an ominous sky? Do they train their cameras on a row of violinists or on a spotlighted vocalist belting out a rock favorite in front of a backdrop?

Since the beginning of time—1956—rock 'n' roll and TV have never really hit it off. But suddenly it's like they've gotten married and can't leave each other alone. KEITH RICHARD (ROLLING STONES)[1]

Dramatizing and pictorializing are always related. When expressing music in visual terms, the director must find images that are synchronous with emotions generated by the music. Such images enrich (and are enriched by) the music, creating an amalgam that is more evocative than either of its elements.

This chapter divides into four major discussions:

- PREPARATION: examining artist, script, and score

- CAMERA AND EDITING: studying a director's techniques in covering classical, pop, country, and rock music

- DRAMATIZING THE MUSIC: creating visual elements that reflect music's emotional content

- STUDIO VERSUS LOCATION: contrasting the advantages and disadvantages of each

---

[1]"Sing a Song of Seeing," *Time Magazine,* 26 Dec. 1983, pp. 54–56.

PREPARATION: KNOWING THE SCORE

There is no feeling worse than walking into a control room inadequately prepared. Even for the most resourceful, most seasoned directors capable of bulldozing their way through any perilous situation, insufficient preparation inevitably undermines the security of a project. It destroys confidence. It consumes precious rehearsal time in missteps that must be corrected. It communicates itself to cast and crew, creating tension, sabotaging their best efforts and vastly increasing the flow of stomach acids.

Preparation of a music show depends in part on the director's familiarity with (and understanding of) music. Obviously, a director lacking knowledge of classical music requires more time preparing a symphony orchestra broadcast than does a musicologist. When I directed in live television I had absolutely no background and little knowledge of the music world. I was able (with help from friends) to hum a tune on key. Management, therefore, with assailable logic, assigned me to direct almost all of the station's musical programs, from symphony orchestra broadcasts to big band concerts to western music variety hours. It was challenging.

Whether you have musical expertise or not, you will need to take certain steps in the preparation of any musical program. These steps concern artist, script, and score.

Artist

When possible, study the artists during an actual performance, whether they be vocalists, rock musicians, or concert pianists. Failing that, try to find videotape or film of programs they have previously presented. Videotape or film is actually preferable to a live performance in that you can run a particular sequence over and over again, familiarizing yourself with the artists, their music, and their style of presentation. Make notes. Ask yourself such questions as:

- Are they colorful or drab? If drab, how will you create audience interest? If colorful, where does the color lie? How will you emphasize it?

- Are there specific personalities that shine? How will you capture their spark?

- Does their physical set-up lend itself to effective camera treatment? How will you change it—without destroying their musical effectiveness?

- If a vocalist, is the vocal style intimate or physical? (How will this affect your camera treatment?) Attractive or unattractive? Are there "good" angles or "bad" angles?

- Are any of the numbers the same ones that will be performed in your show? If so, you are, in effect, watching a rehearsal and can plan your treatment more specifically: camera angles, lighting, setting, and so on.

When possible, meet with your star performers well in advance of the broadcast. Let them know how delighted you are to be working with them and share some of your concepts for the format. At this point, you or a station administrator must discuss certain key issues. Will the show be performed in the studio or at a location? If a studio show, what kind of setting will be most appropriate? Will there be an audience? Who will be the host? Will the show be scripted or off the cuff? (Who will write the script?) How will costs be handled? If the program is to be sponsored, how will commercials be integrated? If your performers have reservations about any of your program ideas, it's better to find out early. Welcome their creative suggestions. Make them feel they are part of the team.

Script

In many cable and local TV station operations, the director is also the producer and therefore responsible for program content as well as its form and style. The preliminary meeting with artists or their manager should prompt them to deliver a suggested list of musical selections as early as possible. You will probably want to discuss an appropriate sequencing of these selections. This sequence provides the skeletal basis for a script.

Many directors believe that their work begins only after a script has been written. While some working directors remain aloof from the writing process, the good ones understand that quality shows begin in the scripting. They know from bitter experience that it's almost impossible to create a fine program from a mediocre script.

If a script is to be prepared for your music program, don't be shy. Contribute ideas before the concrete has hardened. If the writer's concepts are stodgy, impractical, or old fashioned, be tactful in suggesting changes. Some directors have the golden ability of making a writer believe that their ideas actually originated with the writer. Since ego is so inextricably involved in the creative processes, most writers tend to function best when working with their own concepts rather than concepts someone has foisted on them.

Score

It is important that you become familiar with musical selections prior to rehearsal. (When you begin rehearsal, you should already have mapped out a pattern of camera angles.) Listening to cassettes or phonograph records will help immeasurably in your preparation. If possible, get photocopies of the actual scores.

Counting bars is essential in order to cover a musical program effectively. If you cannot read music or count bars, it is imperative that you have someone—an associate director or musician—sitting beside you who can. Lacking musical expertise and denied an associate director, I frequently relied on a stopwatch for timing musical passages. It was helpful but not always dependable, since musical tempos vary. With singers the problem is less acute. Neatly typed lyrics (as they are actually sung) provide an effective directorial road map.

The reason for familiarizing yourself with the music, of course, is so that you will be able to direct your cameras to the right place at the right time. It's embarrassing to cut to a closeup of a piano keyboard at the exact moment a soloist begins to sing.

CAMERA AND EDITING

In photographing a ballet such as *Swan Lake,* some directors prefer to dissolve rather than cut between camera angles. By such transitions from one camera to another, they attempt to enhance the mood generated by music and dancers. All camera and editing techniques carry certain implications; they influence audience reactions; they create a sense of rhythm, mood, or atmosphere. Audiences remain largely unaware of such subtle influences; they occur below the level of full consciousness. It is impossible to provide a comprehensive list of optical implications because they vary from circumstance to circumstance and from program to program. For example, in drama a dissolve often implies the passage of time or marks a change of scene. In a ballet *pas de deux,* it is merely a graceful change of angle.

Transitions between camera angles comprise a director's most elementary technique in dramatizing any message. While digital video effects have revitalized musical transitions (especially in MTV), the cut and the dissolve are still the most often used.

The Cut

A *cut* is clean, crisp, sharp, and incisive. In an uptempo musical number, a straight cut seems to fit the pace and character of the music. In such selections, most directors prefer to cut on the beat so that a sequence of cuts (every two bars, every four bars) almost becomes part of the music; it has a rhythm of its own, reflecting the musical pattern.

A properly executed cut is invisible, whether the musical tempo is fast or slow. When cuts are made on movement, they are virtually undetectable. If a singer whirls and moves downstage during a musical bridge, for example, a cut to a wider angle will go unseen if executed during the whirling motion. Similarly, when a cut is executed as a singer begins a word or musical phrase, the cut will seem invisible.

The theory behind invisible cutting is similar to a technique used by stage magicians. When the magician removes a rabbit from an inner pocket with his left hand, his right hand simultaneously makes a flourish high in the air. The viewer's eye follows the larger action. When a singer or dancer whirls flamboyantly, the observer's eye, drawn to the larger action, is oblivious to the change of camera angle. Similarly, when a singer begins a new phrase, audience attention goes to the new thought he or she is expressing and thus is unaware of an angle change.

Another key principle is also at work. Good editing always follows audience interest. As interest in the performer heightens, spectators want to move closer. Effective editing parallels that increased psychological need for closeness by providing closer camera angles. When cuts are synchronized with audience desires, the audience simply does not see them.

The Dissolve

A *dissolve* from one angle to another is more fluid, less incisive than a cut. It presents a blending or merging between two angles in which the first, for a moment or two, is actually superimposed over the second. In early motion picture scripts, it was called a lap dissolve, suggesting the overlapping of images. Early directors in live television used the command "lap" for such a transition, perhaps because the word was easier to say than "dissolve" (for example, "lap to one," "lap to film").

A dissolve can be any length: almost as quick as a cut or extending as long as a director desires. Television dissolves usually last about two seconds. In drama, extended dissolves often imply a connection between the first image and the second as the first image remains briefly superimposed over the second. For example, when a scene ends on a burning car and the picture dissolves slowly to a hospital bed, to a close shot of the car's driver (the wreck superimposed over her face for a moment, ghostlike), the director perhaps implies that the driver carries the memory of the burning car in her mind; she cannot forget it.

In ballet, a dissolve echoes and reinforces the fluid motion of the dancers, helping to maintain mood. Very slow dissolves during a ballet sequence (especially when photographed against a dark background) provide multiple images of the dancers, enhancing the poetry of their motion, suggesting figures reflected in a pool.

All ballet, of course, is not *Swan Lake*. Modern ballets are often stylized or bizarre in flavor. With such ballets, dissolves might be totally inappropriate, suggesting a fluidity that does not exist in either the action or the music. Whether in music, sports, drama, or special events, camera and editorial treatment must reflect the character and mood of the production.

Shots and Angles

Generally speaking, the impact of a shot varies directly with its closeness. A closeup intensifies the significance of subject matter; a wide (or long) shot tends to diminish it. Close shots gain impact by contrast. Thus, in drama, directors and editors try to save close shots for critical moments, when they are dramatically motivated, aware that if an entire scene is played in close angles, nothing will have impact.

With instrumental numbers, this rule must be modified. It is virtually impossible to assess one portion of a selection as being more "significant" than another. Wide shots should be used sparingly. Their primary purpose is orientation. Close and medium angles usually comprise most of the camera coverage. A wide shot of a symphony orchestra or even a rock group is visually unexciting, although a rock group of three or four members allows the camera to be considerably closer than a seventy-piece orchestra and therefore provides more interest.

Classical Music. Close shots of drummers, violinists, or flautists playing instruments can provide colorful material—but a closeup of a tuba player with inflated cheeks and eyeballs bulging can prove ludicrous, destroying mood and provoking laughter. If laughter does not conflict with the musical mood, however, then such a shot might prove refreshing. For example, if the Boston Pops Orchestra were playing a rollicking polka, humor would not be out of place and such a tuba closeup might add zest to the proceedings. The point, of course, is that the shots must contribute to the overall character or flavor of the music.

If close shots provide interest, extreme closeups often add more. Fingers on piano keyboards, violen frets, harpstrings, or valves on wind instruments are visually dynamic. So are drumsticks rolling on a tympany, bows sawing on a string bass, Chinese cymbals clanging, and even toes tapping out a beat. Don't be afraid to be *bold* with your closeups. Bold angles energize musical selections that otherwise might be visually bland.

Close shots do not always have to include instruments. With a virtuoso pianist or violinist, for example, closeups of the face often provide tremendous visual emphasis, enriching the mood and creating psychological closeness between audience and performer. If you have watched violinist Itzhak Perlman during a concert, you will recall facial expressions of ecstasy or grief, eyebrows occasionally furrowing in the intensity of concentration or lips smiling suddenly in enjoyment of the musical moment—expressions that vastly deepen audience participation and help to communicate the music's emotion.

Shots of the orchestra conductor are effective for three reasons. First, they also communicate emotionality. Second, they provide relief from incessant shots of musical instruments. Third, they provide directors with a convenient "escape hatch" if they get in trouble—if you've miscounted bars and find yourself temporarily lost, cutting to the conductor affords instant salvation. Some conductors, of course, are naturally flamboyant; they dramatize their music with great histrionic flair, providing directors with an unending source of exciting material. Stoic conductors usually end up with considerably less screen time.

In order to photograph conductors effectively, the director must conceal a camera at the rear of the orchestra. Such a hidden camera may also provide effective shots of the audience. Boston Pops programs on PBS often feature group or individual audience reaction shots as a part of their camera coverage, especially if the music is light in flavor and audience members contribute to the ambience through smiling expressions or fingers tapping rhythmically on tables.

Many of the principles discussed in Chapter 3 will be helpful in planning shots of instruments or musicians. The dynamic diagonal line, for instance, occurs repeatedly in side angle shots (such as shooting down a row of violins or horns). These side angles, sometimes called raking shots, derive much of their visual energy from the rhythmic repetition of form as both musician and instrument are repeated in diminishing perspective. It is not always necessary to include an entire row of musicians. Sometimes close raking two-shots or three-shots of instruments (such as string bass or cello) provide bold, effective angles: bows sawing on strings or fingers on strets.

One of my favorite uses of the diagonal line involves the piano keyboard. In most programs featuring a pianist, directors use three or four relatively standard angles: a full profile shot of musician and piano, a close shot of fingers on keyboard, and angles through the raised piano lid, featuring musician but eliminating keyboard. I discovered that two cameras shooting down and close on the piano keyboard (from opposite sides) when superimposed would create crossed diagonal lines of considerable beauty: two keyboards, four hands in motion. Caution: Such an angle contains directorial traps since neither camera may pull back when on the air without revealing the presence of the other. Solution: Either the on-the-air camera must remain briefly on the keyboard to allow the opposing camera to escape or the director must cut to a third camera shooting through the raised piano lid, close on the pianist. In this latter angle, both keyboard cameras can move away unseen.

Thus far we have discussed fixed shots from a stationary camera. Movement may also help to dramatize music. *Dollying* or *zooming* in (or out) creates a visual transition from wide to medium to close. As indicated earlier, such a move ideally should parallel the viewer's increasing interest as it moves from the ensemble orchestra to an individual section or instrument. Conversely, as interest changes from a specific instrument or section to the entire orchestra, dollying or zooming out becomes appropriate.

What is the purpose or reason for such a move when a simple cut achieves the same result, only faster? For one thing, a forward movement does not pretend to be invisible. With dollying in, the audience becomes aware, with some anticipation, that they are being carried slowly forward, from the general to the specific, to a new focus of attention. As much as possible, such movement should be synchronous with the musical tempo. Conversely, dollying out takes viewers from the specific to the general, reorienting and releasing them from whatever tensions may have been generated by closer, more dynamic angles. Dollies or slow zooms outward are often used at the conclusion of a number.

Because *panning* shots are seldom used in classical music programs, they remain fresh and visually interesting. They are simply another way to transfer attention from one orchestra section to another. As with a dolly shot, a slow pan heightens audience interest in its destination. Panning shots become more dynamic when panning, say, from a woodwind section to single violinist, huge in the foreground, the element of surprise adding to the visual boldness.

When photographing a full orchestra, the *trucking* shot remains the most expressive of all camera moves. When used properly, its lateral movement reflects the music's emotional content far more powerfully than either the dolly or the pan. Imagine a raking shot down a row of violinists. Now, as the music begins to swell and soar, the camera begins to glide past row after row of violinists, its sweeping movement propelled by the music, echoing its emotionality. A trucking shot magnifies audience interest because it constantly unveils new imagery, entering camera frame from the side (and thus, at apparently great speed), sweeping dizzyingly past in lateral motion and then disappearing to make way for new forms, new faces, new instruments.

Popular, Country, and Rock Music.   Since these forms are less tradition bound than classical music, directors may be more imaginative in their treatment of them. If camera style becomes a reflection of subject matter, classical music will be relatively conventional, punk or acid rock will be bizarre and uninhibited, with popular and country music somewhere in between.

We will discuss rock 'n' roll as an opposite pole to classical music, setting out a few guidelines for its direction. Popular and country music will not receive special mention here; the camera styles for these, centered in the musical spectrum between classical and rock, may be inferred from the discussion.

MTV, the current cable music television channel, daily offers a virtual textbook of camera gimmickry, distortion or multiple-image lenses, bizarre angles, off-center framing, negative or polarized images, and color enhancement or distortion as visual accompaniment to its music. Watching an hour or two of such often imaginative visual treatment of rock music will stimulate your own imagination and provide potential directors with an ever-enlarging bag of tricks.

Many of the camera and editing rules discussed earlier in the chapter apply equally well to rock. Cutting on the beat, for instance, is good practice for any uptempo selection. With rock, generally more frenetic in tone and tempo than classical or pop, you may want to cut more frequently.

If boldness in closeups seemed essential with classical music, it is imperative in photographing most rock selections. Whereas head, shoulders, and violin would constitute an effective closeup in classical, a head alone is often its rock equivalent. Cameras are frequently hand-held, which allows tremendous freedom of movement. Boldness is sometimes achieved with wide angle lenses, which distort the images for dramatic, occasionally comedic effect. Such lenses magnify foreground and diminish background, creating an illusion of extraordinary depth. The wider the angle, the greater the degree of distortion.

Boldness is also achieved with bizarre angles such as shooting the drummer from extreme low angles so as to frame past an assortment of drums in the foreground. Such bizarre angles frequently shoot up into studio lights, allowing, almost seeking, lens flares, which contribute to the frenetic mood.

Both of these so-called rules, however, must be subordinate to the dramatic principle of progression. Progression simply means *growth* or *development*. In drama it is a climbing action in which events gradually build to a series of crises, each higher than the last. The highest dramatic peak of all usually occurs at the end of a play and is called the climax. The principle of progression occurs again and again in the entertainment world. Preliminary boxing (or wrestling) matches are always followed by the main event. Musical extravaganzas usually climax with a grand finale, the entire cast gathered on stage in an elaborate setting, lights flashing, umbrellas twirling, to sing the show's hit song. Oldtime vaudeville entrepreneurs used to place their headliners in the next-to-closing spot, since that was theoretically the climax.

When sequencing a music show, arranging the order of numbers, try to create a sense of growth in the program. If you're staging a half-hour show with a commercial in the middle, you are, in effect, staging a two-act show. Therefore, each act should end on a high musical peak—and the second peak should be higher than the first since it constitutes the climax of your program.

Chapter 7, Staging the Camera, discusses at some length the concept of camera progression, in which audiences experience a sense of building tension merely from increasingly close angles. Ideally, of course, the increase in tension generated by camera angles should reflect the increased tension generated by actors and the dramatic situation. But the increasingly close angles alone create some illusion of progression.

The director can apply that principle to music. If you begin a number with extremely close shots, you may leave yourself with nowhere to go. If you want to end a number extremely close on hands, instruments, and faces, you must plot your camera progression in advance, calculating where you want to be at the halfway point and how wide your angles must be at the start. Of course, it is often effective to begin extremely close—fingers plucking guitar strings or tapping a bongo drum—so long as you drop back to wider shots for orientation and then build your progression from there.

In directing rock numbers, be adventuresome. Explore new directions. It's no crime to try something wild and fail; it *is* a crime not to try. Even if your sorties don't always work, they will at least add freshness to the look of your show. While some of that freshness is derived from lighting and scenery and use of "borrowed" imagery from videotape and film (which we will discuss shortly), imaginative camera angles and crisp, clean, on-the-beat cutting will make your show professional and viewable.

Vocals.   In the early days of television, Dinah Shore starred in a quarter-hour show twice weekly over NBC. For a few delightful months I was the stage manager of that show. Its director, a sensitive and talented man named Alan Handley, photographed most of Dinah's ballads in essentially the same camera pattern. At the start of each song, camera would be wide. As Dinah wove her spell, creating greater and greater involvement with her audience, Handley moved his camera closer. At the moment of greatest intimacy, of deepest emotionality, the camera was close, a head-and-shoulders shot. Then the song ended. As the audience descended from the mountaintop, the camera drifted back again. In a sense, the director's camera paralleled the movement of the viewer's consciousness, moving closer to the singer as she created her magic and moving away when she had finished.

With genuine talent, it is usually unnecessary for a director to resort to fancy camera angles and gimmicry. Whether it be an actor in a monolog, a comedian, or a singer, if the artist has the ability to capture and hold viewers with the intensity of his or her performnce, then the director will only disturb audience involvement by arbitrarily changing angles.

Students in television production classes tend to become fascinated with hardware. They are dazzled by cameras and microphones and the control room's display of electronic magic. Many come to believe that a show's success depends on the skilled application of technique and technology—that the chemistry between imaginative lighting, optical effects, and a sweeping crane shot will spark audience applause. Understandable—but largely untrue. What appears in *front* of a camera contributes far more significantly to a show's success than the gaudiest display of electronic wizardry. Cameras, lighting, microphones, editing devices, and fancy lenses are only a means of communicating a message. But it's the message that counts, not the communicative devices.

When a vocalist is genuinely talented, don't get in the way. Let the artistry shine through. Yet if the singers are less than talented, they may need some directorial help. Theatricality in the form of visual or audio effects often makes mediocre singers appear better than they are. Echo chambers add resonance to weak voices. A background of dancers, flashy scenery, or lighting effects, or constantly changing camera angles, sometimes dazzle audiences and distract their concentration from a lackluster singer. Spectacle (sound, motion, and color) is often a director's most valuable tool (see Chapter 2).

Enhancing a number through the use of spectacle, of course, is not limited to mediocre performers. Content dictates treatment. A simple, honest ballad suggests simple and honest treatment. A lively show tune or production number suggests a more theatrical staging. If the performer is genuinely talented, that talent inevitably will shine through, regardless of camera cuts, fancy angles, or production gimmicks—or the lack of them. If your budget will allow dancers and elaborate scenery, fine. If not, you may fall back on the hardware that once fascinated you in your TV production classes and utilize chroma key, multiple-image lenses, and fancy camera angles to create your own brand of spectacle.

Be kind to your vocalist. In drama it is often effective to cut to a bold, gritty closeup, revealing every pore and pimple in an actor's face. Not so with singers. During final rehearsal (with singer in makeup), zoom or dolly a camera to a closeup to determine just how close you can get before the shot becomes unflattering. When vocalists sing a love song, it obviously breaks the illusion to reveal gold fillings in their teeth or, on a sustained note, the color of their tonsils. Your singers' success is your success. Make them look good.

Vocalists sometimes sing to their studio audience rather than to television viewers, perhaps because it is easier to communicate with people they can see. If the singers are talented, TV viewers will accept such misplaced attention but usually it is with the feeling that they have become observers rather than participants in the singer-audience relationship. Some vocalists (usually those who play club or concert dates) occasionally leave the stage and sing to individual audience members. Such moves never fail to generate excited reaction from the live audience. But the viewers at home are less enthusiastic. They are no longer recipients of the singer's favors. They feel, with understandable envy, that they are being ignored. Successful TV directors remain conscious of viewer expectations, steering their performers' attention away from studio spectators. The camera lens should be the only audience.

DRAMATIZING THE MUSIC

Just as writers must understand the theme of stories they write, so must directors understand the essential mood, flavor, or motif of a musical program. The central concept may begin with performers, writer, producer, or director. Once it has crystallized in everyone's mind, then the creative wheels may begin to turn.

The developmental pattern (much abbreviated here) might go something like this. Music is selected to fit the concept. Performers, writer, or director may suggest a sequence. The production team (writer, director, producer) discuss production concepts. All understand that these concepts will inevitably change as the show develops, but you have to start someplace. The writer prepares a first-draft script. The production team tears it apart and puts it back together again, searching for better ways to dramatize the initial concept and to cement the program elements. The writer rewrites and polishes the script. The director prepares. Musical rehearsal and timing. Camera rehearsal. Broadcast.

Creating visual imagery that enhances the emotional content of music is something like taking a Rorschach test; no two people react to a given stimulus in an identical fashion. A rock song or a concerto will stimulate a dozen different concepts in a dozen different minds. There will, of course, be thematic similarities, but specific actions, settings, and camera treatment will vary enormously.

During each developmental step, the director and other members of the production team build upon the original concept, enriching it, expanding it, bringing it to life in a number of practical ways.

Dramatizing Rock Music

Dramatizing rock music has become one of the most innovative and creative of popular art forms. Many directors create elaborate sets with dozens of extras in order to dramatize the mood or atmosphere of a particular song.

Treatment of rock music generally falls into two categories: photographing the musicians as they play, and devising free-association imagery that either dramatizes the song's story content (sometimes literally, sometimes with tongue in cheek) or depicts its mood. The two techniques are not always separated. Often they are interwoven, cutting between shots of a drummer and water dripping from a faucet or a beautiful girl riding a white horse. Sometimes shots of musicians are intercut with as many as three or four divergent visual themes interpreting the song's musical or lyrical pattern.

Photographing Musicians.   Camera coverage of rock musicians was discussed at some length in the section on popular, country, and rock music. Directors sometimes employ additional techniques that fall generally into the category of dramatizing although, as stated before, the categories of pictorializing and dramatizing frequently overlap. Traditionally, directorial treatment must depend on the nature of the music. However, certain common stylistic approaches seem relevant to many rock and roll selections, especially those which are bizarre in nature or which wander far from reality.

Directorial treatment of rock music—especially as seen in MTV—often recalls the psychedelic experience. Its style suggests the dream worlds of Dali, Magritte, and de Chirico. It derives its subject matter from the subconscious mind. This concept explains why distortion lenses, light flares, and bizarre camera angles seem to fit the music. Modern directors are limited only by their imaginations in achieving such a dreamlike state. Techniques include:

- Scenery (projected on a screen, matted via chroma key, or actually constructed) such as a jail cell, a mausoleum, an ice floe, or a whore house.

- Colorful locations such as a waterfront, field of daisies, abandoned factory, or ghost town.

- Smoke (generated by a smoke pot or dry ice) clinging to the floor and suggesting that the musicians are floating on clouds.

- Color distortion, achieved either with gels on lights, color correction filters on cameras, or electronic wizardry. Such distortion may be mild or extreme (faces turning green or lavender), the latter suggesting not so much the dream world as the nightmare.

- Split screen, achieved either with optical mattes or with multiple-image lenses. Screen may be divided into as many as sixty-four images.

- Lighting effects, from crisp silhouettes to harsh cross lighting or key lights placed extremely low, throwing huge shadows upon a background. Also, flashing of key lights to suggest lightning (perhaps accompanied by thunder).

- Superimposing effects or imagery over the musicians. Smoke, flames, ocean waves, storm clouds, rose petals, whatever fits the musical mood.

- Electronically reversing polarity, rendering blacks white and whites black: a negative image.

- Shooting through or past foreground objects, such as water dripping down glass beads, racking focus from beads in foreground to musicians in background and vice versa.

- Tilting, polarizing, or stretching the image electronically.

- Star filters to create stars out of highlights (a glittery, sophisticated look) or fog filters to create a soft, hazy, fantasy feeling.

- Computer-generated effects that may twist, bend, flip, or twirl any of the above.

These effects constitute only a fraction of the number available to the imaginative director, to help achieve a dramatization of musical content in photographing rock musicians.

Creating Dramatic Imagery.   The treatment of dramatic imagery often suggests the grotesque or erotic world of the psychedelic trip. It begins, of course, with lyrics and the musical content but then veers into strange and fascinating directions that, when skillfully conceived and performed, add new dimensions to the music.

No book can instruct in the creative processes. Each person possesses a unique reservoir of imagery and develops a distinctive and personal way of reaching his or her subconscious mind in order to tap that reservoir. It might be helpful, however, to trace the free associative wanderings that the mind sometimes experiences in the creation of imagery for a rock song.

Our assignment is to create a visual treatment for a rock ballad, "Burn Me." The lyrics of this song of dubious origin state: "Burn me with your love:/Warm me, take me, bake me/Fill the night with fires that wake me/ Though I run, they overtake me./Baby, burn me with your love."

In creating imagery, the director or writer would probably read and reflect on the lyrics, allowing the music to create a mood. The stream of consciousness elicits a random succession of words and images: A bedroom. Thunder, lightning. Girl awakening in terror. Too obvious, too literal. So is idea of running from flames. Or from some nameless terror. A girl running—perhaps in slow motion, as if in a nightmare. Down long corridor, endless. She falls, can't get up. People in her way, blocking her. They keep pulling at her, trying to stop her. Hideous people. Smiling. Mocking. One of them has the face of Satan. She keeps looking behind her but we never see what's chasing her. Still so damned literal. Yet the idea of running in a nightmare is universal; everyone has experienced it. Red is the dominant color. Wherever she turns, fire symbols confront her. Descent into hell. Advertising sign: picture of the devil, smoke coming out of mouth. Maybe we get some humor in here: kids popping smoke-filled balloons. A street beggar walking on hot coals. Statue in the park smoking a cigarette. Lightning strikes a tree; it erupts in flames. Hard to do. Cost a fortune. Always the Unseen Fear pursuing her. How to end it? Does she get caught? Down subway steps. (Descent into hell.) Trapped against subway wall. White, shiny, tiled. She screams. Busy passersby ignore her. Blank, cold faces—like mannequins. Camera becomes the moving point of view of the Chaser. And we see her illuminated by a red glow that gets brighter and brighter as we move closer. Might work. It's visual, plenty for a director to work with. Rather literal. But it's a beginning.

Dramatizing Classical Music

Unless a concert has an unusually strong thematic flavor, it seems unmotivated and out of character to cut away from the orchestra or soloist for other than audience reaction shots. Purists would frown even on those. When symphony orchestras celebrate a special or festive occasion (for example, Christmas), it is usually with the playing of traditional airs that evoke intense audience emotions. On these occasions, occasional, tasteful use of imagery may be used to complement the music.

Let's use Christmas as an example. Shots of Madonna and Child (oil paintings) or the nativity scene might accompany "Adeste Fidelis"; shots of old English carolers or church bells tolling might accompany "The First Noel." While such scenes might offer visual amplification of the program theme, the focus of interest always must remain on the orchestra or the soloists.

The flavor of the occasion may be echoed in the setting. Again, such visual enhancement should be understated. An orchestra is visually "busy." That is, its elements are numerous and difficult to delineate, especially in a full shot. The "busyness" is compounded by television's 525-line screen that prevents crisp definition. Intricate scenery or fancy trimming exacerbate the problem. Simplicity is the key to the setting.

Because of their size, symphony orchestra broadcasts usually originate in a concert hall or amphitheater. Individual artists perform in both television studios and locations. Recall the piano concerts at the White House by Vladimir Horowitz and others.

Vocalists.   It was once fashionable on television to create little stories out of popular vocals, with scenery, props, and occasionally actors or other singers. The pattern gradually lost favor since many of the "stories" were self-consciously clever or cloyingly cute and took attention away from the singer.

Today scenery and lighting are used to dramatize the mood of the song rather than its story. A garden setting, for example, creates an atmosphere even before the singer walks on stage. The setting also provides the singer with action during the song, which contributes to a feeling of ease, of natural-ness. Many numbers have orchestral bridges in which the vocalist has nothing to sing and therefore must stand, awkwardly waiting to continue. A setting provides a graceful answer—walking in the garden, smelling flowers, feeding a bird in a birdcage, or swinging gently in an old-fashioned swing.

If an entire show is built around a vocalist, locations provide enormous color and scope. One Perry Como television special, for example, opened with its star aboard a small boat in the New York harbor and featured as its background the Statue of Liberty.

STUDIO VERSUS LOCATION

There are two initial options for your show's setting: studio or location. Directing a show in the studio offers many practical advantages. You have far more control of all production elements. In a musical show, sound must be a major consideration. Studios are acoustically superior to most locations. You are not bothered by airplanes flying over, trucks rumbling by, or police sirens. Sound in open air shows tends to lose "liveness" since there are no reflective surfaces to create reverberations. Conversely, indoor locations are often filled with hard surfaces, bouncing sound back and forth unmercifully, creating disturbing echoes. Both problems may easily be solved by prerecord-ing sound tracks and allowing vocalists to lip-sync their performance. In the Perry Como special described previously, such prerecording allowed total camera and performer mobility. TV audiences seldom wonder where the orchestral background is coming from.

Lighting is less of a problem since modern lighting units are relatively small and easily transportable. Still, on location you probably won't have the flexibility or lighting quality that you have in a studio. The same holds true in other areas. If a prop or costume is missing, someone must return to the studio to get it. Or run to a store to purchase another. Everything seems to take longer on location simply because you are working in someone else's backyard.

On studio shows, directors sit in a control booth, separated from cast and crew. On location, separation becomes isolation. Miles of cable connect cameras, microphones, and production lines (usually) to a control truck. The isolation is so complete that directors must depend almost entirely upon their floor managers. They don't have the luxury of bellowing into a studio address system. (An abrasive habit, even in the studio!) If the floor managers are not alert and authoritative, a dark cloud of frustration and helplessness settles over the director. Like trying to pick up a needle with ice tongs.

But locations also offer major advantages. When the location sufficiently enriches a show, complementing it in mood and character, then advantages far outweigh discomfort or inconvenience. No matter how skillfully designed the setting, no matter how artful the lighting or sound, a studio show always looks like a studio show; it has a slickness, a glossiness that, with less than first-rate talent, smacks of plasticity.

Some years ago I directed "The Tex Williams Show," a western musical variety program that for a time originated at Knott's Berry Farm in Buena Park, California. The show first was staged in the streets of the western ghost town, surrounded by hundreds of ebullient fans. The ghost town background was ideal for a western variety show, and the fans lent tremendous color and excitement.

Later, because the show blocked traffic, interfering with sales in many of the Knott stores, they decided to move us. The Knott organization built us a small but handsome western street of our own in an open area with a grandstand large enough to accommodate triple the number of spectators. We broadcast the show every Sunday afternoon for over a year from that location. Ultimately, probably because of location costs, the show moved to studio E at NBC. It expired a couple of months later.

"The Tex Williams Show" started as a colorful, slambang western, energized by the proximity of fans and by the earthy, good-humored atmosphere of the ghost town. You could almost smell the hot buttered popcorn. If a stagecoach came rattling down the street during a comedy routine, so much the better! If a baby cried (and one always did—right in the middle of a soulful ballad!), it simply contributed to the noisy, familial, cotton candy atmosphere.

When the show moved to the more sedate arena, separated now from its audience, the production values vastly improved; we had better control of sound and camera. Yet the show lacked excitement. It no longer rubbed elbows with its fans. Even though it originated at Knott's Berry Farm, it had become a studio show, operating in front of painted sets in a traditional audience-stage pattern. Some of the warmth had disappeared. And with it, some of the show's appeal. The final move to a television studio completed the sterilization process.

When the right chemistry exists between a show and its location, magic happens. The show emerges with character and colorations never possible in a studio. Put Luciano Pavarotti in a cathedral singing Christmas songs and the TV screen lights up the room. Put Barbra Streisand in Central Park surrounded by thousands of adoring fans and television justifies its ancient movies and its hours of violence. Put the Rolling Stones in the Los Angeles Coliseum or Police at the US Festival and you create vibrations impossible to achieve in any TV studio.

CHAPTER HIGHLIGHTS

- Since music evokes emotion, music programs pose a special challenge to directors: how to complement that emotionality in visual terms. Answers arise from use of technical elements—camera, editing, and lighting—and from appropriate visual imagery.

- As with other program forms, music shows require careful preparation. Directors should familiarize themselves with performers and the music selections they will play or sing. When scripts are used, directors should involve themselves in the creative processes early, working with the writer to assure that the presentation will be optimum.

- In directing music shows, the ability to count bars is almost a requisite. Lacking such ability, directors must rely on a musically oriented associate or a stopwatch.

- Use of camera and editing should match, as much as possible, the flavor and mood of the music. Cuts are crisp, sharp, and incisive, ideally suited to uptempo music. Since dissolves are more fluid, more langorous, they create visual poetry for certain dance numbers and romantic ballads.

- With symphony orchestras—as with most groups—wide angles usually are dull. Close angles create visual impact. Raking (side angle) shots down a row of musicians create an effective visual rhythm. The faces of some virtuosos communicate the music's emotion far more than shots of instruments. Moving shots that parallel the music's content—trucking or dolly shots—create visual excitement. Because panning shots are seldom used, they remain relatively fresh in music shows.

- With rock music, MTV provides a virtual textbook of techniques for directors. Since the music is often bizarre and adventuresome, directors are encouraged to echo that sense of adventure in their camera treatments. The dramatic element of progression is still at work, however: The program should build to a climax.

- With genuinely talented vocalists, directors should keep production elements simple, allowing the talent to shine through. With less-than-gifted performers, directors should try to fortify performances through addition of such theatrical elements as dancers, fancy settings, and background singers.

- Although their themes may be similar, two directors will rarely create identical imagery for musical selections. In music video, camera coverage embraces two areas: the musicians themselves and imagery that dramatizes a song's lyric or musical content. Both usually are treated imaginatively, almost with a sense of the psychedelic, resorting to free association imagery and optical and color distortion.

- Music shows may originate in a studio or on location. Both offer advantages and disadvantages. Studios provide greater security; the director has better control of all production elements, including sound, lighting, and effects. But locations sometimes offer excitement, an opportunity for original visual treatment and an ambience that is seldom possible in a studio.

Books that may be helpful

Baker, G. P. *Dramatic Technique*. New York: Houghton Mifflin, 1919.

Bare, Richard L. *The Film Director*. New York: Macmillan, 1971.

Beaver, Frank E. *Dictionary of Film Terms*. New York: McGraw-Hill, 1983.

Berger, John. *Ways of Seeing*. New York: Penguin Books, 1977.

Brady, Ben. *The Keys to Writing for Television and Film*. Dubuque, Iowa: Kendall/Hunt, 1982.

Burrows, Tom and Wood, Donald. *Television Production—Disciplines and Techniques*. Dubuque, Iowa: Wm. C. Brown, 1978.

Clurman, Harold. *On Directing*. New York: Macmillan, 1972.

Cole, Toby and Chinoy, Helen Krich, eds. *Actors on Acting*. New York: Crown Publishers, 1949.

Cole, Toby and Chinoy, Helen Krich, eds. *Directors on Directing*. Indianapolis: Bobbs-Merrill, 1976.

Dmytryk, Edward. *On Screen Directing*. Woburn, Mass.: Focal Press—Butterworth, 1984.

Egri, Lajos. *The Art of Dramatic Writing*. New York: Simon & Schuster, 1946.

Elisophon, Eliot. *Color Photography*. New York: Viking Press, 1961.

Field, Syd. *Screenplay*. New York: Dell Publishing, 1979.

Fischer, Heinz-Dietrich and Melnik, Stefan Reinhard, eds. *Entertainment—a Cross-Cultural Examination.* New York: Hastings House, 1979.

Funke, Lewis and Booth, John E., eds. *Actors Talk about Acting.* New York: Avon Books, 1963.

Giannetti, Louis D. *Understanding Movies.* Englewood Cliffs, N.J.: Prentice-Hall, 1972.

Gradus, Ben. *Directing: The Television Commercial.* New York: Hastings House, 1981.

Henning, Fritz. *Concept and Composition.* Cincinnati, Ohio: North Light, 1983.

Lewis, Colby. *The TV Director/Interpreter.* New York: Hastings House, 1972.

Livingston, Don. *Film and the Director.* New York: Macmillan, 1953.

Pincus, Edward. *Guide to Filmmaking.* New York: Signet, 1969.

Reisz, Karel. *The Technique of Film Editing.* New York: Hastings House, 1968.

Reynertson, A. J. *The Work of the Film Director.* New York: Hastings House, 1970.

Rose, Tony. *How to Direct.* London and New York: Focal Press, 1954.

Schramm, Wilbur. *Men, Messages, and Media: A Look at Human Communication.* New York: Harper & Row, 1973.

Sherman, Eric, ed. *Directing the Film—Film Directors on Their Art.* Boston: Little, Brown, 1976.

Sievers, David W., Stiver, Harry E., Jr., and Kahan, Stanley. *Directing for the Theatre.* Dubuque, Iowa: Wm. C. Brown, 1965.

Silver, Alain and Ward, Elizabeth. *The Film Director's Team.* New York: Arco Publishing, 1983.

St. John Marner, Terence (in association with London Film School). *Directing Motion Pictures.* New York: A. S. Barnes, 1972.

Stanislavski, Constantin. *An Actor Prepares.* Translated by Elizabeth Reynolds Hapgood. New York: Theatre Arts Books, 1936.

Trapnell, Coles. *Teleplay.* New York: Hawthorn Books, 1974.

Truffaut, François. *Hitchcock.* New York: Simon & Schuster, 1967.

Wurtzel, Alan. *Television Production.* New York: McGraw-Hill, 1983.

Zettl, Herbert. *Sight, Sound, Motion: Applied Media Aesthetics.* Belmont, Calif.: Wadsworth, 1973.

Zettl, Herbert. *Television Production Handbook.* Belmont, Calif.: Wadsworth, 1984.

Glossary

A.D. Assistant director or associate director.

Adda The commercial name for a computer that creates and stores video graphics.

Automated Dialog Replacement (ADR) A computerized system for "looping," recording new dialog to replace unsatisfactory dialog—synchronized with an actor's lip movements.

Angle (Camera angle) The position from which a camera photographs action (for example, high angle, low angle). See Chapter 7.

Antagonist The opposing person, force, or element that prevents a hero (protagonist) from reaching a goal, thus creating drama's primary conflict.

Arc A camera movement that curves. May be circular, semicircular, or very slight.

Art Director The person who designs sets, coordinating visually related production materials.

Aspect Ratio The screen proportion: three units high by four units wide in TV, wider for most feature films.

Audio The sound portion of a television program. Usually monitored by an audio engineer in TV and a mixer in film.

Availables A listing of all stories possible, for inclusion in a news program.

Backlight The light source behind a photographic subject, creating illusion of dimension, separating subject from background.

Back Story   A character's background or history, often useful when creating a dimensional character.

Back Timing   A process for ensuring the correct program length: timing each element and then determining where the program should be, moment by moment, as it progresses.

Beat   In a script, a momentary pause. In theater, the separate actions or phases of a scene.

Blocking   The director's manipulation of performers or camera within a set: their movement, relative positions, business, etc. See Chapters 6 and 7.

Boom   (Microphone boom) A long metal arm holding a microphone, manipulated to follow performers about a set, picking up dialog out of camera range.

Business   Personal actions by a performer within a scene (for example, combing hair, cleaning a gun, sewing, ironing, reading a newspaper).

"Busy"   Term used to describe subject matter, often a background, that has an intricate or multidetailed pattern, dizzying in its complexity.

Canted Angle   Sometimes called a "Dutch" angle in which the horizon tilts, suggesting disequilibrium—as with drunkenness or insanity.

Cartridge   ("Cart") An audiotape recording on a loop that rewinds as it plays.

Cassette   A plastic case containing either a video or audio tape recording.

Character Generator   A device that reproduces letters or numbers electronically on a TV screen, such as statistics during a sportscast.

Chroma Key   A special effect that replaces a background color (usually blue) with selected video material (for example, a scene or graphic).

Chyron   Commercial name of a computer that generates and stores graphics.

Cinematographer   (Director of photography) Person in charge of a camera crew, responsible for lighting, composition, and exposure.

CK   (Corner Key) Letters indicating that a graphic will be keyed into a corner of frame.

Claustrophobic Frame   An angle that is uncomfortably close on subject matter, restricting the audience's view.

Closeup   (Close shot) A close camera angle on a person or object, delineating detail and intensifying dramatic values. See Chapter 6.

Color Correction Filters   Filters that change a scene's color values, usually subtly, for aesthetic effect.

Complementary Angles   A pair of camera angles that reveal similar or reverse perspectives on subject matter (for example, over-the-shoulder shots, one favoring actor A, the other favoring actor B).

Composition (Visual)   A harmonious arrangement of two or more elements, one of which dominates all others in interest.

Computerized Graphics   Pictures, effects, or titles generated by a computer (for example, Quantel, Adda).

Control Room (Booth)   A room from which a director and certain technicians control the rehearsal and broadcast (or videotaping) of a show.

Coverage   All of the camera angles needed by a director for the effective editing of a scene (a full shot, over-the-shoulder shots, closeups).

Covering   Photographing the action, usually in a comprehensive angle.

Crane   A metal boom arm with a camera mounted on one end, allowing vast, sweeping upward or downward movements.

Cross   An actor's move across a stage or set.

Crossing the Line   An abrupt reversal of character positions within a frame. Cause: photographing characters from opposite sides of an imaginary line that bisects them. (See Chapter 6.)

Cut   An instantaneous change of camera angle effected by joining together separate film or videotape segments or by switching electronically between cameras.

Cyclorama (Cyc)   A large cloth background for performances, often blue in color.

Dailies   A screening of film or videotape shot (usually) the previous day.

Depth of Field   The range of a picture that is in sharp focus. "Deep focus photography" offers sharp focus throughout.

Desensitizing   Diminishing impact of subject matter upon an audience because of repeated viewings.

Digital Leader   Numbers appearing at one-second intervals at the head of videotape or film. A visual countdown used for cuing.

Digital Video Effects (DVE)   An electronic device for inserting graphics—or other material—into a video picture. Operated by a technical director.

Director   A person who shapes a program message through the manipulation of technical and artistic elements, seeking to maximize their effect upon an audience.

Dissolve   An optical transition between scenes or camera angles; a blending or overlapping of images as one "melts" into the other.

Dolly   A four-wheeled camera vehicle that allows movement in all directions. A dolly shot moves forward or backward in relation to subject matter.

Downstage   That part of a stage nearest the audience (or camera).

Dubbing   The combining of dialog, music, and sound elements into a single track (or magnetic three-stripe) for optimum dramatic effect.

Editing   The cutting or splicing together of film or video elements. Editing usually occurs in postproduction.

Effects Bus   That part of an electronic switcher that controls visual effects such as mattes, keys, wipes, dissolves.

EFX   Abbreviation for "effects."

Electronic Field Production (EFP)   Video recording of drama or feature stories away from a studio. EFP usually requires postproduction editing.

End Cue   *See* Out Cue.

ENG   Electronic news gathering, utilizing portable camera, sound, and VTR units to record or transmit news or feature stories.

Establishing Shot   A comprehensive angle that provides excellent audience orientation.

Exposition   Information that the audience needs to know in order to understand a story. Usually revealed through dialog or visual clues.

Fade In/Out   Transitions from black to full picture, from full picture to black. Fades often signify a curtain or commercial break. A fade out/fade in within a dramatic work signals a major time lapse.

Fax   Abbreviation for "facilities."

Feed Lines   Lines of dialog that serve no real dramatic purpose other than to cue another actor's response (for example, "And then what happened?").

Filter   A glass or gelatinous material placed in front of a camera lens that changes the optical or color quality of an image.

Flare   A halation or bright flash when camera is aimed at a light source.

Floor Manager   The director's assistant in live TV. When directors are confined to a control booth, the floor manager becomes their arms, legs, and voice on the stage.

Fog Filter   A camera filter that creates a soft, luminous image with varying degrees of diffusion. Used extensively in TV commercials.

Format   The pattern or form of a script or program.

Frame   The basic visual unit, a single picture. Also, the camera's framing of a picture; the field that it encompasses.

Freeze Frame   An optical effect in which moving subject matter suddenly becomes stationary, frozen in position. Also, the final frames of a commercial, after the audio portion has concluded.

Gizmo   *See* Limbo.

Golden Mean   Believed by some to represent a basis for perfect visual design. See Chapter 3.

Graphics   Visual materials for TV (for example, titles, sketches) drawn by artists or generated by computers.

Hand-Held Camera   Technique used by directors to evoke feeling of news or documentary coverage, to create appearance of gritty reality.

Heavy A villain: evil or amoral, often sadistic.

High Angle Shot Camera angle in which the camera looks down, used primarily for orientation or to make characters appear inferior or weak.

Honey Shots Shots of pretty girls—usually cheerleaders—sprinkled through a sports telecast to add sensual appeal.

Identification The viewer's emotional involvement with (usually) the protagonist in a drama, in a sense *becoming* the protagonist.

INDX An acronym for Independent Exchange, an exchange of visual news material relayed to independent TV stations via satellite.

Jump Cuts Cuts between too-similar camera angles in which characters or scenery change screen positions disconcertingly. Also, cuts between noncontinuous action (as when frames have been deleted).

Keying *See* Matte.

Limbo An area used for shooting commercial inserts or small displays, usually with a neutral-colored, seamless backing. Also, a "gizmo."

Location An actual setting away from the studio (for example, a beach, a factory, a desert). In TV, a location sometimes is called a remote or a nemo.

Logo A commercial name, insignia, or trademark, usually distinguished by unique artwork or lettering.

Long Lens A lens with telescopic properties, bringing distant objects close. Long lenses flatten space, diminish distance, reducing the speed of objects moving toward or away from camera.

Long Shot A wide angle, orienting audiences.

Looping A postproduction technique for replacing dialog on film or tape, synchronizing new dialog with lip movements of actors. Used when original sound track is flawed.

Low Angle An angle created when a low camera shoots up at objects or characters, making them appear strong, dominant.

Magazine format A program embracing different feature stories (for example, "60 Minutes").

Master Angle A single camera angle in which the action of an entire scene is played. Usually a full shot.

Matte To cut one picture or title into another electronically. Also referred to as keying.

Medium Shot A camera angle somewhere between a long shot and a close shot. When photographing performers, usually a waist or a hip shot.

Microwave Link Using a parabolic "dish" to transmit a picture from a remote truck to a TV station—or from a station to its transmitter.

Monitor   A control booth or studio TV screen that reveals some aspect of program content (for example, preview, nemo, on the air).

Montage   A term that originally referred to the editorial assembling of film elements. Montage today describes a rapid succession of images that convey a single dramatic concept (for example, a whirlwind courtship).

M.O.S.   Letters standing for "Midout Sound," signifying any sequence that is filmed silently. An affectionate carryover from early Hollywood and the German director who first spoke the words.

Movieola   A motor-driven device for viewing and editing 16mm and 35mm film.

MTV   (Music Video) Short filmed or taped musical numbers that convey the story, mood, or emotion suggested by a song. Often bizarre or highly imaginative in their imagery.

Neutral Density (ND) Filter   A camera filter that reduces the quantity of light transmitted without affecting the quality of the image.

On the Nose   A term used to describe dialog or action that is blunt, obvious, and heavy-handed.

Out Cue   The final words in an SOT segment, alerting the director to cue the upcoming sound source.

Overhead Shot   An angle from an overhead camera, creating a privileged, godlike perspective. Sometimes used in musicals to accentuate patterns formed by dancers.

Over-the-Shoulder Shot   A camera angle framed past the foreground head and shoulders of character A, with a frontal view of character B.

Panning Shot   A camera move created when the camera head turns horizontally with its base remaining stationary. From the word *panorama*.

Point-of-View (POV) Shot   A subjective camera angle that becomes the perspective of a character, looking at the world through his or her eyes.

Postproduction   The period following completion of principal photography, a time usually devoted to editing, scoring, dubbing, and so on.

Pot   An abbreviation of *potentiometer,* a device that controls sound volume on an audio control panel.

Preproduction   The preparatory period before a film or TV program begins principal photography, devoted to script examination, casting, set design, search for locations, and so on.

Producer   The executive in charge of a production but who is subordinate to an executive producer.

Production Board   A flat, rectangular board prepared to facilitate scheduling and budget. Cardboard strips listing scenes, performers, extras, and so on are affixed to board, describing work to be accomplished each production day.

Production Values The elements that add color and richness to a movie or TV production (for example, distant locations, extravagant costumes, expensive sets).

Progression The classical climbing action of drama; a growth in dramatic tension. Increasingly close camera angles also represent progression.

Protagonist The hero in drama; a character with whom an audience becomes emotionally involved; a person with a problem.

Racking focus Changing a camera's focus from foreground to background (or vice versa). Audience attention tends to follow the focus change.

"Radio" Lines Lines of dialog that comment on what is happening—action that the viewer can see—and that are, therefore, unnecessary.

Raking Shot An angle in which a succession of objects or characters are photographed from the side so that viewers see them in depth.

Rhythm In visual composition, the pleasing repetition of imagery (for example, a succession of arches). Also, repetition of phrases, actions, or musical themes in drama, each recurrence enriching the story values or emotion conveyed.

Riser A raised platform.

Roll Cue A word or action that signals the director's command to roll videotape or film. The command itself.

Rough Cut An editor's first assembly of film or tape. A director's first opportunity to appraise the completed project.

Rundown Sheet The sheet of paper that describes stories to be included in a news program—or a sequence of events.

Scoring Adding music to a program that will enrich its dramatic or emotional content.

Screen Direction The consistent pattern of movement from angle to angle: left to right or right to left. See Chapter 7.

Script The basis for most movies and TV programs. A scenario that creates drama through plot, characters, and dialog—or that defines a sequence of events.

Selective Focus Placing camera focus on a point of greatest dramatic significance; viewer attention tends to follow focus.

Set-up (Camera set-up) A camera position with its accompanying arrangement of lights.

Shot Sheet A list of shots that each camera operator is expected to provide for a program.

Slow Motion A technique for slowing action so that it gains dramatic significance. In sports, slo-mo is used to reveal action details.

Socius Function   The element of companionship provided by TV and other entertainment.

SOT   Sound on tape.

Source Music   Music that originates within a scene rather than from a composed score (for example, a radio, a hi fi, a dance band).

Special EFX (Effects)   Trick photography, optical effects, or those devised on the set (for example, smoke, explosions, bullets hitting a target).

Spectacle   An element of audience appeal, generally utilizing sound, motion, or color.

Spine   A character's or story's basic need, goal, or drive.

Stage Manager   *See* Floor Manager.

Star Filter   A filter that reproduces light sources or flares in a star pattern, creating an upbeat, glittery effect.

Storyboard   A series of frames or sketches indicating key dramatic points in a script, scene, or commercial. Usually includes dialog beneath sketches.

Style   A director's personal pattern of treating material, including staging of camera and performers, script elements, music, and so on.

Subjective Camera   When the camera becomes a character, photographing action from that person's point of view (POV). Suggesting a character's mood or emotions through more generalized camera treatment.

Suspense   Usually associated with films generating anxiety or apprehension; actually a component of all well-conceived drama.

Switcher   The electronic device used for cutting between cameras or for creating dissolves or other optical effects. Also, the person who operates such a device (that is, a technical director or TD).

Tally Light   The red light on a video camera indicating when it is on the air.

Technical Director (TD)   Person in charge of the crew in a live or videotape operation. Edits and creates video effects through an electronic switcher.

TelePrompter   A device that displays news or other copy for a performer to read. Often reflected in glass angled before the camera lens so that the performer may look directly into camera.

Tilt   A shot created when camera tilts up or down, camera base remaining fixed.

Timing Cut   A cut from one angle to the next that eliminates or shortens tedious or unnecessary dramatic material.

Tracking Shot   A camera shot that moves with performers, usually in their tracks, ahead of them or behind them.

TRT   Total running time, usually of a videotape segment.

Trucking Shot   Term often used interchangeably with *tracking shot*. Camera moves with performers, usually from a side angle.

Unit Manager   The person in charge of assembling "below-the-line" elements: camera crew, electricians, carpenters, and so on. Responsible for schedule and budget.

Uplink   Used to transmit a video signal from an earth station to a satellite.

Upstage   That part of a stage farthest from the audience (or camera).

VTR   Videotape recorder or recording.

Wide Angle Lens   Camera lens commonly used for orientation shots. Extremely wide angle lenses create distortion; foreground objects appear large, bizarre, comedic. Wide angle lenses accentuate the illusion of depth.

Wrap   To conclude production activities for the day and go home. "That's a wrap": words that a cast and crew are always happy to hear.

Zoom Shot   A change of angle that, through a lens adjustment, moves quickly or slowly from a wide to a close angle, or vice versa.

INDEX